Manufactured in the United States of America

Published by
Kennikat Press Corp.
Port Washington, N.Y. / London

Library of Congress Cataloging in Publication Data
Main entry under title:

In search of the promised land.

(National University publications: Interdisciplinary
urban studies)
Bibliography: p.

1. Afro-Americans—History—Addresses, essays, lectures. 2. Afro-Americans—Social conditions—Addresses,
essays, lectures. 3. Afro-Americans—Economic conditions—Addresses, essays, lectures. 4. City and town
life—United States—History—Addresses, essays, lectures. I. Kornweibel, Jr., Theodore.
E185.I5   973'.0496073   80-19237
ISBN 0-8046-9267-X

IN SEARCH

OF THE

PROMISED LAND

ESSAYS IN
BLACK URBAN HISTORY

edited by
THEODORE KORNWEIBEL, JR.

National University Publications
KENNIKAT PRESS // 1981
Port Washington, N.Y. // London

IN SEARCH
OF THE
PROMISED LAND

Kennikat Press
National University Publications
Interdisciplinary Urban Series

General Editor
Raymond A. Mohl
Florida Atlantic University

To My Mother
And to the Memory of
Kate

CONTENTS

PREFACE

For several years I have had students read many of the articles contained in this volume for various Afro-American studies and urban history courses. What I really needed was an anthology that would focus on the total Black urban experience in America from colonial times to the present, and that which would avoid a preoccupation with "ghettoes" and negative social phenomena. The matter of perspective was crucial, for both the general public and academia have indulged in more than enough pessimistic hand-wringing over the trials and problems of contemporary urban Black communities as well as "analyses" of the purported "breakdown" of major Black institutions. In assembling this volume, I have sought to include articles which, while not ignoring negative trends, would focus the reader's attention on the more positive and proactive aspects of both individual and group life over several generations of urban experiences. The creative responses of these communities, in building social structures and organizational networks, have too often been ignored or deemphasized, and it is my hope that this volume will begin to redress the balance. I only regret that additional articles in every category could not be included; the reader should be aware that recent scholarship is adding significantly to the field. Finally, such a book has long been needed, because Blacks were this country's largest non-English immigrant group prior to the Revolution, and along with the first English settlers, among the original urban generation in America.

Several individuals have assisted in the completion of this project, and I wish to give them my thanks. Professor Daniel E. Weinberg reviewed the introductory materials. Typing was done by Mrs. Anne M. Porter and Mrs. Gladys L. Richardson, as well as by the Word Processing Center of San Diego State University. Several student assistants in the Department of Afro-American Studies performed helpful tasks: Terri Anne Rucker, Mary Ann Burnett, Don Phin, Alisa Bass, Wanda Marchbanks, Sabrina Kincade, Stephanie Evans, and George Earby. Most of all, I wish to acknowledge the spiritual support of my wife, Catherine, and my daughter, Kate, who have always encouraged me and believed in me. They know how much I owe to them, and from whence we all draw our ultimate strength.

IN SEARCH
OF THE
PROMISED LAND

CONTRIBUTORS

Neil Betten
Department of History
Florida State University, Tallahassee

John W. Blassingame
Department of History
Department of Afro-American
    Studies
Yale University

Robert Blauner
Department of Sociology
University of California, Berkeley

Lawrence B. de Graaf
Department of History
California State University,
    Fullerton

Reynolds Farley
Department of Sociology
Director, Population Studies Center
University of Michigan

E. Horace Fitchett
Professor of Sociology (Retired)
Howard University
Washington, D. C.

Theodore Hershberg
Department of History
School of Public and Urban Policy
Director, Philadelphia Social History
    Project
University of Pennsylvania

Theodore Kornweibel, Jr.
Department of Afro-American
    Studies
San Diego State University

Raymond A. Mohl
Department of History
Florida Atlantic University,
    Boca Raton

Gary B. Nash
Department of History
University of California,
    Los Angeles

Elizabeth H. Pleck
Fellow, The Bunting Institute
Radcliffe College

William L. Richter
Bill's Farrier Service
Tucson, Arizona

1

THE URBAN PARAMETERS

"The city" brings to mind many images for modern Americans. For those members of an older generation whose parents or grandparents migrated from Europe, cities may represent the doorway to opportunity and upward mobility. To younger white Americans, cities may hold out the promise of fast living, a "swinging" popular culture, and chic reconverted brownstones in "fashionable" neighborhoods. To rural people of whatever ethnic background, the city may symbolize decadence, rootlessness, and aimlessness, on the one hand, or escape from the stagnation of country life on the other. Many Americans having little contact with cities see them in terms of cold statistics on crime and welfare. To many Blacks, as well as to recent immigrants from foreign lands, the city has meant both a refuge and the chance for a new start with new rights and opportunities. Undoubtedly this brief catalogue does not represent every possible view. Cities have been all things to all people, and the goal of this volume is to sift out their meaning for Afro-Americans.

What is a city? Even urban specialists have difficulty agreeing on a single satisfactory definition, so it may be more helpful to list some common characteristics shared by urban areas. Cities have more dense, compact populations than either rural or suburban areas. Residents are concentrated in part because large-scale activities are centralized in cities: trade and commerce; manufacturing; communications; government and administration. Occupations in cities tend to be both more specialized and more remote than rural occupations. On the farm, a worker may perform a wide variety of tasks, from plowing to harvesting to transportation and marketing; in the process, he may see the product from its beginning to its completion. Much city work, however, involves very narrow and specialized skills, and many workers perform only a small portion of the total labor needed for production or the provision of services. Finally, urban life-styles and habits differ markedly from rural ones. The adjective "urban" implies a sophisticated cosmopolitan outlook. It is no accident that cities are more often centers of art and culture. Although rural areas typically have more close-knit social networks, city life breeds an outlook broader than the parochial vision of nonurban areas.

In this volume "city" and "urban" are used interchangeably. But the process of "urbanization" needs explanation. This refers to the phenomenon whereby a city's population increases at a faster rate than the surrounding area. Broadening this still further, we can speak of America as an urbanizing nation. The historical trend has been for urban areas to grow faster than—and often at the expense of—rural areas. The United States has never been more urbanized than it is today, and this pattern of an increasing concentration of population in cities has characterized nearly two centuries of national development. Urban populations can increase through three means. If the birth rate among those already resident in a city is greater than the death rate, urban growth will result. A similar result occurs when more people migrate into a city than leave it. Finally, a city may add to its population by expanding its geographical boundaries through annexation of surrounding communities. Black urbanization has been largely the product of the second factor—immigration.

The scope of Black urban history encompasses far more than economic and population studies, however. For not only do people mesh and interact in large-scale activities, they also become members of subcommunities and frequently contribute to subcultures. An understanding of the Black urban experience requires attention to Afro-American churches, social networks, neighborhoods, businesses, life-styles and class structure. So while much of the history of Blacks in cities is a record of struggle against adversity, there is also the story of creative community building. We should be aware of the tendency, especially among social scientists, to adopt an unbalanced negative view. By studying all types of individuals, all life-styles, and all socioeconomic groupings, one may more successfully avoid a perspective fixated on pathology. Struggle, conflict, and thwarted progress have been elements of the Black urban existence, but there is a reverse that needs equal emphasis. Many Black responses to the city display what psychologists call a proactive stance—creative searching for solutions and growth—as opposed to a more passive, reactive posture.

We may study Black urban history from two focuses. One approach highlights what is distinctive about that experience: what happened to Blacks in the cities, and what responses were made to city life that were unlike those of other groups. We will pose this sort of question in the last section of this volume, "Blacks and the American City: Conceptual Perspectives." The second approach seeks to identify what Blacks have shared in common with other city dwellers. We may begin here by asking why Blacks have located in the cities of America. Some came involuntarily, as slaves. Since servitude was practiced in all thirteen of the British North American colonies, this meant that slavery existed in every American city during the colonial period. Bondage was abolished in the northern states soon after 1800, but it continued in the South until 1865. So for more than two centuries slavery was practiced in American cities, and there is nothing directly comparable to it in the European immigrant experience—not even indentured servitude. But if we focus on those who came to the cities voluntarily, there is much that Blacks shared in common with non-Black urban residents. Persons of all ethnic groups came seeking opportunities not possible in the rural areas of the United States, Europe, or Latin America. Wider employment, expanded social opportunities, "freedom," have been the goals of nearly all city-bound people. This held true even for escaping slaves before the Civil War, for the city held out possibilities for self-liberation and a new identity that rural areas could not match.

Another way in which Blacks have shared common experiences with other groups pertains to their place in the urban social structure. Nearly every ethnic group in the nineteenth and twentieth centuries found an urban niche first as common, unskilled, and undifferentiated labor. In other words, Blacks and others formed the basis for an urban working class. What is distinctive is the degree to which Blacks, more than any other "immigrant" group to the city, have become captive in the lower economic class position and have been denied mobility upward and out of the city. Urban life also encouraged both Blacks and immigrant groups to preserve and capitalize upon their ethnicity. Businesses, schools, theaters, churches, and fraternal lodges became ethnic institutions, with national or racial ties being the primary cement bonding customer to entrepreneur or member to member. In the anonymity of the city, where individuals may find themselves stripped of past experiences and habits, the preservation of one's previous identity becomes all the more important. Eastern European Jews in American cities established societies based on the town or region from which they had emigrated. Blacks from St. Helena Island in South Carolina, upon migrating to New York City, set up social clubs on the basis of their place of birth. For both groups, geographical origin thus became the foundation for nonbiological kinship.

Finally, it can be observed that the sociological impact of the city, on Blacks as well as on individuals from foreign lands, has been similar. All groups went through a migration experience. All encountered stresses or changes in family ties, marriage rates and ages, childbearing and child-rearing practices, norms, and social roles for males and females. This is not to say that the impact was always the same for every group; rather, it is to stress that no group escaped the crucible of the city, in which old demographic and social patterns were tested, tried, and transformed. The city did not totally obliterate one's "old country," whether it was Russian Georgia or Georgia, USA, but no one was the same upon acculturation to urban life.

THE URBANIZATION OF NEGROES
IN THE UNITED STATES

REYNOLDS FARLEY

The distribution of the Negro population with regard to urban or rural residence has followed a curious pattern in the United States. Negroes originally were brought to America in the seventeenth century to work in cities as laborers or house servants. During the latter part of that century and the next, the number of Negroes in the emerging cities grew as more workers were needed and European immigrants became difficult to obtain.

Agricultural prosperity during the eighteenth century opened a new economic niche for Negroes, and many slaves entered the southern colonies. After the Revolution, the invention of the cotton gin and the settling of the Gulf Coast states increased the need for slaves. In northern cities the Negro population grew slowly, if at all, as European immigrants filled the need for unskilled labor. Southern cities contained some slaves and free Negroes, but by the time of the Civil War the Negro population was concentrated in rural southern areas.

Immediately following the Civil War, many Negroes moved to southern cities. However, the lack of prosperity and industrialization meant that only a small proportion of all Negroes could support themselves in an urban setting. In the North, European immigrants continued to fill the low skill jobs. Thus at the turn of this century, Negroes were almost as concentrated in the rural South as forty or one hundred years earlier.

Reprinted with permission from the *Journal of Social History*, 1 (Spring 1968), pp. 241–258. Footnotes and several of the tables appearing in the original publication have been deleted in the present volume, and should be consulted for full documentation of the author's conclusions.

Careful analysis does reveal a beginning of the out-migration of Negroes from the South during the years following the Civil War, an out-migration pattern which became substantial after 1900. Practically all of those leaving the South migrated to cities in the North or West. Economic changes have encouraged Negroes to leave the South since early in this century. For a long time, small and marginal farms—typically operated by Negroes in the South—have been disfunctional. The boll weevil devastated farms, thus lessening the need for agricultural workers and encouraging Negroes to leave the South. World War I necessitated greater industrial production, but cut off the supply of immigrants. Industries began to recruit southern Negroes, thus precipitating further urbanization of Negroes. During the Depression years the movement of Negroes to cities slackened, but World War II and the continuing prosperity of the postwar era meant a resumption of predepression trends.

As a consequence of these shifts, today Negroes are more urbanized than the white population. Rates of population change since 1960 suggest a continuing movement of Negroes away from rural areas to cities. Since the southern Negro population is still large and rapidly growing, we might expect a continuation of these trends in the foreseeable future.

This article examines the process of urbanization of Negroes and attempts to elucidate some of the factors responsible for this process.

NEGROES IN PRE-REVOLUTIONARY CITIES

The earliest settlements in what is now the United States—Salem and Boston in Massachusetts, Newport on Narragansett Bay, New Amsterdam, Philadelphia, and Charleston on the Carolina coast—grew into trading centers in the seventeenth century. Each served an interior hinterland and, because they were ports, traded with England, the West Indies, and Africa. At an early date a need arose for manual labor. In Boston, an attempt was made to enslave Indians, but their hostility and unwillingness to remain slaves made this an inefficient system. Indentured servants provided much labor, but they were costly to obtain and maintain, and they would work for only a specified number of years, usually five or seven. Furthermore, they had legal rights and might sue their masters if they believed themselves to be mistreated. Negroes as a source of labor possessed distinct advantages. They were held perpetually, replaced themselves, and probably were cheaper to support. Thus, the importing of Negro slaves began early in the seventeenth century. Negroes arrived in New Amsterdam in 1626, one year after the founding of the village. Boston received its first Negroes in 1638, eight years after the founding of the city.

The Negro population of the American colonies grew slowly during the latter seventeenth century. However, early in the eighteenth century, both European and New England traders recognized that profits were to be made in the slave trade. As commercial activities expanded in the American cities, the need for labor also grew. The continental wars and their American counterparts—King William's War (1689-1697), Queen Anne's War (1701-1713), King George's War (1740-1748), and the French-Indian War (1754-1763)—made it difficult to obtain immigrants from Europe. As a consequence, the number and importance of Negro laborers rose, and in each city some few Negroes became artisans. This produced a situation such that by 1750 many northern cities or colonies had a greater percentage of Negroes in their population than they do at present. For instance, in 1748 about 10 percent of Rhode Island's population was Negro. The census of 1965 indicated that only 2.5 percent of the present population of Rhode Island is Negro. Eleven percent of Boston's population was Negro in 1752. This percentage fell for many years, and in 1960, 9 percent of Boston's population was Negro. In New York, better than one fifth of the population was Negro in 1746 compared to 14 percent in 1960.

In northern cities, the Negro population apparently reached a peak around 1750 and remained stationary or declined thereafter. A number of reasons can be given for this. As agriculture expanded in the South, imported slaves brought greater prices in that region. After the Treaty of Paris in 1763, it became easier to secure immigrants from Europe, workers who were generally more skilled and possibly more industrious than Negro slaves. Perhaps most important was a growing opposition to and indignation about the holding of slaves. Religious and legal regulations in Massachusetts set so many strictures on slaveholding that no slaves were found in that state when the first census was taken in 1790. The opposition of Quakers prevented there ever being numerous slaves in Philadelphia and, to a lesser extent, in other cities. In contrast, the number of slaves in the South increased during the eighteenth century as agricultural production and the plantation system expanded. Among the first crops to require gang labor was rice, which was introduced to the Carolina lowlands in the 1690's. Shortly thereafter, indigo, a crop which had sowing and harvesting seasons complementing those of rice, was introduced; this enabled a planter to use one labor supply for both crops. Cotton later became the principal crop, necessitating more slaves.

Only one city developed in the South during the colonial period—the port of Charleston. The sparse evidence available suggests that many slaves were used in this city to perform unskilled labor. There are reports of Negro craftsmen and the emergence of a system for hiring out slaves.

The census of 1790 indicates half of the population of this city was Negro; about 90 percent of these Negroes were slaves.

URBANIZATION OF NEGROES IN THE PRE-CIVIL WAR PERIOD

During the period between the Revolutionary and Civil wars, Negroes did not become highly urbanized. In fact, in most cities—both North and South—the proportion of Negroes fell, and in many towns the actual numbers of Negroes declined.

TABLE 1: NEGRO POPULATION, DISTRIBUTION BY REGION, 1790-1964

	SOUTH	NORTH-EAST	NORTH-CENTRAL	WEST
1790	91.1%	8.9%		
1800	91.6	8.3	0.1	
1810	92.1	7.4	0.5	
1820	92.7	6.2	1.1	
1830	92.8	5.4	1.8	
1840	91.9	5.0	3.1	
1850	92.1	4.1	3.8	
1860	92.2	3.5	4.2	0.1
1870	90.6	3.7	5.6	0.1
1880	90.5	3.5	5.8	0.2
1890	90.3	3.6	5.7	0.4
1900	89.7	4.3	5.7	0.3
1910	89.0	4.9	5.6	0.5
1920	85.1	6.5	7.6	0.8
1930	78.8	9.6	10.6	1.0
1940	77.1	10.6	11.0	1.3
1950	68.0	13.4	14.8	3.8
1960	60.0	16.0	18.3	5.7
1964	54.4	18.1	19.4	8.1

Table 1 shows that from 1790 to 1860 and long afterwards, over 90 percent of the Negro population resided in the South. Within the South almost all Negroes were to be found in rural areas. Of course, the South was a predominantly farming area, but the reasons for the small number of Negroes in southern cities before the Civil War merit exploration.

Often the question was raised as to whether Negroes were capable of performing any tasks other than the highly routinized jobs of a field hand. A widespread belief held Negroes to be so mentally inferior and so inclined to laziness that they could not be taught the rudimentary skills for labor in an urban environment. Some commentators claimed Negro workers in southern cities were indolent and performed but one-third or one-half the work done by comparable northern workers. However, many reports counteract this view. Throughout the South, Negroes filled skilled and unskilled positions in cities. In many cities occupations such as those of barbers, blacksmiths, or cabinetmakers were dominated by Negroes; industry also employed Negroes widely. By 1850, almost all employees of the Virginia tobacco factories were Negroes; in Richmond, the Tredegar Iron Works used slaves in all nonsupervisory positions. In many areas, groups of white mechanics both complained of competition from slaves who would work at less cost and petitioned for protection against such Negro competition.

Wade argues effectively that the real reason for the decreasing Negro population of southern cities was the inability of slavery as a system to survive in cities. In rural areas, slaves lived on isolated plantations; their activities were known; and they were subject to the control of the master or overseer. While some ran away, apparently most were apprehended. In a city such a system of control was impossible. Slaves typically lived in their own quarters, earned some or all of their own keep, and spent their leisure time as they saw fit. This meant that slave discipline was difficult or impossible. Furthermore, free Negroes or even abolitionists could mingle with slaves, educate them, and encourage them to be less docile. Consequently, the institution of slavery with its master-slave relationship did not easily fit an urban framework.

Denmark Vesey's planned insurrection in Charleston and Nat Turner's rebellion in Virginia led to new efforts to control Negroes—either free or slaves—in cities and to restrict their freedom through legal and extralegal means. As a result, the Negro population in most southern cities declined during the first sixty years of the nineteenth century.

Different reasons account for the slow growth of the Negro population in northern cities. Northern states had abolished slavery by 1818, but Negroes were generally unwanted. Most states instituted Black codes to restrict Negroes and then enacted measures to forbid Negro immigration and to encourage emigration from northern cities and states. For in-stance, a Massachusetts vagrancy law of 1788 called for the expulsion of all Negroes who were not citizens of Massachusetts. Ohio, from 1804 to 1807, passed a series of Black codes demanding that Negroes register, present proof of their freedom and good behavior, or be expelled. Both Indiana and Illinois included provisions in their constitutions making it illegal for Negroes to migrate into the state. Connecticut, along with other states, restricted the education of Negroes. In Pennsylvania judicial decisions upheld the denial of political and civil rights to Negroes. Mob action or violence was directed at Negroes in many cities. White citizens of Cincinnati, concerned about the increasing Negro population and rising welfare costs, tried with some success to evict Negroes by force in 1829. In Philadelphia, anti-Negro rioting occurred in 1834, 1835, 1838, and 1849; in Pittsburgh in 1839 and 1842.

Although the need for unskilled labor rose during this period, Negroes were generally limited in the jobs they might seek and in some instances were displaced by European immigrants. In New York, Irish immigrants rapidly came to monopolize the market for manual labor, and excluded Negroes. Job opportunities for Negroes apparently contracted as immigration increased. Similarly in Philadelphia, the Irish undermined the economic position of Negroes during the 1840's and 1850's.

The harshness of living conditions for Negroes in northern cities insured that their death rate would be high and their rate of natural increase low. A Philadelphia study of 1847 found many Negroes to be living in such cramped and unsanitary conditions that practically all infants died shortly after birth. In New York, as in other cities, contagious diseases afflicted the Negro population and limited its growth.

URBANIZATION OF NEGROES IN THE POST-CIVIL WAR PERIOD

For a long period subsequent to the Civil War, most Negroes remained in the South. During this period, the South failed to industrialize as rapidly as the North, and the typical industry of southerners—both Negro and white—was that of agriculture. From 1860 to 1900, the percentage of the nation's population in the South held steady at one-third, but the South's share of manufacturing output was not proportional. In 1860, 11 percent of the total value of products originated with southern manufacturers. In 1870, this fell to 7 percent; in 1880, 7 percent; in 1890, 9 percent; and in 1900, 11 percent. As a consequence, the South did not urbanize as rapidly in the later nineteenth century as did the other regions of the country. As recently as 1950, the majority of Southerners lived in rural areas; the Northeast became predominantly urban in the 1870's; and the north-central and western regions during World War I. This slow growth of urban centers in the South meant that most Negroes lived in rural areas. The census of 1890, the first to give a rural-urban breakdown of the Negro population, found 80 percent of all Negroes and 85 percent of the southern Negroes in rural areas (see Table 2).

In spite of the concentration of Negroes in rural areas for a lengthy span after the Civil War, there was a substantial movement of Negroes to cities immediately following the war. After emancipation, many Negroes left their farms of residence and flocked to cities, particularly those containing Union Army camps. For some, this freedom of movement was a certification of emancipation; others expected the federal government to support them, on the assumption that the end of slavery meant they no longer would have to struggle for a living. Most southern towns, however, were severely devastated by the Civil War. Rail lines were destroyed, and many of the factories found in southern cities were either wrecked or dependent upon the highly disrupted agricultural sector. The presence of unskilled and destitute Negroes in cities complicated

TABLE 2: PERCENTAGE OF NEGRO
POPULATION, URBAN, 1890-1960

	TOTAL USA	SOUTH	NORTH AND WEST
1890	19.8	15.3	61.5
1900	22.7	17.2	70.4
1910	27.4	21.2	77.5
1920	34.0	25.3	84.5
1930	43.7	31.7	88.1
1940	48.6	36.5	89.1
1950[a]	62.4	47.6	95.2
1960	73.2	58.4	95.2

[a]Beginning in 1950, a new definition for urban was used which included places of less than 2,500 if located in urban territory.

attempts at reconstruction. The Freedmen's Bureau tried to resettle Negroes in rural areas. Certain federally held lands in the South were turned over to the Bureau to be distributed to Negroes, but these tended to be marginal lands and apparently few Negroes benefited. In another effort to encourage Negroes to leave cities, the Freedmen's Bureau arranged and acted as overseer in a contract labor system and paid transportation costs as well.

The efforts of the Freedmen's Bureau may have been partly successful in resettling Negroes, but the Negro population of most southern cities jumped sharply following the Civil War. Such an increase was unprecedented and never duplicated. As noted in the previous section, the proportion of Negroes fell until 1860. In contrast, the Civil War decade witnessed a very sizable increase in the proportion of Negroes in each of these cities.

Little change in the proportion of Negroes occurred in latter decades of the nineteenth century, which suggests that the urban Negro population grew about as rapidly as the urban white population. In most cities, Negroes filled the need for unskilled or semiskilled labor and for house servants. In Memphis, many worked as stevedores; Negroes were employed in construction work in other cities. After Richmond industries resumed production, Negroes were employed at many jobs held by slaves prior to the war. In North Carolina cities many Negroes labored in tobacco factories. By 1890, there developed in many southern towns

TABLE 3: NET MIGRATION OF NEGROES BY REGION, 1870-1960

	NORTH-EAST	SOUTH	NORTH-CENTRAL	WEST
1870-1880	26	− 68	42	
1880-1890	61	− 88	28	
1890-1900	136	− 185	49	
1900-1910	109	− 194	63	22
1910-1920	242	− 555	281	32
1920-1930	435	− 903	426	42
1930-1940	273	− 480	152	55
1940-1950	599	− 1,581	626	356
1950-1960[a]	541	− 1,458	560	347

[a]Figures for 1950-1960 were obtained from different sources than those for earlier decades. The figures for the earlier decades refer to Negro population while those for 1950-1960 refer to nonwhite population.

a small middle-class Negro population. A few Negro doctors and lawyers and a large number of teachers were to be found in the larger cities. In some places, Negro banks and newspapers operated. And yet the census of 1890 shows that practically all Negroes who held nonagricultural jobs worked as laborers, porters, or house servants. Contemporary descriptions of the Negro areas of southern cities indicate most Negroes lived at near-subsistence levels, often in dilapidated, unsanitary houses.

OUT-MIGRATION OF NEGROES FROM THE SOUTH

Although most Negroes remained in the South following the Civil War, out-migration trends did develop, which became more obvious and involved significant proportions of the Negro population in this century. Since 1850, the census has included a question asking the respondent's state or country of birth. By comparing state-of-birth information and making appropriate allowances for mortality, it is possible to estimate the volume of out-migration from or immigration to a region for decennial periods. Such estimates of net migration of Negroes are shown in Table 3.

In the last ninety years, there has been a continual and generally increasing outflow of Negroes from the South and corresponding gains in the Negro population in other areas.

Immediately following the Civil War, out-migrants from the South were few in number. Some did move to the plains states, particularly Kansas, in the expectation of receiving free land. Beginning in the late 1880's, a shift in the direction and an increase in the volume of Negro migration occurred—the movement was from the South to northern cities. In fact, Negroes leaving the South since 1880 have consistently migrated to cities. In 1890, the first date for which the requisite data are available, three-fifths of all nonsouthern Negroes lived in towns, and by 1910 this figure approached four-fifths.

Many reasons can be given for the out-migration of so many Negroes, reasons demographers typically categorize as push factors and pull factors. Among the most important push factors were the limited economic opportunities for Negroes in the South. Apparently the employment of Negroes in agriculture on either a wage, sharecrop, or tenancy basis was not satisfactory to either Negroes or white land-owners. The depression of the 1890's and the gradual spread of the boll weevil from the Southwest across the cotton lands to the Southeast further exacerbated the economic status of Negroes and encouraged many to leave. The amount of land farmed by Negroes in the South apparently reached a peak in 1910 and has consistently declined since that date. Despite growth of the Negro population in the South, the number of Negro farmers has declined since 1920. As mechanization and modernization of agriculture occurred, the Negro farm population has continued to drop. From 1960 to 1965, the Negro farm population declined 41 percent while the white farm population fell 17 percent.

Another push factor was the abuse of Negroes in the South. Vann Woodward argues that southern states typically instituted or reinstated Jim Crow practices and laws toward the end of the nineteenth century. For some period during Reconstruction, Negroes participated in politics, utilized their civil rights, and assisted in the expansion of educational opportunities. Beginning with Mississippi in about 1875 and concluding with North Carolina in 1900 and Virginia in 1902, one state after another discovered some subterfuge to exclude Negroes from voting or political activities, to limit their civil rights and restrict their opportunities. As a consequence many Negroes left the South. Shortly after the turn of this century, New York, Philadelphia, and other northern cities apparently contained more than a few trained Negroes who had attempted to build careers in the South but found themselves limited by new Jim Crow laws. Some studies have claimed that rural areas in which attacks on Negroes, such as lynchings, were commonplace lost Negro population most rapidly.

The major pull factor responsible for migration was the promise of economic prosperity in the North. And yet this pull factor probably did not operate until the time of World War I. To be sure, Negroes had been used as strikebreakers by certain northern industries for a long period of time. Yet descriptions of Negro workers in the era before 1917 suggest there was little competition between white and Negro workers. Certain occupational niches, such as domestic service, Pullman car porters, and some construction and slaughterhouse jobs provided employment for almost all Negroes; other jobs were typically closed to Negroes.

During the years from 1910 to 1914, an average of over 900,000 Europeans migrated to this country each year. In the following five years, the average fell to about 100,000 per year, due to World War I. In spite of this drop in immigration, the number of workers in manufacturing rose, as did the output of the manufacturing sector. One of the main sources of additional workers for northern industries was southern Negroes. Many firms sent labor recruiters to southern areas and paid the transportation costs of Negroes who would move to such cities as New York, Philadelphia, or Chicago. Thus from 1910 to 1920 over half a million Negroes left the South for northern cities.

The immigration laws of 1921 and 1924 effectively limited immigration from abroad, and during the twenties the out-migration of Negroes from the South increased. The depression years dampened the out-migration streams, but World War II and the postwar prosperity witnessed a resumption of the movement of Negroes away from the South. During the forties, Negro migrants to the West became numerous, apparently a response to military and industrial growth along the western seaboard.

One additional pull factor should be noted: at various times northern Negro newspapers undertook campaigns to encourage Negroes to migrate North. Perhaps the most outspoken of these campaigns was carried out by the *Chicago Defender,* a paper with a wide circulation in the South. The South was pictured as a land of oppression where the Negro had no access to jobs or schools and where he might be lynched without provocation. The North, on the other hand, was seen as a land of opportunity where jobs were available, schools open, and civil rights respected.

For more than sixty years, these push and pull factors have affected the distribution of the Negro population. Three major consequences may be noted:

First, the Negro population is now less concentrated in the South and more evenly distributed nationally. For the first 120 years of this nation's history, nine-tenths of all Negroes resided in the South. In the next fifty-year span the proportion in the South fell to slightly over one-half. The appropriate figures indicating these changes are shown in Table 1.

Second, the Negro population has become a primarily urban population both within and outside the South. Table 2 presents the percentages of the Negro population that were urban from 1890 to 1960, the only dates for which this information is available. From an early date Negroes in the North and West lived in cities. Urbanization of Negroes occurred more recently in the South, but there is no doubt that southern Negroes are becoming increasingly concentrated in cities.

Third, the racial composition of the large northern cities first, and later the large western cities, changed due to the immigration of Negroes. The proportion of Negroes in these cities climbed in the past and will continue to do so in the foreseeable future. Within southern cities there has been much less change in racial composition.

In recent years, many northern cities have lost large numbers of whites, but gained many Negroes as a consequence of both immigration and high rates of natural increase. Because of these changes in such northern cities as Cleveland, Newark, and Gary, more than one-third of the population is nonwhite. In other cities, such as Philadelphia, St. Louis, and Detroit, more than one-fourth of the residents are nonwhite.

PROSPECTS FOR THE FUTURE

The southern Negro population is still a large and growing population. Despite sixty years of out-migration the number of Negroes in the South has grown from about 8 million at the turn of the century to 11.25

million in 1960. The loss through migration has failed to equal the gains due to natural increase, and the fertility of southern Negro women seems to insure rapid future growth.

Within the South the rural Negro population will continue to decline. The rural farm population is sure to drop as aggregation occurs in agriculture. The rural nonfarm Negro population may increase as it did from 1950 to 1960. As larger southern cities expand and smaller cities obtain industrial plants, many Negroes can begin to work at nonfarm jobs while living in rural areas or small hamlets. As the cities of the South grow, the Negro urban population in this region will also increase as it has in the past.

Though there has been a long history of Negroes leaving the South, it is extremely difficult to predict the volume or direction of such migration in the future. If the out-migration rates of the 1950's persist into the 1960's, the number of out-migrants will be larger. One might argue that there are persistent social and economic systems which facilitate the migration of many Negroes away from the South to the cities of the North and West. However, increased economic opportunities in some regions of the South, such as Florida and Texas, may combine with decreasing economic opportunities in northern cities to diminish the out-migration of Negroes from the South.

2

SLAVES AND FREEMEN
IN COLONIAL CITIES

From the beginning of the British North American colonies, white immigrants established towns and cities. For some, this was a conscious duplication of prior experience in Europe. For others, the lure of upward mobility and wealth through an urban commercial life was the primary motivation. For America's largest non-English immigrant group prior to the Revolution, there was, however, rarely an element of choice. Black slaves were imported into cities in all the colonies, often within a few months or years of their founding. A smaller number of free Blacks also chose urban residences. So the Afro-American population has been an integral part of the city growth of the nation from its beginnings.

To understand this Black urban experience before the Revolution, it is first necessary to describe the colonial city. If a population of three thousand is used as a benchmark, then there were only sixteen cities in 1775. Most of these—Boston, Marblehead, Salem, and Newburyport, Massachusetts; Portsmouth, New Hampshire; Newport and Providence, Rhode Island; Hartford and Norwich, Connecticut; Albany and New York City; and Philadelphia—were located in the middle colonies and New England. The only southern cities were Baltimore, Charleston, Savannah, and Norfolk, Virginia. All these cities depended on commerce, and many were sea or river ports. Due to plantation development, the growth of southern cities was retarded. Particularly in Virginia and Maryland, each large plantation was a commercial center, and large planters acted as merchants and middlemen for more modest farmers; thus towns and cities were slower to develop.

What was the eighteenth-century American city like? Economic life was strictly regulated by English legislation which decreed which industries might be developed and which were reserved for the mother country. Prices, the quality of merchandise, profits, and permission to sell certain goods were commonly regulated by government. Legislation also fixed penalties for idleness and assigned responsibility for the construction of public works and the staffing of the night watch. So we must understand Black life in colonial American cities within this less than free milieu. The freedoms of Blacks were restricted, but so, too, were the freedoms of the white population. And Blacks comprised just one element of what the upper strata of society would have defined as the lower members of the class spectrum. All cities had their "inferior" sorts: Blacks, Indians, indentured servants, common seamen, the demimonde. Those who taunted the British into committing the Boston Massacre came from this class; John Adams wrote that the colonial provocateurs were "a motly rabble of saucy boys, negroes and mulattoes, Irish teagues and outlandish jack tarrs." Disorder and lawlessness were a common and unresolved vexation to the more established classes in colonial cities, and attempts to curb the activities of Blacks must be set in a class context. Blacks experienced certain discriminations that no other group faced, but in many areas of life their experiences were common to other members of the urban lower classes.

Blacks were imported into New England, some to work in agriculture, but most to fill the general labor shortage in both town and countryside. Their numbers varied in inverse proportion to the supply of European labor available. Those who were settled in urban areas, both free persons and slaves, generally worked as domestics, unskilled laborers, or artisans. Proportionally more Blacks entered the artisan ranks than in middle colony towns, where there was a more steady supply of skilled German immigrants. Labor was often in short supply in three of New England's largest "industries"—rum distilleries, spermaceti works, and commercial shipping—and Blacks were to be found there in considerable numbers. New England was chronically short of seamen, and many free Blacks entered this occupation; for enterprising slaves, seafaring was an avenue to escape and eventual freedom.

Local authorities, and whites in general, looked with apprehension on the Black population within their towns and cities. Each New England colony had its slave code and other controls which applied to both free Blacks and slaves, but attempts at strict enforcement were not greatly effective. Blacks were rarely completely docile, and often refused to carrying identifying passes or ignored laws forbidding them to patronize or congregate in grog shops. Those who were most discontented struck back; arson was their most common weapon. Yet when grave difficulties arose with the Indians, controls over the Afro-American population were relaxed, for fear of a Black-Indian alliance. In extreme emergencies, free Blacks as well as slaves were drafted into the militia, and several persons of color were among the ranks of the minutemen at Lexington and Concord.

Daily life for both free Blacks and slaves was in many ways not different from that of other lower economic groups. Puritan-influenced New England attempted, with diminishing success, to structure society along patriarchal lines, linking every individual, including slaves, to a household. In church-dominated towns, there was considerable pressure to bring Blacks within the orbit of formal religion. But such attempts at "integrating" the Afro-American population into daily life ran counter to their desires for autonomy and a racial group existence. Blacks constructed a communal life out of funerals, special annual holidays, and informal gatherings to shop, eat, and drink. No separate churches or fraternal societies were established in New England cities until after the Revolution, but the germ was growing prior to that time. The most elaborate aspect of communal life was the yearly holiday in which Blacks were permitted to elect their own governors, judges, and sheriffs. Acting with the permission of the white authorities, these officers were permitted a limited jurisdiction over their fellows, including the imposition of mild punishments.

Free Blacks in New England cities enjoyed slightly more legal rights than those in other colonies. When convicted of crime, they received the same punishment suffered by whites. But this was about the limit of "equality." Like free Blacks elsewhere, they could not vote or serve on juries and were commonly segregated in both sanctuary and cemetery. Few free Black children attended school and fewer yet alongside whites. Slavery in New England, in both the cities and countryside, was milder than in other colonies, because the Black population was low: the economy could not absorb a large number of slaves. Consequently New England whites did not live in as much terror of a slave uprising simply because they did not have high Black population densities.

Life for Blacks in seaport cities of the middle colonies was often similar to that in New England. But where there existed an adequate supply of skilled foreign immigrants, as in Pennsylvania, opportunities for slaves or free Blacks to enter the artisan category were fewer. In most middle colony towns apart from the seaports a large majority of Blacks were domestic servants in homes of the wealthy or upwardly mobile members of the middle class. As in New England, most slaveholders owned only one or two bondsmen. In Philadelphia, colonial America's largest city, slaves were only imported in considerable numbers when the supply of immigrant indentured servants was cut off during wartime. And even then, there was no "industry" in the modern sense, since most manufacturing was carried out in family shops by individual craftsmen. So Black labor was not a significant element of the commercial process. New York was the second largest city, and being a seaport, offered opportunities for a floating pool of Black workers similar to New England port cities. But since New York performed even less "manufacturing" than New England or Philadelphia, there were few opportunities for the growth of a Black artisan class.

Day-to-day existence for the Black population in the middle colonies, particularly in smaller and inland cities, had its peculiar difficulties. Although spared the rigors of plantation slavery, Blacks found domestic work nonetheless harsh, with close proximity to whites, little time to oneself, and few opportunities for a varied social life. Usually comprising no more than 1 or 2 percent of the town's population, Blacks often found their numbers too small to provide mates for all who wished to marry. Stable marriage was difficult, for often husband and wife were owned by different slaveholders; if free, partners frequently found employment with two different employers. Even in Philadelphia, with a comparatively large Black population, males outnumbered females, which provided a further impediment to marriage. It is no wonder, then, that urban Black populations in this era were unable to reproduce themselves through natural increase.

Communal life in the middle colonies was similar to that in New England. Again, no all-Black churches or benevolent societies existed. Yet before we conclude that Blacks' social existence was pathetically meager, we should acknowledge that historians may yet find evidence of a richer group experience. In large cities, like New York, Philadelphia, and Boston, there were a handful of Black-owned groceries and taverns; such stores were likely to be a focus for the local community. And despite the absence of formal Black churches, we must assume a degree of religious communalism. We have records of urban Blacks gathering for the funeral of one of their fellows. It is possible that individuals seeking a comfortable and relevant worship experience held praise meetings, apart from the scrutiny of whites, similar to those beginning to be held on southern plantations. So we may yet learn of a richer group life in the cities of the New England and middle colonies.

Only two cities of considerable size and commercial importance—Charleston and Baltimore—developed in the southern colonies prior to the Revolution. Charleston serves as the clearest example of the possibilities for Black autonomy in a southern urban setting, although one must emphasize that this city's precise characteristics were not duplicated elsewhere.

Charleston was an important seaport and trade center, whose population growth was fueled by Blacks—mostly slaves—imported from the West Indies, by English from the mother country, by English from the West Indies who brought with them Caribbean slaveholding practices, and by French émigrés from both the homeland and the West Indies. White migrants from the West Indies brought with them relatively open attitudes toward racial intermixture, which resulted in the growth of a free mulatto class with its own institutions and identity separate from slaves. Another feature of Charleston sets it apart from cities of the northern colonies: by the late eighteenth century, the city's population was divided almost exactly between white and Black. In no northern city did the population ratio come close to this figure.

Economic opportunity, for both free Blacks and slaves, was considerably greater than in northern cities. In addition to unskilled labor and domestic service, a significant number of Blacks learned the artisan crafts. Many white artisans entering colonial South Carolina did not intend to practice their skills; instead, they wanted to emulate the rich whites, buy land and a slave or two, and attempt to become planters. So great was the reluctance of whites to practice skilled trades that by the mid-1700's the white artisan class had virtually disappeared from Charleston: by that time, also, Blacks—both slaves and free—were proficient in every craft, from fine goldsmithing to more mundane skills. Such trades provided avenues for some slaves to purchase their freedom by "hiring out." Through this arrangement a slave owner would permit a skilled slave to find his own employment with the only stipulation that a certain amount of the earnings be turned over to the master monthly. Anything earned beyond that amount was recognized as the property of the slave. An industrious bondsman could hope to save for the eventual purchase of himself and family members.

Social and communal life for Blacks in pre-Revolutionary Charleston was richer and more varied than in northern cities. The most common form centered on informal activities, particularly in the numerous back-alley grog shops which catered to both slaves and freemen. Greater opportunities for selecting a mate and marrying also existed. And the urban population was ever growing, with a continual infusion of runaways as well as slaves accompanying masters who had come to Charleston for the social season or to escape the malarial plantations. Free mulattoes, who tended to look down upon slaves and free persons of unmixed African ancestry, were by the late eighteenth century beginning to organize their own exclusive religious and social groups.

Control over the Black population in Charleston was never as rigorous as whites would have desired. South Carolina had an extremely severe slave code, but it was impossible to enforce regulations against parading, assembling after dark, or the selling of alcoholic beverages to slaves. No American city in colonial times had an efficient police force, and it proved impossible to curb nighttime activities of the large numbers of slaves and free Blacks. Uprisings or, more frequently, rumors of insurrection periodically stirred the white population, but Charlestonians found it tiresome to be on eternal guard. One should not imply from this that Blacks' lives were easy or without threat and anxiety, but neither a consistent will nor a mechanism existed whereby the Afro-American population could be effectively policed and subordinated.

Williamsburg, the capital of colonial Virginia, provides a contrast to the bustling commercial and artisan atmosphere of Charleston, although by strict definition Williamsburg was only a town, having a mere fourteen hundred permanent inhabitants in the mid-eighteenth century. This population was, like that of Charleston and other southern towns, almost evenly divided between Black and white, and nearly all persons of color were slaves. The town's economy depended on the House of Burgesses (the legislature), the College of William and Mary, and strictly local trade. Slaveholding was widespread among whites, with over 80 percent of households owning an average of four or five bondsmen. Most Blacks thus served in domestic occupations, although there was a small group of artisan slaves, sometimes apprenticed to free white craftsmen. But clearly slaves were not as economically important in Williamsburg as they were in Charleston.

The daily life of domestic servitude was no light burden, even though town life was on the whole less harsh than plantation existence, for it took an endless amount of drudgery to make an eighteenth-century household function smoothly. But there were social outlets to balance the tedium of daily labor. A population of seven hundred Blacks provided a sturdier base for community life than the much smaller numbers found in northern towns of comparable size. Williamsburg Blacks functioned as a well-knit community in hiding runaways. Large numbers of slaves were married to persons in other households, and this tended to create a network of extended "kin." Leisure time for slaves was in theory only guaranteed on Saturday nights, Sundays, and holidays, yet gatherings for drinking, singing, dancing, and socializing took place with less supervision than in plantation districts. Urban slaves enjoyed a greater independence of personal life by evading or defying laws forbidding the consumption of alcohol or unsupervised assemblies. We have no record of formal Black churches or schools, but it is reasonable to assume that some group life did center on educational and spiritual endeavors. And, as in Charleston, there was, on the whole, no great amount of white paranoia about slave revolts prior to the Revolution, and in any case, no strong police force to keep Blacks in total submission. Finally, we should make brief mention of New Orleans, not an "American" city until 1803. Under the rule of France, and briefly of Spain, Blacks were granted more formal legal rights than in Anglo-American cities where a much more rigid color line prevailed. Nor were social differences between mulattoes, free Blacks, and slaves as pronounced in English colonial cities as they were in New Orleans, although its Black social structure bears some resemblance to Charleston. But in terms of rights to purchase one's freedom, inherit a legacy, receive justice in the courts, and serve in the militia, the legal heritage of France created unique traditions that would characterize New Orleans throughout the slavery period and into freedom.

SLAVES AND SLAVE OWNERS
IN COLONIAL PHILADELPHIA
GARY B. NASH

Although historians have recognized the importance of slavery in the social and economic life of colonial America, they have associated the institution primarily with the plantation economy of the southern colonies. Textbooks in colonial history and Black history rarely mention urban slavery in the northern colonies or take only passing notice of the institution and conclude that the small number of slaves in northern cities served as domestic servants, presumably in the households of the upper class. The history of slavery in the colonial period is particularly obscure for Philadelphia, the largest city in British North America on the eve of the Revolution. In the extensive literature on William Penn's colony the inquiring student finds only the most impressionistic information regarding the number of slaves in the city, the pattern of slave ownership, the use of slaves, and the interplay of demand for Black and white bound labor. None of the historical accounts of Philadelphia published in the last century deals directly with slavery, thus leaving the impression that the institution was incidental to the development of Philadelphia as an urban center.

To some extent this gap in our knowledge can be explained by the traditional dependence of historians upon literary evidence. In the case of Philadelphia they have been unusually handicapped by the fact that

Reprinted with permission from *William and Mary Quarterly*, 3d. ser., 30 (April 1973), pp. 223–256. Footnotes and tables appearing in the original publication have been deleted in the present volume, and should be consulted for full documentation of the author's conclusions.

not a single official census was taken in the city during the colonial period. Although census data revealing the racial composition of the population are intermittently available for New York from 1698 to 1771 and for Boston from 1742 to 1770, historians of colonial Philadelphia have had to rely on the widely varying comments of residents and travelers to estimate the slave population. Thus, the opinion of Governor William Keith, who reported in 1722 that Pennsylvania had few slaves "except a few Household Servants in the City of Philadelphia," and the view of Andrew Barnaby, who recorded nearly forty years later that "there are very few Negroes or slaves" in Philadelphia, and the comment of Benjamin Franklin, who wrote in 1770, that in the northern cities slaves were used primarily as domestic servants and that in North America as a whole "perhaps, one family in a Hundred . . . has a slave in it," have taken on unusual weight in the historical record. To be sure, visitors to Philadelphia occasionally conveyed a different impression. For example, after visiting the city in 1750, Peter Kalm, the Swedish botanist, noted that in earlier decades slaves had been bought "by almost everyone who could afford it, the Quakers alone being an exception." Kalm added that more recently Quakers had overcome their scruples "and now . . . have as many negroes as other people." But Kalm's view seems to have been regarded as a minority report and is seldom cited by historians.

Despite the absence of census data, other kinds of evidence are available to indicate that slaveholding in Philadelphia was far more extensive than has generally been believed. It is known, for example, that in December 1684, just three years after the coming of the Quaker founders of the colony, a shipload of 150 African slaves arrived in Philadelphia. Transported by a Bristol mercantile firm, the slaves were eagerly purchased by Quaker settlers who were engaged in the difficult work of clearing trees and brush and erecting crude houses in the budding provincial capital. So great was the demand for the slaves, according to one prominent settler, that most of the specie brought to Philadelphia by incoming settlers was exhausted in purchasing the Africans. Thus at a time when the population of Philadelphia was probably about two thousand, 150 slaves became incorporated into the town's social structure. Although little evidence is available to indicate the extent of slave importation in the next few decades, a survey of inventories of estates from 1682 to 1705 reveals that about one in fifteen Philadelphia families owned slaves in this period.

It is unlikely that slaves entered the city at more than a trickle in the next few decades, at least in part because of the high import duties imposed after 1712. But the reduction of the import duty to £2 per head in 1729 and the lapse of any duty after 1731 seem to have triggered a significant increase in slave importations. Although most Quaker merchants withdrew from the trade in the 1730's, after a period of controversy within the Society of Friends regarding the morality of importing and trading slaves, merchants of other religious persuasions gladly accommodated the growing demand for slave labor. Some indication of this new importance of slavery can be inferred from the burial statistics which were recorded in Philadelphia in 1722, 1729, 1731–1732, and 1738–1744, and published annually beginning in 1747. Whereas only 26 Negroes died in Philadelphia in 1722, 97 were buried there in 1729, 102 in 1731, and 83 in the following year. These figures tend to confirm the observation of Ralph Sandiford, an early Quaker abolitionist, who wrote in 1730 that "we have *negroes* flocking in upon us since the duty on them is reduced to 40s *per* head for their importation." Indeed, the proportion of Black deaths in the annual death toll during the early 1730's was the highest in the city's history.

Following a period of relatively heavy imports in the early 1730's, the traffic in slaves seems to have slackened considerably. Correspondingly, the number of black deaths declined in the late 1730's and did not again reach the level of the period from 1729 to 1732 until after 1756. This leveling off of the slave trade at a time when the city was growing rapidly cannot be satisfactorily explained in economic terms since the high import duties of the earlier period had not been reinstituted. Instead, it must be attributed to a preference for German and Scotch-Irish redemptioners and indentured servants who flooded into Philadelphia between 1732 and 1754. Although these immigrants had been attracted to Pennsylvania in substantial numbers since 1716, their numbers increased dramatically beginning in 1732. The relative decline in Black deaths between 1732 and 1755 suggests that city dwellers with sufficient resources to command the labor of another person usually preferred German or Scotch-Irish indentured servants to Black slaves when the former were readily available, even though indentured labor was probably somewhat more expensive.

The beginning of the Seven Years' War in 1756 marked the onset of a decade in which slavery and slave trading reached their height in colonial Philadelphia. This can be explained largely by the sudden drying up of the supply of indentured German and Scotch-Irish laborers who had disembarked at Philadelphia in record numbers between 1749 and 1754. Historians have never made clear the reasons for this stoppage, although most have implied that the wartime disruption of transatlantic traffic put an end to the Palatine and Scotch-Irish emigration. The answer, however, originates on land, not at sea. Beginning in the fall of 1755, the English commanders in the colonies began recruiting indentured servants in order to bolster the strength of the British units, which were reeling under the attacks of the French and their Indian allies on the western frontier. About two thousand Pennsylvania servants had been recruited by the end of 1755 according to one estimate, and the problem was serious enough by early 1756 to warrant a strong message from the Assembly to the governor warning that "if the Possession of a bought Servant ... is ... rendered precarious ... the Purchase, and Of Course the Importation, of Servants will be discouraged, and the People driven to the Necessity of providing themselves with Negroe Slaves, as the Property in them and their Service seems at present more secure."

Rather than reversing the policy of luring servants into the British army while offering partial financial recompense to their owners, Parliament legitimized and extended the practice in a law which was carried to the colonies in July 1756 by Lord Loudoun, the new British commander-in-chief. By this time Benjamin Franklin was issuing firm warnings to the English governments and predicting what had already happened: the continuing enlistment of servants, he wrote, "will ... intirely destroy the Trade of bringing over Servants to the Colonies, either from the British Islands or Germany." As Franklin explained, "No Master for the future can afford to give such a Price for Servants as is sufficient to encourage the Merchant to import them" when the risk of losing a newly purchased servant to the British army remained so great. With little hope for a reversal of English policy, Pennsylvanians seeking bound labor turned to Black slaves. According to one of Philadelphia's largest merchants, writing in September 1756, "all importations of white Servants is ruined by enlisting them, and we must make more general use of Slaves." If those with capital to invest in human labor had heretofore preferred white indentured labor to Black slave labor, even at some economic disadvantage, by late 1756 their options had been narrowed and they turned eagerly, in the face of the rising cost and unpredictability of white labor, to African slaves.

The shift to Black slave labor is reflected both in the shipping records and in the annual bills of mortality in Philadelphia. Importation of slaves, which according to a recent study had averaged only about twenty a year in the 1740's and about thirty a year in the early 1750's, began to rise sharply. Although precise figures are not available, it appears that at least one hundred slaves entered Philadelphia in 1759. By 1762, probably the peak year of slave importations in the colony's history, as many as five hundred slaves may have arrived, many of them directly from Africa. In each of the following four years, between one and two hundred disembarked.

Corroborating evidence of this rapid expansion of slavery is provided by the burial statistics of Blacks during these years. Whereas burials had averaged fifty-one a year from 1738 to 1742, sixty-four a year from 1743 to 1748, and fifty-five a year from 1750 to 1755, they rose sharply to an average of ninety-one annually from 1756 to 1760, when unprecedented numbers of slaves were sold in the city, and remained steady at an average of eighty-seven a year in the next three five-year periods.

What makes this rapid growth of slavery in Philadelphia especially noteworthy is that it occurred at precisely the time the pre-Revolutionary abolitionist movement, centered in Philadelphia and led by John Woolman and Anthony Benezet, was reaching its climax. Attempting to end the slave trade through appeals to conscience at a time when white indentured labor was becoming unreliable and expensive, these ideologues found their pleas falling on ears rendered deaf by sudden changes in the economics of the labor market.

The rapid wartime growth of the slave trade ended as fast as it had begun. By the beginning of the 1760's, with the war subsiding and British recruiting sergeants no longer at work, the influx of German and Scotch-Irish redemptioners and servants recommenced. Scotch-Irish immigration, which throughout the colonial period flowed predominantly through Philadelphia, had begun an upward swing in 1760; within three years ships crowded with Palatine immigrants were also disgorging their passengers on the Philadelphia docks. Concurrently the slave trade tapered off. The import duties, reported annually to the Assembly by the customs officer at Philadelphia, indicate that from September 1764 to September 1768, when German and Scotch-Irish immigration had almost reached prewar levels, slave imports dropped to an annual average of sixty-six. Between 1768 and 1770 they declined to less than thirty per year, and by the end of the latter year the Pennsylvania slave trade had all but ceased. Given the choice once more between Black slaves and white indentured servants, Philadelphians and other Pennsylvanians chose the latter to satisfy their requirements for bound labor.

For the years from 1767 to 1775 the size and composition of the Black population in Philadelphia can be charted with unusual precision because abundant records with which the social historian can work have survived: transcripts of the tax assessors' reports for 1767, 1769, 1772, and 1774, an enumeration of taxable slaves in the city in 1773, and constables' returns for 1775. Unlike earlier tax lists, which indicate only the total ratable estates of the city's inhabitants, the assessors' reports for these years record each category of assessable wealth, including land, buildings, ground rents, slaves, servants, and livestock. In addition, the constables' returns of 1775 list all heads of household and include for each house the number—and in most cases the ages—of all tenants, hired and bound servants, slaves, and children. As specified by law, the tax assessors listed only slaves between twelve and fifty and servants between fifteen and fifty years of age as assessable property, so the totals obtained from these lists must be adjusted to account for slaves and servants outside of these age limits.

The tax assessors' reports of 1767 indicate a total of 814 slaves between the ages of twelve and fifty in the city of Philadelphia. If we include as a part of urban Philadelphia the district of Southwark, which lay along the Delaware River immediately south of the city and contained many of the shipyards, ropewalks, tanneries, sail lofts, and ship chandlers' offices associated with the maritime commerce of the city, the number of slaves is swelled to 905.

To this number we must add slaves who were under twelve or over fifty years of age. Unfortunately almost no data for determining the age structure of the slave population in Philadelphia are available for the years before 1775. It is virtually certain, moreover, that by 1775 the age distribution had changed markedly after a decade of declining importations. It is reasonable, however, to infer the age distribution of Philadelphia slaves from coeval census data for New York City slaves. In the enumerations of 1731 and 1737, 23.5 percent and 25.3 percent, respectively, of the slaves in New York City were under ten years of age. In the census reports of 1746, 1749, 1756, and 1771, the Black population was divided into those sixteen and over and those under sixteen. The under-sixteen segment was, respectively, 48.7, 43.7, 41.2, and 36.2 percent of the whole slave population. These figures indicate that the proportion of children was declining and that Negroes of twelve years or younger made up about 25 to 30 percent of the slave population of New York City in the decade before the Revolution. Census data for eight counties of New Jersey between 1726 and 1772 and for the entire province of New York between 1703 and 1771 show a fairly low range of variation in the age distribution of slaves and thus reinforce one's confidence in estimating that about 30 percent of the slaves in Philadelphia were too young to be included in the tax assessors' reports in 1767.

Slaves over fifty years of age are estimated to have composed 5 percent of the Philadelphia slave population in 1767. The Philadelphia constables' reports of 1775, which give the ages of most of the city's slaves, reveal that 7.6 percent of the slaves were over fifty. Because the age structure of the slave population probably advanced from 1767 to 1775 as a result of a low birth rate and a marked decrease in slave importations, this figure was probably nearer 5 percent for the former year. Comparable data from New York City shows that 6.7 percent of male slaves were over sixty in 1746, 3.7 percent in 1749, 6.0 percent in 1756, and 2.8 percent in 1771.

After adjusting the total of 905 taxable slaves to account for those of nontaxable ages, we can estimate that in 1767, at a point only a few years after what was probably the apogee of slaveholding in the colonial period, almost 1,400 slaves served their masters in Philadelphia. In a total population of about 16,000, slaves represented one-twelfth of the city's inhabitants.

As importations of Black slaves subsided following the reopening of the white indentured servant trade, the slave population in Philadelphia entered a period of substantial decline. Between 1767 and 1773 the number of slaves between twelve and fifty years old in Philadelphia decreased from 905 to 669 and the approximate total number of slaves from 1,392 to 945. The number of slaves dropped again, although slightly, in 1774 and then decreased sharply in the following year.

How is one to explain this precipitous decline of the slave population, which between 1767 and 1775 reduced the number of slaves in the city by more than half? Given the intensity of the abolitionist campaign during these years, one might suspect that the manumission of slaves was the major factor. Benjamin Rush's assertion in May 1773 that three-quarters of his fellow Philadelphians "cry out against slavery" seems to confirm such a view. But even among Quakers, the only vigorous opponents of slavery in Philadelphia, manumissions were rare until late in 1775, a year after the Yearly Meeting of the Society of Friends took a strong stand against slaveholding and began systematic visitations to Quaker slaveholders in order to encourage private manumissions. In fact, as the carefully kept Quaker records reveal, only eighteen slaves were manumitted in Philadelphia between 1766 and 1775, and of these fourteen belonged to "persons not in Membership with Friends."

The real explanation of the rapidly declining number of slaves was the inability of the slave population to reproduce itself in a period when slave importations had virtually ceased. This is made manifest by correlating the data from the annual mortality bills and the constables' reports of 1775. The mortality bills reveal that between 1767 and 1775, 679 Blacks, almost all of them slaves, were buried in the "strangers Burialground"—an average of about seventy-five per year. In an era when slave importations were inappreciable, one side effect of this heavy death toll was to alter the age structure of the slave population. Many female slaves passed beyond the age of fertility and were not replaced by younger slave women. This further depressed a fertility rate which even in periods of substantial importation was far below the white birth rate for two major reasons. First, the male slaves outnumbered female slaves in almost all places and times during the colonial period, and Philadelphia, so far as can be ascertained from the limited data, was no exception. Second, in a city where more than half of the slaveholders owned only a single adult slave, sexually mature male and female slaves infrequently lived together under the same roof, thus further reducing the incidence of conception.

The low fertility rate of slave women in the northern regions in general was noted by several eighteenth-century amateur demographers. Franklin, for example, remarked in 1751 that only by constant importation was the African population maintained. Edward Wigglesworth, professor of divinity at Harvard, ventured the same opinion in 1775, writing that "a large annual importation from Africa [was required] to keep the stock good." That these impressions of knowledgeable observers applied with special force to Philadelphia after slave importations dropped off in the late 1760's is evident from the age structure of slaves listed on the constables' reports of 1775. These lists give the ages of 89 percent of the city's slaves of whom only 10.7 percent were under ten years of age. Data for other areas indicate approximately the same age structure. From 1767 to 1775, when the slave population averaged about 1,000, 679 Blacks had been buried in Philadelphia and fewer than 100 Black children had been born and survived infancy. This excess of deaths over births can only be explained by an extremely low birth rate, a drastically high infant mortality rate, or a combination of the two.

While the slave labor force was contracting rapidly, the number of free Blacks in Philadelphia grew slowly. Free Blacks had lived in the city at least as early as 1717 when the Anglican church recorded the baptism of a free Black woman. Although it is extremely difficult to trace the growth of the free Black community during the next half century, some scattered evidence is available to throw a glimmer of light on these Philadelphians. Between 1748 and 1752 fourteen free Blacks, some adults and some children, were baptized in the Anglican church. And in 1751, the *Pennsylvania Gazette* printed the complaint of one Philadelphian who upbraided a number of free Blacks, who "have taken Houses, Rooms, or Cellars, for their Habitations," for creating disorders with "Servants, Slaves, and other idle and vagrant Persons." By 1768 eight free Black children were attending an Anglican school established ten years before for the education of Blacks, and in 1770 a Quaker school for Blacks had enrolled thirty-six children of free Blacks. Twenty-seven free Blacks are mentioned in the Anglican baptism records between 1756 and 1765, and in the following decade forty-one additional free Blacks were cited. From this scattered and incomplete evidence it seems likely that the free Black population was about 150 in 1770. Occasional manumissions in the early 1770's may have swelled the number of free Blacks to about 250 on the eve of the Revolution. These population estimates can be combined with the statistics compiled from the bills of mortality to approximate a crude death rate for 1767, when slavery was near its peak in Philadelphia. By calculating the slave population at 1,392 and adding 100 free Blacks, an estimated Black population of 1,492 is obtained. With Black burials averaging 102 annually in Philadelphia in the five-year period 1765 to 1769, this indicates a crude death rate of 68.4. Although this figure seems startlingly high, it is not out of range with the death rate of Negroes in pre-Revolutionary Boston where between 1742 and 1760 the crude mortality rate varied between 54 and 67. Moreover, there is good reason for the Black mortality rate in Philadelphia to have exceeded that of Boston: despite Benjamin Franklin's vigorous denials, Philadelphia seems to have been an unusually unhealthy island in the middle of the generally salubrious northeast coastal plain.

By examining the tax assessors' reports of 1767, it is also possible to draw a collective profile of slave-owning Philadelphians for that year. The assessors' reports disclose that of the 3,319 taxpayers in the city 521 (15.7 percent) owned slaves. Because taxpayers who owned only slaves under twelve or over fifty years of age do not appear on the assessors' returns as slave owners, this total must be increased somewhat. The constables' reports of 1775 show that almost 14 percent of the slave owners in that year owned only slaves whose ages fell outside the taxable limits. If this pattern applied in 1767, more than seventy slave owners would not be revealed by the assessors' returns and the total number of slave owners should be increased to about 590. A still more accurate measurement of how extensively slavery permeated the social structure can be made by keeping in mind that the number of taxpayers and the number of householders were by no means the same. Of the 3,319 taxpayers in 1767, 337 were assessed a poll tax, indicating that they were single freemen, usually living at the home of their parents or renting lodging in the house of another. Others—perhaps as many as 10 percent—were tenants. It is clear from the tax assessors' reports that very few tenants or persons assessed a poll tax owned slaves. By conservative estimate, then, the number of householders could not have numbered more than about 80 percent of the number of taxpayers. Calculating the number of households in Philadelphia at about 2,655 (80 percent of the total number of taxpayers) and the number of slave owners at about 590, we can estimate that slaves resided in the homes of more than one in every five families in Philadelphia in 1767.

To understand how many Philadelphians participated in the institution of slavery, one must also take into account the shifting composition of the slave-owning group in the city. Although only fragmentary evidence remains by which to trace the sale or transfer after death of slaves, some indication of the turnover in slave ownership can be inferred by comparing the tax assessors' reports of 1767 and 1769. On the 1769 list, 125 persons appear as slave owners who had not been assessed for slave property in 1767. Including these "new" owners, over 700 Philadelphia families, representing about one-quarter of the households in the city, were involved in slavekeeping in the closing years of the 1760's. However moderate the treatment of slaves and whatever the quasi-familial status of some bondsmen and women, the master-slave relationship and the ownership of other human beings as chattel property were extensively woven into the fabric of city life. If John Woolman was correct in believing that slaveholding, even by the kindliest of masters, did "yet deprave the mind in like manner and with as great certainty as prevailing cold congeals water," and that the absolute authority exercised by the master over his slave established "ideas of things and modes of conduct" that inexorably molded the attitudes of children, neighbors, and friends of slaveholders, then Philadelphia, at least for a brief period, was indeed deeply involved in the "peculiar institution."

In sharp contrast to the towns of the colonial South, most slave owners in Philadelphia held only one or two adult slaves. Of the 521 slave owners appearing on the 1767 tax list, 57 percent owned only a single slave between twelve and fifty years of age and another 26 percent owned but two. If slaves under twelve and over fifty years of age were included, these figures would be somewhat, but probably not significantly, changed. In all likelihood, this pattern of ownership reflects the limited possibilities for employing slaves in gang labor in a city where most of the productive labor, outside of ship building and a few enterprises such as bakeries, brickyards, and ropewalks, was still carried out in the small shop of the individual artisan.

That slave owning in Pennsylvania was predominantly an urban phenomenon is made apparent by comparing the number of slaves in the city with figures for outlying rural areas. In Chester and Lancaster counties, the most densely populated and agriculturally productive areas in the colony, slaves numbered only 289 and 106 respectively on the assessors' lists of 1759. Only 4.2 percent of the taxpayers in Chester County and 1.2 percent in Lancaster County owned slaves in that year. Although it might be expected that the large importations of the early 1760's would have increased the incidence of slaveholding somewhat in these areas, this did not in fact happen. By 1773-1774 the number of slaves reported by the tax assessors in Chester and Lancaster counties had dropped to 237 and 52 respectively, while the number of taxable white inhabitants was increasing sharply between 1760 and 1770—from 4,761 to 5,484 in Chester County and from 5,635 to 6,606 in Lancaster County.

Even in Philadelphia County, immediately to the north and west of the city, slave owning never approached the level obtained in the city. In 1767 only 206 of 5,235 taxpayers (3.9 percent) owned a total of 331 taxable slaves. Thus the incidence of slaveholding in the city was about four times that of the surrounding countryside. No tax lists for Philadelphia County are extant before 1767, making it impossible to determine whether slaveholding was increasing or decreasing at this time. But it appears that slaveholding was near its peak in 1767; by 1772 the number of slaves had dropped from approximately 502 to 457 and two years later had declined to 410.

The tax assessors' lists also reveal that slaves composed more than three-quarters of the unfree labor in the city in 1767 and that slaveholders outnumbered servant holders more than two to one. The five-year period between 1755 and 1760, when almost no indentured servants entered the colony and most of those already there completed their terms of servitude, serves to explain this emphasis on Black labor. That 104 ships arrived in Philadelphia with Scotch-Irish and German immigrants in the six intervening years before the tax list of 1767 was drawn suggests that for at least a brief period in the early 1760's slaves may have represented as much as 85 to 90 percent of the city's bound laborers. After 1767, however, with slave importations reduced to a trickle and white indentured servants crowding into the city, the composition of the unfree labor force underwent equally sudden changes, reverting to what was probably the pre-1755 pattern. By 1775, white servants, who less than a decade before had composed less than one-quarter of the unfree labor force, constituted 56 percent of Philadelphia's bound workers.

A different pattern prevailed in the rural areas of Philadelphia County. Whereas white indentured servants made up only 22 percent of the unfree labor force in 1767 in the city, they constituted almost half of the bound laborers in the surrounding county. Seven years later this pattern had changed only slightly in Philadelphia County, where the incidence of both servant holding and slaveholding was always much lower than in the city.

What also claims our attention is the fact that at a time when the population of the city was growing rapidly the demand for bound labor, either Black or white, was shrinking. Between 1767 and 1775, when urban Philadelphia grew from approximately 16,000 to 20,000, the number of servants and slaves declined from 1,737 to 1,542. Whether this was a long-range trend reflecting changes in the organization of work and the growing profitability of wage versus bound labor is impossible to determine without examining a series of postwar assessors' reports. But it is possible that on the eve of the Revolution a plentiful supply of free wage laborers, created by rural overpopulation in the hinterland, decreased the demand for bound labor in Philadelphia. Or the sources of indentured labor in Germany and Ireland may have been drying up. Whatever the reasons, those with money to invest in human labor were turning more and more in the last third of the eighteenth century from the bound to the wage laborer.

By analyzing the 1767 tax list, it is also possible to establish the correlation between economic status, as measured by assessable wealth, and slave ownership. As might be expected, slave owners were concentrated in the upper wealth bracket. Only 5 percent of Philadelphia's 521 slave owners in 1767 came from the bottom half of the white wealth scale, and these 26 individuals owned only 28 of the 905 taxable slaves in the city. Almost two-thirds of the slave owners had sufficient wealth to place them in the top quarter of the property owners and one-third of them, holding 44 percent of the city's slaves, came from the wealthiest tenth of the population. This unsurprising correlation between wealth and slave ownership parallels the Boston pattern of 1771.

Slave owners in the city were distributed through the top half of the social scale to a far greater degree than in the rural areas. Whereas the top 10 percent of the taxpayers in Philadelphia owned 44 percent of the city's slaves, the upper tenth in Philadelphia County owned 77 percent of the slaves, in Chester County 58 percent, and in Lancaster County 60 percent. This tendency for slaveholding to be heavily concentrated in the upper reaches of rural society but to be diffused through the middle strata of urban society is probably best explained by the greater prosperity enjoyed by those at the middling levels of city life. In Philadelphia County, for example, the top tenth of the wealth holders included all those with estates of £24 or more. In the city, by contrast, a taxpayer needed at least £60 of taxable property to count himself or herself in the wealthiest tenth of the community. Put differently, more people in the city than in the county had amassed sufficient wealth to afford a slave, and it seems likely that this contributed to the much higher incidence of slave holding and servant holding in Philadelphia than in outlying areas.

The correlation between wealth and slave ownership can be misleading, however. At first glance it seems to indicate that slaveholding was restricted to the elite in Philadelphia and thus, like the building of stately townhouses and the flourishing of the arts in the third quarter of the eighteenth century, was a part of cultivating the genteel life. This view is reinforced by scanning the list of slaveholders, which is studded with names of prominent pre-Revolutionary Philadelphians—merchants, professionals, proprietary officeholders, and political magnates such as John Baynton, Thomas Bond, Thomas Cadwalader, Benjamin Chew, John Dickinson, Benjamin Franklin, Joseph Galloway, Thomas Lawrence, Samuel McCall, Samuel Mifflin, Robert Morris, Edward Pennington, Edmund Physick, Edward Shippen, Joseph Shippen, Robert Waln, Thomas Wharton, and Thomas Willing. But an analysis of the occupations of slave owners reveals that slaves were owned by a wide range of artisans and even by men such as mariners and carters who commanded little leverage in the social and political life of the city and could hardly be considered proto-aristocrats.

About one-third of the taxable slaves in the city in 1767 was owned by merchants and shopkeepers. Many of these slaves were doubtless household servants, while others were being held for sale by merchants engaged in the slave trade or were contracted out for day labor. Ninety-five slaves (10.5 percent) were held by thirty-nine "professional" men— sixteen doctors, ten lawyers, nine officeholders, two conveyancers, a clergyman, and a teacher. Innkeepers or tavernholders owned thirty-four slaves, and widows and "gentlemen" accounted for thirty-one more.

Nearly half of the city's slaves are included in these categories. But the other half were owned by artisans, men associated with maritime enterprise, or, in a few cases, by laborers. Almost every occupational category in the city included at least one slaveholder, and some, such as bakers, metalworkers, woodworkers, and ropemakers, were heavily represented.

That slave labor was used extensively by artisans and craftsmen is also revealed by the small number of Philadelphians who held four or more slaves of assessable age—men, in other words, who were employing labor on a fairly large scale by pre-Revolutionary standards. Only 32 of 521 slaveholders in Philadelphia were included in this group. Of these, eight were merchants, including such prominent figures of Philadelphia society as William Allen, perhaps the wealthiest man in Philadelphia, Isaac Coxe, Samuel Howell, John Hughes, later appointed stamp distributor, Archibald McCall, Samuel McCall, Samuel Mifflin, and Thomas Willing. Six lawyers, including John Dickinson (whose eleven slaves made him the second largest slaveholder in the city), John

Ross, and John Lawrence were also among this group, as were two proprietary officials, James Tilghman and Benjamin Chew. But among the other large slaveholders were five bakers, three ropemakers, a sailmaker, a goldsmith, and a ferryman whose slaves apparently operated the ferries that plied the Delaware River between Philadelphia and Burlington, New Jersey. The largest slave owner in Philadelphia was John Phillips, whose thirteen slaves manned the city's largest ropewalk in Southwark.

Perhaps most surprising is the large number of ship captains and mariners who owned slaves. Almost 10 percent of the slave owners were men whose work took them to sea. It is possible that these Philadelphians purchased female slaves to assist their wives with household tasks while they were away. But given the racial attitudes of colonial Americans and the general apprehension of slaves that existed in all urban centers, it is more likely that most of these seagoing Philadelphians purchased slaves to work on board ship. The substantial number of mariners and ship captains who owned slaves suggests that the American merchant marine may have been far more heavily manned by Black labor than has been previously recognized. It is especially likely that slaves owned by mariners were Black sailors. The constables' reports reveal that all but two of the thirty-two mariners owning slaves were married, but twenty-three of them owned no house, renting their quarters from others. Nine of them had no taxable assets other than their slaves, suggesting that these mariners, who were generally located in the lower reaches of society, had used the small amount of capital they possessed to purchase a slave and thus increase their share of the profits from Atlantic voyages.

Mariners were not alone in preferring slave labor to real estate as a field for investment. Of the 521 slave owners, only 190 (36.4 percent) owned a house or property in Philadelphia. The other 331 rented their dwellings, preferring to put excess capital into the acquisition of a slave or two rather than purchasing or building a house. Of course both the incidence of slave ownership and home ownership increased with the level of wealth in Philadelphia so that many men in the top echelon owned both real and human property. But for a significant number of middle-class Philadelphians with limited capital to invest, acquisition of slaves took precedence over the purchase of a house. Indeed, for one-eighth of the slaveholders their human property represented their only taxable assets. Typical of these Philadelphians were men and women like Charles Jenkins, a mariner living in Southwark; John Dowers, a sailmaker in Mulberry Ward; William Benning, a staymaker in Walnut Ward; and Widow Sinclear who kept a tavern in Walnut Ward. Thus a great many of Philadelphia's slave owners appear to have been small entrepreneurs who lacked the assets to purchase or maintain a slave merely for the social prestige it would confer. Instead, most of these city dwellers seem to have purchased slaves, particularly after the white indentured labor supply became uncertain, as a means of carrying on their crafts and small-scale industries and thereby improving their fortunes.

Correlations between slave ownership and religious affiliation are difficult to establish because church membership records are incomplete for the pre-Revolutionary period. But the Society of Friends was assiduous in record keeping, and therefore it is possible to identify almost all of the Quaker slaveholders and determine whether the incidence of slaveholding among Friends differed from that of non-Friends. This is of special significance because for Quakers buying, selling, or even owning a slave involved a direct conflict of economic interest and ideology. Whereas an Anglican, Presbyterian, German Lutheran, Methodist, or member of any other religious group in Philadelphia could participate in the institution of slavery secure in the knowledge that it was justified both by his church and by the prevailing philosophies of the Western world, Quakers could not. Since the 1690's individual Quakers had been developing piecemeal the argument that slave owning was sinful and only by dissociating themselves from it could they cleanse themselves of impurities. Individual arguments of this kind were followed by official action. Periodically after 1730 the Philadelphia Yearly Meeting advised its members not to buy or sell slaves. More importantly, prodded by the tireless work of John Woolman, the Yearly Meeting agreed in 1758 to exclude Friends who bought or sold slaves from meetings for business and to refuse their contributions as tainted money. Although it would not institute a policy of disownment, as Woolman urged, the Yearly Meeting appointed a committee which, with the assistance of Friends appointed by the various Quarterly Meetings, was to visit all slaveholders and convey the message that slave ownership, although not yet cause for disownment, was no longer consistent with the Quaker view of just relations among the brotherhood of man. Woolman himself took up the task of making independent visits to dozens of Philadelphia slave owners, asking them to look into their hearts to ascertain whether their ownership of slaves did not reveal an immoral lust for gain. These visitations, together with the official pronouncements of the Yearly and Quarterly Meetings, involved every Quaker slaveholder by the late 1750's in a situation where economic interest and ideology were in direct conflict. Increasing the tension was the fact that the uncertainties and rising price of white bound labor, owing to the recruitment of indentured servants by the British army beginning in late 1755, created new inducements for the purchase of Black labor at the very time that the Quaker leaders were taking fresh steps to end the involvement of Friends in the institution of slavery.

The best method of estimating the size of the Quaker segment of the entire Philadelphia population, in order to lay a basis for comparing the ratio of Quakers to non-Quakers on the list of slave owners in 1767, is to establish the number of Quaker and non-Quaker deaths during this era. On the annual bills of mortality, Quaker burials represented between 12.4 and 13.9 percent of the total number of white burials in the city for every five-year period from 1755 to 1774; for the period as a whole Quaker burials represented 12.8 percent of the same total. In the list of slave owners in 1767, it is possible to identify 88 members of the Society of Friends, or 16.9 percent of the total of 521. Although the burial statistics indicate only the approximate size of the Quaker community, it seems safe to conclude that Friends were somewhat over-represented among Philadelphia slaveholders in proportion to their numbers. Confirmation of this extensive involvement by Friends in slavekeeping can be found in Quaker documents themselves. To be sure, a prominent Philadelphia Quaker, James Pemberton, wrote in 1762 that the "In[i]quetous [slave] traffic hevy of late [has] lamentably Increas'd here, tho' the members of the Society Appear entirely clear of being Concernd in the Importation and there are few Instances of any purchase of them." But only three months earlier the Philadelphia Yearly Meeting had regretfully noted an "increase of Slaves among the members of our religious Society" in its report to the London Yearly Meeting. And among the slave owners identified in the 1769 assessors' reports are the names of at least seven Quakers who had not owned slaves two years before. The evidence is substantial, then, that when faced with a direct choice between forgoing the human labor they needed or ignoring the principles enunciated by their leaders and officially sanctioned by the Society through its Quarterly and Yearly Meetings, the rank and file of Philadelphia Friends chose the latter course. More than twenty years of abolitionist campaigning by men such as Woolman and Benezet, and the increasing commitment of the Society of Friends to ending slavery, culminating in the decisions of 1758, failed to stem the influx of slave labor into Philadelphia, to bring about more than a handful of manumissions, or even to prevent an increase in slave ownership among Quakers. Not until about 1764, by which time white bound labor had become as available as before the war, did Quakers stop buying slaves; and not until the eve of the American

Revolution was the ideological commitment of the Quaker leadership able to prevail over the membership at large in the matter of manumission.

The religious affiliations of non-Quakers cannot be readily identified, given the fragmentary state of church records for several groups such as the Baptists, Roman Catholics, and Swedith Lutherans. But an analysis of surnames in the list of 521 slaveholders indicates that at least one group eschewed slaveholding to a remarkable degree. This was the German element in Philadelphia, composed of German Lutherans and German Calvinists. German Lutherans ranked just behind the Anglicans as the largest religious group in the city and, combined with German Calvinists, accounted for 23 percent of the burials in Philadelphia between 1765 and 1769, a five-year period bracketing the tax assessment of 1767. Although they contributed virtually nothing to the antislavery literature of the period, they seem to have had a strong aversion to slaveholding. Only 17 of the 521 (3.3 percent) slave owners can be identified as Germans—an incidence of slaveholding that clearly distinguishes them from all other ethnic and religious groups in the city. This abstinence from slaveholding can only partly be explained in economic terms, for while it is true that the Philadelphia Germans were concentrated in the lower half of the wealth structure, thus putting the ownership of a slave beyond the means of many, a sizable number of Germans enjoyed a modest affluence. Perhaps of equal importance was the aversion to slaveholding which the immigrants from the Palatinate expressed beginning with the Germantown petition of 1688 against slavery and continuing through Christopher Sauer, the German printer in Philadelphia who almost always refused to accept advertisements for runaway slaves or slave sales in his German-language newspaper at a time when Benjamin Franklin had no compunction about printing them in the *Pennsylvania Gazette*. The Philadelphia Germans had no reservations about purchasing indentured servants, most of whom were their countrymen, but they drew the line there and only rarely ventured to purchase African slaves.

On the eve of the American Revolution, the slave population was dwindling as a result of a small number of private acts of manumission and, more importantly, because of the virtual cessation of the slave trade and through natural decrease. As the Second Continental Congress convened in Philadelphia, slavery was moving slowly into its twilight period in the largest city in British North America. But the long history of slavery in the city and the wholesale substitution of Black for white bound labor in the late 1750's and early 1760's demonstrate that even in the center of colonial Quakerism the appeals of antislavery ideologues went largely unheeded whenever they interfered with the demand for bound labor. In an era of economic expansion Philadelphians, including Quakers, avidly sought slave labor when their manpower requirements could not be otherwise met, and not until white indentured laborers became available in sufficient number to supply the needs of the city did the abolitionist appeals produce more than a few dozen manumissions.

3

BLACKS
IN ANTEBELLUM CITIES

Southern cities in the first half of the nineteenth century differed widely from one another. Some, like Charleston and New Orleans, were urban centers of longevity, with complex social structures incorporating Blacks, mulattoes, and whites of varying status. They were, in addition, truly cosmopolitan cities, rich in culture and tradition. Other cities were of recent origin, having just emerged from towns or crossroads market-places to become important centers of local commerce or, like Baton Rouge, government. St. Louis, lying on the frontier, was a sometimes raw, rapidly growing city which nonetheless had a history going back to French domination of the Mississippi Valley. All the region's cities were changing over time, some growing, others declining as the general population moved southwestward from the old Upper South into the newly settled Black Belt and trans-Mississippi territories in the last four decades of the slavery period.

The Black presence in the cities was an essential one, even as the white population viewed the Afro-Americans in their midst with ambivalence. Without the presence of Black artisans, both slave and free, the commercial and industrial prosperity of many urban centers would have vanished. In some places Black artisans competed with, and drove out, white skilled craftsmen, although in growing smaller cities, like Baton Rouge, there was more than enough work to go around and few if any labor conflicts arose. The practice of hiring out continued to be widespread, although whites increasingly saw this arrangement as subverting the efficient control of slaves. Southern cities also depended upon Black domestic workers for the daily tasks of household management and service, as well as for visible demonstrations of whites' social status and wealth. Ownership of slaves was fairly widespread, more common than in the rural areas, although the average urban slaveholding was usually five or less per household.

Industrial slavery was prominent in several southern cities. In Charleston, the municipality owned slaves and employed them in construction, refuse collection, and street repairs. Some cities staffed their fire departments with slaves. Black labor, both slave and free, was common on the docks of both ocean and river ports. In Richmond, the Tredegar Iron Works, one of the country's largest foundaries, owned dozens of slaves who lived in barracks and performed, at considerable profit to the owners, nearly all the tasks done by free white men elsewhere. In other cities slave labor was used extensively in ropewalks, cotton presses, and tobacco factories. Altogether about 5 percent of the South's slaves worked in nonagricultural and nondomestic occupations.

A major problem confronting all antebellum southern cities was social and police control of the Black population. Where formal segregation made no sense in the enforced intimacy of the plantation, some method of structuring race relations seemed both rational and desirable in urban areas where many owners, consciously or otherwise, abdicated firm day-to-day control over their bondsmen. As hiring out increasingly permitted a slave to find his own lodging away from his master, apprehensive whites began to demand that more strict municipal control be imposed to compensate for the eroded supervision by masters. But municipal regulation, except in periods of crisis, was commonly lax. No American city was efficiently policed, since most relied not on a trained police force but instead on a revolving patrol or night watch. Consequently, imposing controls on a Black population determined to achieve an autonomous group life proved impossible to achieve consistently. Whites suspected that unsupervised gatherings of slaves and free Blacks in taverns and groceries led to escapes and the exchange of stolen property. Other worries centered around religious gatherings where, it was suspected, revolts might be hatched. An equal worry were the innumerable interracial contacts in the city. Historians have perhaps placed too much attention on interracial sexual relations, but this is because contemporary whites were so vocal in denouncing such associations while continuing to practice them. But the issue was beyond regulation because segments of the white population—upperstatus males seeking concubines or mistresses, middle-class persons earning profit in selling spirits, and lower-class individuals of both sexes desiring the company of fellow gamblers and imbibers—were determined to ignore municipal fiat.

Group life for the Black population of several cities was rich and varied simply because of the large number of persons of color, whether slave or free, gathered into a small geographic area. Where the city's history went back several generations, there was likely to be a complex Black social-class structure. In Charleston and French-influenced cities like New Orleans, Mobile, and Natchez, there was a mulatto aristocracy based more on ancestry and color than on occupation and wealth. Not only did this add diversity to the community, it produced class differences in terms of allegiance to established (white) society. Members of the colored upper crust of Charleston believed they were contributing to order, stability, and progress when they exposed a slave revolt being plotted. Obviously, considerable social distance separated the lives and status of such persons and the majority of urban Blacks still in slavery.

The opportunities for both personal and group autonomy were far greater in southern cities than in the plantation areas. Gaining one's freedom through self-purchase, if one were allowed to hire one's time, was an option for the most skilled craftsmen. Escaped slaves slipped into the anonymity of urban life to forge new identities and pass for free. The possibilities for mutual action and cooperation among slaves or between slaves and free Blacks were far greater than in the rural areas. If one had an inclination toward an entrepreneurial career, opportunities presented themselves to artisans catering to the white community's needs and to shopkeepers and tavern proprietors serving members of their own race. And only in the cities of the South, not in the rural areas, could formal Black churches and literary and fraternal societies flourish. These provided fertile ground for community leadership and social-class differentiation.

Despite these opportunities uniquely present in southern cities before the Civil War, restrictions circumscribed many areas of life. Legislation concentrated on the duties and obligations, not the privileges of free Blacks, and many provisions of the slave codes applied to them. But enforcement of slave codes was more difficult in the cities, and even punishment by individual masters tended to be more moderate as white peer pressure curbed cruel or sadistic chastisement. Supervision could be rigid and punishment swift in times of rumored or actual slave insurrection, but in periods of outward calm the white population neglected day-to-day vigilance. This only contributed, however, to the marginality of free Blacks. Viewed by whites as inveterate saboteurs of the smooth functioning of the slave system, free Blacks strove either for identity with urban slaves or, in the case of the more prosperous and upwardly mobile, social distance between themselves and their brothers in bondage.

Blacks in the cities of the North, in the first half of the nineteenth century, did not suffer slavery as did their kinsmen in the South: slavery was abolished throughout the North soon after 1800. But urban life nonetheless was structured by discrimination, unequal competition, and a lack of political rights. Two generalizations are useful here. First, the poverty of Blacks was similar to that of recent immigrants from Europe. Both groups found themselves at the bottom of the social, economic, and political ladder. But one key difference separated them: the immigrant could lose his accent, put aside his Old World folkways, and become a white American and enjoy a fair chance of achieving upward mobility. For Blacks, however, meaningful mobility was stymied by the badge of skin color. Second, this handicapped position of Blacks in northern cities deteriorated markedly, particularly after 1830. Deterioration can be measured in increased racial violence against Blacks, population declines in several cities, disfranchisement where once the vote had been exercised, increased residential segregation, mounting stresses on the family, and growing pressure from foreign immigrants willing to compete for low-paying unskilled jobs.

Economic hardships had a direct impact on the Black family. Although, as today, a majority of urban Black households in northern cities were two-parent nuclear units, it was much more likely that female-headed families would be found among the poor. This reflected the lack of decent economic opportunities for unskilled Black males. It was often easier for women to find steady, full-time employment, even though it was commonly in low-paying domestic service. The result of this was an unbalanced sex ratio in most cities, with a surplus of females. Thus, for young Black males the difficulty in finding long-term employment made the likelihood of establishing stable marriages less promising. Most males worked in either unskilled or semiskilled employments. As the century progressed, the ranks of Black skilled artisans declined; skilled and semiskilled immigrants increasingly pushed Blacks out of craft positions. And in most cities Black workers were almost totally barred from factory employment. Black business provided no more cause for rejoicing, for only a tiny minority made comfortable livings. Successful entrepreneurs catered primarily to well-to-do whites, but this patronage was not founded on any secure allegiance and, in the case of caterers and barbers, could be whittled away easily. Most businessmen eked out a "mom-and-pop" existence in tiny shops providing occasional services and retail goods to the impoverished Black population. And rare was the Black professional—physician, lawyer, teacher—who could establish a comfortable and stable middle-class income and life-style. In short, as northern cities grew in size, expanded their occupational structure, became more diversified economically, and began to industrialize, few of the new opportunities trickled down to the Black population.

To focus only on the economic decline of northern Blacks ignores creative efforts to build a viable community and to deal with important issues of civil rights and southern slavery. Blacks in a number of cities greatly expanded their churches, founded schools, and established a wide variety of voluntary associations like literary, temperance, abolition, and mutual-aid societies, militia companies, and masonic and other fraternal organizations. All these provided experience in leadership, autonomy in decision making, the opportunity for recreation, entertainment, and social interchange, as well as insurance against an uncertain future. Yet this communal development excited the envy and suspicion of whites. During the 1830's an alarming number of antiabolition riots occurred in major cities like Cincinnati, Boston, New York, and Philadelphia, often with the approval of influential whites. Clearly many northern whites dreaded the possibility of nationwide freedom for the Black population, fearing that emancipation would cause hundreds of thousands of ex-slaves to flood North. These apprehensions were only one aspect of northern racist thought, which was based on assumptions of the innate biological inferiority and depravity of Blacks. To "protect" society against this alleged menace, northern states by the early 1800's had passed "Black Codes" designed to drastically limit the legal and social rights of Blacks and, if possible, so discourage them that they would leave for other cities, states, or even Africa. Blacks in many cities and states of the North organized politically to put pressure on white legislators to abolish the Black Codes, but only limited success was gained. In New England alone could Blacks vote without legal restriction by the time of the Civil War, so effective political leverage could rarely be mobilized. But this did not discourage northern Black militancy. From the 1830's onward, conventions met to discuss discrimination and chart strategies both for political change and internal self-development. Urban Blacks were prominent in these meetings. That they were unable to bring about fundamental change says less about the strength of Black activism and more about deeply entrenched racism in the North.

THE TRADITIONS OF THE FREE NEGRO IN CHARLESTON, SOUTH CAROLINA

E. HORACE FITCHETT

The free Negro in the slave system was an anomaly. The system was designed for free white men and Negro slaves. In a large measure the position of the emancipated Negro, prior to the Emancipation Proclamation, was comparable to that of the slave. Some of them preferred slavery to the type of freedom which they received. They were by law deprived of education, of suffrage, and of freedom of movement; they could not testify in court against a white man, and from time to time they were prohibited from assembling in groups of more than seven without the presence of a white man. However, before the slave structure was disrupted by the Civil War there were approximately one half of a million people of this class in the United States. In a few communities, particularly along the seacoast, they developed into a respectable, economically independent, class-conscious group. This is notable in the case of Charleston, South Carolina.

In this discussion I shall answer briefly the following questions: 1. How did this group arise? 2. What was its economic position and how was it attained? 3. What relations did this class of people sustain with out-group members and in its own group? 4. Were there any evidences of deviations from the approved patterns of behavior? If so, what form did they take? 5. What was the nature of the process of accommodation and social adjustment to the social system?

When the first census was taken in 1790 there were 8,089 white persons, 7,684 slaves, and 586 free Negroes in Charleston, South Carolina. Hence, the latter group constituted 3.58 percent of the total population. Many of the members of this group had no memory of a slave background or tradition. This was particularly true of the mixed

Reprinted with permission from the *Journal of Negro History,* 25 (April 1940), pp. 139–152. Footnotes appearing in the original publication have been deleted in the present volume, and should be consulted for full documentation of the author's conclusions.

bloods. Dr. Reuter advances the generalization that: "There seems to be no historical exception to the rule that when peoples come into contact and occupy the same area there is a mixture of blood that results, ultimately, in the establishment of a new modified ethnic type." This condition is no less true of Charleston than of other areas. Documentary evidence may be presented to support this generalization. In 1720 one slave master, James Gilbertson, a planter, made the following provisions in his will for a mulatto woman and her children:

My will is that my mulatto woman Ruth shall be free immediately after my Decease, & also my will is that her three female children Betty, Molly, and Keatty shall be free at the age of one and Twenty years, my will is also that Ruth have the feather bed W:ch the Indians did Cutt up, also a pot and her maintenance upon my plantation during her natural life.

In 1834, a prominent Charlestonian, a native of France, acknowledged in his will that the children of his housekeeper and slave were his off-spring, and his executors were instructed to provide for the mother and her children out of the estate. He states:

I do hereby recognize and declare that the issue of my slave and house-keeper, Celestine, are my children and I will order and direct that my executors herein named, or such person or persons that may qualify on this will, shall and do, as soon after my death as may be convenient, send the said woman Celestine and all her said issue my children, out of this State to some other State, territory or country, where they can severally be made free and their liberty secured to them respectively; and I will, order and direct that said executors or such person or persons that may qualify and act on this will shall defray the expense of trans-portation or conveyance of the said Celestine and her issue to said State, territory or country as expressed from the funds of my estate.

In 1826 one of the wealthiest and most influential citizens of Charles-ton made the following stipulation in his will for his mulatto man:

In consideration of the good conduct and faithful valuable service of my mulatto man Toney by Trade a millwright I have for some years past given him to himself one half of his time say from the middle of May to the middle of November every year. It is my will and desire and I do direct that the same indulgence be given to him for six years from the time of my death during which time he may instruct other servants in his Profession to supply his place and at the expiration of six years from the time of my death I will and direct that his whole time be given up to him ... after the expiration of six years he may be emancipated and set free or allowed to depart from this State as [he] may ... think proper.

These wills are typical of many of those which I examined. They not only provided for the freedom of a slave but also for his economic security. In a very real sense they imply that these persons were not slaves. They were in some instances recognized as the offspring of the upper-caste member; they were allowed freedom of action and movement; and they were accorded special ·privileges. Thus they were not treated as slaves nor did they conceive of themselves as slaves. Indeed, in some of the wills the testator indicated that the servant should not be considered a slave. Such was the desire expressed in the will of Mrs. Bonneau in 1807. Moreover, some of these persons obtained their freedom so early in the history of the country that the conditions of slave status could easily have been lost to their descendants. Their emancipation was indeed coeval with that of many of the white servant class. In the *South Carolina Gazette* for January, 1738, the following advertisement was made for a white servant girl:

Runaway the 28th of December last, a white woman servant, about 16 years of age, named Anne Brown, born in London and can talk a little French, belonging to Edw. Townsend of Savannah, Georgia. Whoever brings the said Servant to Charleston shall have £5 in currency reward.

There were also cases in which free Negroes entered Charleston from other states. Such was the case of Richard Holloway, whose citizenship papers were dated January 21, 1794. He is designated in this document as a seaman, a native of Essex County, Maryland, and a mulatto about twenty years of age.

In general it is fair to say that the free Negro arose out of: 1. Children born of free colored parents; 2. Mulatto children born of free colored mothers; 3. Children of free Negro and mixed Indian parentage; 4. Manumitted slaves.

In the latter part of the eighteenth and during the first part of the nineteenth centuries there emerged in Charleston a relatively economically independent group of free Negroes. They were primarily the artisans of the system. Records show, moreover, that they engaged in business transactions which made the system a going concern. In 1819 they were listed in thirty branches of work. Among them were eleven carpenters, ten tailors, twenty-two seamstresses, six shoemakers and one owner of a hotel. Thirty years later they were listed in fifty different types of work. In 1859 there were among them fifty carpenters, forty-three tailors, nine shoemakers, and twenty-one butchers. In these trades some of them became wealthy. In the above mentioned year, "353 persons paid taxes on property and one-hundred-and-ninety were slave holders.

The property on which they paid taxes was assessed at $724,570 and the amount paid on slaves aggregated $1,170." If we divide this group of taxpayers into three approximately homogeneous classes, we find that there were 192 who paid taxes on property whose assessed value ranged from $1,000 to $5,000; this group owned 105 slaves, or an average of .54 slaves each. In the second division there were 21 persons who paid taxes on property whose assessed value ranged from $5,000 to $10,000, and they owned 68 slaves, or 3¼ slaves each. And in the third bracket, there were 9 persons who paid taxes on property whose value ranged from $10,000 to $40,075. This group owned 54 slaves, an average of 6 slaves each. In this class one individual paid taxes on $23,000 worth of real estate and 14 slaves; another $33,000 worth of real estate and 5 slaves; and a third paid taxes on $40,075 worth of real estate and 14 slaves.

Moreover, the wills and deeds which they made indicate that they engaged in some of the most important business ventures of the system. In 1815, Jehu Jones bought a hotel at public auction for $13,000. This hotel was located on the most important street in the city and in close proximity to the most fashionable Episcopal church in the community. It was patronized by the elite of the white society, including the governor of the state.

In 1853, Joseph Dereef, another wealthy person of color, sold a piece of property to the city council for $3,600 for the extension of a street. In 1870 his brother, R. E. Dereef, sold a part of his wharf to the South Carolina Rail Road Company for $17,000. In 1833 Thomas Ingliss made provisions in his will for the support of a relative from the stocks which he held in the Mechanics Bank of the city.

One of the characteristics of the free Negro of Charleston, which attracts the attention of the sociologist, is that it was a class-conscious group; and identified its interest, loyalties, and manners with the upper-caste members of the society insofar as that behavior did not offend or disturb the status quo. They organized themselves into societies with high eligibility requirements. These associations were ostensibly charitable and benevolent, but in reality they were social and status organizations. In 1790 the Brown Fellowship Society was formed. The preamble of this organization stated that its members were bona fide free brown men of good character. The fee of admission was $50.00, and the membership was restricted to fifty members. The society provided for the education of the children; assistance to the orphans and widows and burial grounds for their dead. They maintained a clubhouse where meetings were held monthly, and on each anniversary provisions were made for special observance. This institution had a continuous existence for more than a hundred years. In fact vestiges of it are still in evidence. There is left the cemetery, with large imposing tombstones and vaults; so is the foundation of the hall in which they met. It still has a secretary and a president. In spite of the fact that other Negro organizations, including a church, were abolished during crisis periods in this slave community, the Brown Fellowship Society kept alive. The members and their organization were careful and cautious in their conduct. We only need to remember the conflicting philosophies and the revolutionary movements of the underprivileged groups of this period to appreciate how delicate and precarious the position of this group was. At their meetings they prohibited any discussion of local or national problems. Rule XVIII of the by-laws states: "All debates on controverted points of divinity or matters of the nation, governments, states or churches, shall be excluded from the conversation of this society, and whoever shall persist in such shall be fined...." The secretary of the organization kept very careful minutes of the proceedings of the meetings, and on one occasion when the mayor of the city asked to inspect them, because of a recently enacted law to prohibit more than seven Negroes to assemble at a time, the group was praised highly for its records and avowed objectives. So they were informed that the law was not intended for them. Among other things the minutes showed that a member had been expelled from the society on April 17, 1817, for violating its rules.

Now the question may be asked, What were the attitudes of this class to other groups in the community? As I envisage it, their behavior was a replica of that class in the white society which they aspired to be like. Their attitudes towards their slaves ranged from exploitation to humanitarianism. Again the wills which they left give us some indication of their position. In 1825 William Pinceel made the following stipulation in his will:

I give and bequeath unto my Son Emanuel forever my Negro boy slave named Joe. I also give and bequeath unto Said Son for life my Negro boy slave named Tom and immediately after the death of my said Son, should the said Negro boy have conducted himself towards my Said Son as a faithful servant, then I direct that he be emancipated, but should he not have conducted himself then I give the said Negro boy to such person as my Said Son nominate and appoint in his last will and writing.

The following will was made by a schoolteacher in 1831. He taught in Charleston between 1815 and 1830, and was one of the most active members of the Brown Fellowship Society:

I desire that soon after my decease instruction shall be given to have all my stock and other things appertaining to my plantation in the country together with the plantation itself sold and the money arising from the same shall go to defray all expenses, taxes & provided however the said plantation cannot be sold at a fair price and it can be worked by the hands now there viz. Scipio, Abram, and Peggy so as to pay expenses taxes and so forth in such case the same shall not be sold but retained for the benefit of the family if at all event, the Negroes on said plantation whose names are above mentioned be disposed of there shall be an exception of Scipio whom it is my wish shall be retained together with my slaves in town viz.: Fanny and Mary to be subservient to the wishes of my beloved wife Jennet Bonneau and children.

Some of these masters also left their slaves or former slaves provided for economically. In 1859 John L. Francis left $1,000 to one servant and $200 to another, together with his wardrobe.

The emphasis which the free Negro of this class placed upon mixed blood, free ancestry, economic position, and a devotion to the tenets of the slave system set them apart from and above other classes in the community. Moreover, their in-group tendencies were so strong that the free Black people of the city were constrained to organize themselves into a society of free Blacks. The first rule of this society says that it will "... consist of a number of respectable Free Dark men, as a majority may determine: not less than seven or more than thirty-five which number of seven shall be considered a quorum to transact business at any time...."

It is fair to say that the upper-caste free Negro served as a custodian of the system. He interrupted plans which the detached, discontented, underprivileged Negroes designed to overthrow or to offend the mores of the system. In 1822 the intended Denmark Vesey insurrection was circumvented by a member of this class who instructed an informed slave to go and tell his master. The insurrection had been in the process of development for four years and was considered one of the most intricate ever undertaken in this country. It had as its model the uprising of the Blacks in San Domingo. Its leader had traveled through the islands as the slave of a slave trader. Upon receiving his freedom he settled in Charleston and assumed the position of the leader of the slaves. It is estimated that from six thousand to nine thousand slaves were identified with this movement. Only about thirty of the leaders were executed for the plot. On the other hand the slave who divulged the plans was emancipated by the state of South Carolina and paid an annual stipend for the rest of his life. Meantime the free Negro received $1,000 and exemption from taxation for the rest of his life.

There are other evidences of unrest, but I shall take time to mention only a few of them. Between 1832 and 1853 approximately 400 free Negroes left South Carolina for Liberia, Africa. They were impelled by the claims of the American Colonization Society on the one hand and the insecurity of their positions on the other. In a mass meeting which was held by this group in 1831 in the interest of emigrating to Africa, the theme was that "in Liberia you will enjoy moral and political freedom." In December, 1832, 146 persons of this class departed from Charleston for Liberia. As far as I have been able to ascertain none of them were members of the Brown Fellowship Society.

The relations which the aristocratic free Negro sustained in his own family and among other members of his group deserve study and analysis. They provided for the education of their children; they married inside a restricted class; dowries were apparently provided for the daughters; and great care was taken in the protection and transmission of property and slaves.

In 1794 George Bedon indicated in his will that:

. . . it is my particular desire and request that my two Sons . . . should be brought up in a Christian like manner and kept to school for the benefit of an Education until they arrive at the age of fifteen years then my two sons to be bound out during the term of six years to some handicraft trade under a kind and able master and in like manner my daughter until she arrives at the age of fourteen years to be bound to a discreet and careful Mantua-maker a person of good character who will be so kind as to take care of an orphans morals as well as to teach her the trade.

In 1861 Jacob Weston, one of the wealthier members of this caste, stipulated in his will that his wife and son should live in England after his death and that the son should be educated there. It was indicated that they be maintained out of the family estate. The same testator designated that the support of his wife should be revoked if she married again.

As was the practice generally, so it was in this group that marriage and courtship relations were expected to have the approval of the parents of the interested parties. The following letter was written in 1832, in reply to one which a young man had sent to the parents of his friend:

Charleston, March 19th, 1832

DEAR SIR:
It affords me the pleasure of giving you the approbation of Mr. Kougley and myself towards the affection you have for my daughter Cecelia. It has met her approbation for your visiting the house on her

account, as to your standing in life we are perfectly acquainted with, as to objections we can have none, therefore we must join both hand and heart in wishing you all the prosperity and happiness this world can afford. I hope it is with the approbation of your family that you have addressed my daughter with respect, Dear Sir

We are yours,

JACOB AND MARY KOUGLEY

The Marriage Book of St. Phillip's Church, founded in 1672, shows that 168 mulattoes were married by the rectors of that institution between 1828 and 1860. There were a considerable number of marriages among the families who were either business partners or who were identified with the same social and fraternal organization; in other words, by usage and expectation, selections were made from in-group members. Records show that even the slaves of business partners entered into marriage relations. On November 16, 1837, Mingo, the slave of R. E. Dereef, was married to Hatira, the slave of Robert Howard. These men were partners in the wood business.

The exhibition of a feeling of class-consciousness and the effort to maintain group solidarity were best exemplified in the activities of the Brown Fellowship Society. Through this medium social relations were cultivated, a system of education fostered, provisions for caring for the sick, the orphan and widow were made; and many men of wealth acted in an advisory and legal capacity as executors of the last wills of the members of the group. When the Society was one hundred years old, its name was changed to the Century Fellowship Society. Early in the twentieth century an auxiliary organization was formed which they named the Daughters of the Century Fellowship Society. The object of this branch of the association was "... the erection of a hall to the memory of the men who won a page in the social history of the eighteenth century." On the 117th anniversary of the organization, the president, in his annual address, epitomized the career of his caste in the following words: "Fortunately there were the classes in society, and as our forefathers allied themselves with them, as a consequence they had their influence and protection and they had to be in accord with them and stood for what they stood for. If they stood for high incentive so did our fathers. *If they stood for slavery so did our fathers to a certain extent. But they sympathized with the oppressed,* for they had to endure some of it. . . ."

In conclusion, the free Negro of Charleston answers nicely to the "marginal man" concept. By virtue of his biological characteristics; because of his partial accessibility to two social worlds; as a result of his feeling of superiority to one of these worlds, and his position of inferiority to the other, he was either constrained to become a misfit or to carve out a position which the community accepted and which he respected. Because of the nature of the social system he became a member of a separate caste which incorporated the interests, loyalties, and usages of the upper-caste members of the society insofar as this behavior did not offend or disturb the hierarchical arrangements. In this position he was able to circumvent the harsh ordinances which were designed to perpetuate the slave economy and to assuage the circumstances of his existence.

It is fair to say, however, that when the system was disrupted during the Civil War, this group provided the leadership, and the basis of organized, stable life, for the Negro community.

This study has shown that (1) intimate human relations, whether between subordinates and superiors or between persons of equal rank, result in irresistible and inevitable *claims* and *obligations* of each upon the other. In this case these relations gave rise to the emergence of a large group of free Negroes in the slave society. (2) City life with its heterogeneous population and its consequent conflict and fusion of cultures, with its competition and division of labor, tends to secularize human relations and institutions, and to facilitate freedom of movement, action, and thought. Hence, if the city economy is to move on with efficiency, even the lowest servant in it must have economic value, and this is inevitably interlaced with the process of mobility. The city offered the free Negro his best opportunity for economic success. It is further shown that (3) in a society in which a group's position is not definitely defined by the mores and traditions, efforts will be made to copy the patterns of conduct of those groups which have prestige, recognition, and security. Lastly, it is shown that (4) the extent to which this class of Negroes in Charleston differed from similar groups in the total slave economy marked the extent to which the modes of life and patterns of conduct in the community as a whole, differed from the rest of the slave communities. The difference, in other words, is one of degree rather than kind.

SLAVERY IN BATON ROUGE, 1820-1860

WILLIAM L. RICHTER

In the middle 1830's, a traveler described the streets of the river towns above New Orleans as "solitary" with "closed stores and deserted taverns" which added "to their loneliness." The river trip north was boring, with miles of cane fields, levees, and, most of all, monotonously flat land. When he saw the hills one hundred miles above New Orleans, they appeared to him "like an oasis in the desert." Located on those hills was the town of Baton Rouge, "a delightful residence," neat, well-built, of Spanish and French architecture, with streets parallel to the Mississippi River and forty feet above the water.

Baton Rouge was founded about 1808, south of the United States fort on the bluffs. The town was laid out in several sections named after the men who established them. Included were Gras, Duval, Leonard, Hickey-Duncan, Mather, and Beauregard towns, which were incorporated into "Baton Rouge" in 1817.

In 1837, the state penitentiary was completed east of Baton Rouge, and in 1849 the state capitol was moved to the city. The first bluff on the south end of Baton Rouge was donated to the state, and the new capitol was erected there. Admirers described the building as a "grand, gloomy, and peculiar . . . ancient castle" standing in "solitary majesty,"

Reprinted with permission from *Louisiana History*, 10 (Spring 1969), pp. 125-145. Footnotes and tables appearing in the original publication have been deleted in the present volume, and should be consulted for full documentation of the author's conclusions.

with "stately minarets and towers." Mark Twain was perhaps more realistic in calling it a sham castle which epitomized the Southern Romanticism gleaned from the pages of Sir Walter Scott. For a state capital, Baton Rouge in 1860 was far from rich. A cyclical economy rose and fell with the picking of cotton and cutting of cane. To alleviate the problem in part, Baton Rouge merchants concentrated on volume business in the peak periods. The achievement of this goal depended upon the road system on the east bank of the Mississippi and the envisioned Plank Road to Clinton to the north. To tap the west bank, the city sponsored the Baton Rouge and Grosse Tete Railroad in the 1850's. The railroad was designed to cut competition from Plaquemine and even Donaldsonville. The wharf at Baton Rouge was changed from the worst on the Mississippi to one of the best. The one problem for the city merchants that was never completely solved was convincing the large planters that they should buy from Baton Rouge, because the majority of them bought directly from New Orleans and thus bypassed the local middleman. In 1860, Baton Rouge was a typical medium-sized town in the South. Its 5,428 people, Black and white, were "on the make"—eager to advance themselves and their town.

Negro slaves were an important minority of Baton Rouge's population. In total numbers, the slave population grew from 266 in 1820 to 1,247 in 1860. The growth was steady, and the largest addition was made in the decade of the 1840's, followed by the 1850's. Female chattels between the ages of twenty and fifty outnumbered bondsmen of the same ages after 1830, but after 1840, there were never over fifty-one more females than males of working age. The closeness of the figures for males and females was due to the demands of mechanics and industry for male slaves. Twenty percent of the slaves were mulatto in 1850. This figure rose to 29 percent in 1860.

The rise and fall of slave numbers in relation to the total population seemed to depend on the Panic of 1837, and the increased numbers of whites who moved to the city in the 1850's. At the same time, the increase in slave population tapered off because of the demand from the plantations, and because of the inability of townsmen to buy much more than one slave at a time. Most obvious, however, was the reshuffling of the existing slaves among increasing numbers of new slaveholders. Only 20 percent of the people owning slaves in 1850 can be found in the 1860 census. The number of new slaveholders rose in the decade of the fifties faster than the number of slaves, and the number of whites owning one slave doubled; whereas the number owning more than twenty chattels decreased by two-thirds. Such statistics indicate that there was an appreciable amount of mobility in the slave system.

Although the percentage of slaves in the total population fluctuated in the antebellum years, the number of whites who owned slaves remained about one-third of the population after 1840. Ninety percent of the slaveholders held fewer than ten slaves; an average slaveholder owned five slaves. Only once, in 1850, did more than three persons hold more than twenty slaves. By 1860, two of the six had left town or died, two had sold half of their bondsmen, and two retained the same number of chattels. Almost all of the large slaveholders were "gentlemen" by occupation. Fifteen slaves were the property of free men of color in 1860, an increase of 50 percent from the 1830 figures. In only one case did it appear that a free colored slaveholder owned other than the members of his own family.

Few Negroes were able to escape the toils of bondage in Baton Rouge, although there were several individual emancipations by benevolent masters. Emancipation became more difficult, and in 1857 impossible to achieve, because of the beliefs of Southerners as to the true nature of the Negro. The attitude of white Baton Rouge was typical of the South. Baton Rouge citizens thought their chattels to be childlike, inherently inferior, incapable of living as free men, irresponsible, and in need of discipline. Due to the proximity of the Sugar Islands, Louisianians were particularly sensitive to the Haitian revolt and British emancipation. Jamaica was a prime example of the maxim that to extinguish the civilizing force of slavery would cause the Negro to "relapse into the barbarism of his race." Negroes had been slaves since the beginning of time. The *Baton Rouge Gazette* pointed to the capture of black ant pupae by red ants as conclusive evidence that nature fitted any black species "for no other end than to fill the station of slavery."

While burdened with a negative stereotype, slaves were very important to the economic life of the community. They provided a means of income for their owners in various ways, including sales, industrial work, hiring out, domestic services, and apprentice duties. Although there was no exact record, the sharp decline in demand for more male slaves in Baton Rouge during the decade of the 1850's, as well as the high prices in the surrounding parish for field hands, indicated a possibility of speculation in slave prices by the town dwellers. The 1860 census shows two men, a "trader" and a "speculator," with eleven and twelve slaves respectively. Neither of these men nor his occupation was listed in previous records. Bondsmen were being sold in the country for $1,800, and one "not likely" boy brought $1,600 on the block. Sales were so popular that the members of the state legislature were often missing from their seats. Projected prices by local authorities ranged from $2,000 to $2,500 for male chattels, causing widespread "negro fever."

Despite the profits to be made in the sale of male slaves to the country, Baton Rouge developed an industrial demand for sawyers and foundrymen that seemed to offset some of the plantation demand. In fact, industry was attractive enough to cause Frederick Arbour to invest his money and thirty slaves in sawmilling. John Hill and William Markham had twenty-one slaves working in their foundry. In each case, slaves constituted over half of the workers in the industry.

Slaveholders in Baton Rouge, as in other Southern cities, hired out their slaves. The hiring-out system operated in two ways. Either the slave was bound over to another white, or the slave was allowed to hire his own time. In Baton Rouge, there was no evidence of a central hiring place or use of identification badges. In fact, the slaveholders probably would have rebelled against such laws. For example, one Louisiana law denied Negro slaves the right to hire their own time. The *Gazette* had called for its enforcement by the mayor, but when the mayor did enforce the law, the local populace brought pressure to bear, forcing a concession by the city government. The slave was allowed to hire his own time for a one-week contract, but in all cases, he had to have the master's written permission.

Although hiring time was an important use of slave labor, most Baton Rougeans employed their own slaves in domestic or "apprentice" work. (At least 70 percent of the slaveholders had only one slave at each census.) Females were almost exclusively used in domestic work as cooks, maids, and nurses. Male slaves were most often general laborers, or helpers for carpenters, bakers, butchers, painters, wagonmakers, or shoemakers. When slaves were employed in other than menial tasks, they often met opposition in the form of law. Any shop that sold liquor was off-limits to Negro clerks. Restaurants run by free men of color or slaves were closed as nuisances and gathering spots of potential trouble. Chattels were not permitted to sell any goods without written permission from their masters. The penalty was twenty-five lashes and forfeiture of the goods. The profits, however, must have balanced the risk of capture, for punishment and reiteration of the laws failed to stop the illicit trade.

Although slaves were used in many skilled and menial tasks, the white mechanics of Baton Rouge felt little competition from them. The major reason for lack of complaint may have been the fact that mechanics hired and owned large numbers of slaves. It was not uncommon for carpenters to employ from three to ten slaves. Instead of creating competition, the slaves actually enabled a white mechanic to handle more than one job at a time. In this respect, Baton Rouge differed from the larger cities in the South, as described in Richard C. Wade's *Slavery in the Cities*. If slaves did not compete with the Baton Rouge mechanics, the skilled workers were far from happy because of the competition from the state penitentiary. Both Black and white convicts were leased to a company which, in turn, had the right to hire out prisoners who were sentenced to hard labor. The lessees, McHatton and Ward, made the prison into a profitable business venture in several ways. They had the prisoners working on their plantation, hiring out to various townsmen, operating the lessees' cotton and woolen factory, as well as operating the bagging and rope plant located on the penitentiary grounds. Twenty years of protest resulted only in closing the penitentiary store and ending the sale of prison goods in town establishments. From the investment of $4,000 for their lease, McHatton and Ward realized $7,000 profit in 1860 alone. The alleged lowering of wages and prices was the mechanics' constant complaint against cheaper prison labor and goods.

Contrary to the pattern found by Wade in large Southern cities, the free colored population was specifically exempted from the complaint against "Black Mechanics." The free men of color were a fair form of competition for they, too, had "families to support and taxes to pay." The reason for Baton Rouge's judicial attitude toward the free man of color was that he did not compete with the white mechanics in the town economy. The free colored worked as laborers and cigarmakers; by 1860 they had begun to take over the barbering trade. Another field open to them was that of managing Negro boardinghouses. The restrictions against the free Negro operating groceries, restaurants, and grog shops seemed more concerned with keeping liquor out of any Negro's hands than with overt job discrimination.

The free colored persons were, however, only a small part of the Negro population of Baton Rouge. Their slave brethren constituted one-fourth of the total inhabitants of the town, and were the subjects of a massive list of state and local laws. These laws required the slave to be mentally alert at all times so that he might not find himself in a compromising situation. For example, a slave had to use great care in suppressing emotion while around whites. The slightest word, quick movement of a hand or arm, or a wrong look could lead to chains, lashes, or even instant death from the offended townsman. Slaves were corrected occasionally for abusive language or actions; but the profanity and misbehavior of soldiers in town on leave from the fort created nearly as much concern.

Insulting language was a trivial problem compared to the fear and potential destruction by fire in Baton Rouge. According to Kenneth

Stampp, arson was believed to be one of the chattel's favorite devices for revenge, but there was no overt suspicion of the slave population voiced during the fire outbreaks. Yet so great was the danger of fires to the town, and so common was their occurrence, that a $500 reward was posted for the arrest and conviction of arsonists. Shortly thereafter one Negro was arrested for firing the house of a white who had refused to allow "the boy" to stay with his bondswoman, but this appears to have been an isolated instance, after which there was no call for extra surveillance of the Negroes to prevent further incidents.

Theft was often directly traceable to the colored population, even if fire was not. Negro slaves broke into stores at night, once robbed a white man in his hotel room, and often tried to break into houses. One loyal slave exchanged shots with two Negroes who were lurking in his mistress's back yard. A popular joke of the time was the conversation between two slaves over a new hat. When asked how much the prized article cost, the "owner" replied, "I don't know, *de shop keeper wasn't dar.*" Any Black was under suspicion. The town constable was in the habit of arresting colored persons on his "intuitive knowledge of their intentions." Many of these arrests resulted in the return of stolen goods. Of the fourteen court cases involving chattels between 1838 and 1842, eleven concerned theft—a fact which testified to the magnitude of the problem.

Most crime, including arson and theft, occurred at night when the streets were deserted. To combat nightly lawbreakers, Baton Rouge relied on an institution called the "patrol." Established as early as 1822, the patrol had to be re-created seven times before 1860. Each time it failed to function correctly. Public apathy was stifling. The only other local organization with less public support was the state militia. In theory, the patrol was to serve from nine o'clock at night to five o'clock the next morning. More often than not, the patrols ended up in a local tavern after a few hours of work, and later added to the revelry in the streets. In short, the Baton Rouge patrol was far from being "hated and feared" by anyone, Black or white. Reliance for protection from crime shifted instead to a system of streetlights, which was set up in 1829. Twenty years later, the lights were in general disrepair because no one had the responsibility for taking care of them.

The lackadaisical attitude toward patrol responsibilities did not mean that slaves were not caught and punished. Although the records are scarce, punishment for slave offenders was generally corporal, harsh, and thorough. The common penalty was twenty-five lashes and a fine to pay for court costs. If the master of a convicted slave did not pay the court costs, the slave could work off the debt at fifty cents per day. It is interesting to note that the jailer had an unlimited expense account for "cowhides."

Punishment for the individual slave's crimes was determined by the slave courts. Although only a brief record of court cases is available, these facts are evident. Out of nearly eight hundred cases over a four-year period, forty-five concerned Negroes, but of those, only fourteen concerned slaves. Also, both slaves and free colored received acquittals as well as convictions. Several tentative conclusions might evolve from this information. Either the slaves were punished more often privately by their masters than publicly by the state for criminal acts, or the chattels behaved well and stayed within the law. Also, as poorly as they may have been staffed with legal minds, the slave courts did try to find justice rather than convict solely on the matter of race. The idea that slaves were innately inferior and criminally inclined should no longer be accepted. But the opposite notion of the unjust southern white is no more satisfactory. In actuality, the truth lies somewhere in between.

Slaves convicted for lesser crimes and lodged in the parish jail were liable to employment on city and parish public works. If the Public Works Commissioner, G. M. Kent, needed more than the seventeen slaves he owned and conveniently hired to the city, the vagrants in jail were available. At fifty cents credit per day to their fine (up to $150), vagrants became a popular and cheap source of labor for the town's board of selectmen. The jailer, J. J. Odum, averaged $60 a month for "state work."

Interestingly enough, the slave population of Baton Rouge did not seem to fear jail as punishment. The jails had a reputation for good food, easier work hours than their usual jobs, and an inability to insure maximum security. A total of forty-nine slaves escaped from jail between 1828 and 1841. Authorities concluded that the problem was created by a wooden building which housed the jail. Better law officers and a new brick jail finally ended the rash of escapes.

The large number of slaves in the Baton Rouge jail was traceable not to the lawlessness of the local colored population, but to the fact that Baton Rouge was the central holding pen for runaways in middle and east Louisiana. Not only was the parish jail full of runaways, but the surrounding woods were full, too. The anonymity of town life drew many runaways into Baton Rouge. In the city were food, friends, shelter. A smart slave could hide in relative comfort rather easily. One slave, who said he was from Franklin County, Mississippi, was found in the belfry of the Methodist church. His hideout contained kitchen furniture, extra clothes, dried beef, a revolver, and a knife. The town felt there were, no doubt, "other runaways in the neighborhood, who take advantage of nighttime to prowl about town and commit depredations." A bondswoman named Jane disappeared into the town's hideaways and was still at large two years later. Her master, a prominent citizen, believed she was receiving aid from unknown persons. Despite the large number of runaways lurking in and about town, the fear of an insurrection inside the town was negligible throughout the antebellum period. Partly because of the presence of the United States Army in the fort, Baton Rougeans felt rather safe. The real fear in their hearts was that an insurrection in the Felicianas might send a band of armed Negroes south on Plank Road. The town dwellers never expressed doubt of their servants and relied on the censorship laws and laws against slave education to keep their Negroes free from "evil" ideas; however, many masters taught their slaves to read and write anyway, and some learned by stealth.

Although there were incidents that can be pointed to as criminal acts, more often the court reports in the newspapers mentioned "a dearth of interesting items in the Police Courts." In 1857 the parish grand jury found only thirty-eight true bills; most of these were against whites for carrying concealed weapons. A year earlier, the newspaper reported ninety-six cases, of which the entire Negro population could account for about half. Baton Rouge generally had few serious crimes.

The law disobeyed most was the curfew. In response to complaints by citizens that Negroes "perambulate the streets freely at all hours of the night . . . ," the local officials passed a nine o'clock curfew. The signal was the ringing of the Catholic church bell, or in the event that the bell was not rung, the beating of tattoo at the fort. The penalty for violation of curfew was a night in jail, ten lashes for the slave, and a two-dollar fine for the slave's owner. In 1839, an amendment of the law provided for ringing the bell at noon, at eight o'clock every night, and at four in the afternoon on Sundays. Any town slave out after the eight o'clock bell received the usual penalty. Slaves not living in town who remained in the streets past four o'clock on Sunday received fifteen lashes.

The law was exact and left no doubt as to intent. Seldom, however, was it enforced. It is probably that the bell was rung indiscriminately and that few people knew why it was rung. In 1858, one white man appealed to the local editor to inform the town of the purpose of the bell. He had heard it ring at eleven o'clock the night before, and had thought a fire was in progress.

Not only was the curfew haphazardly enforced, but also masters were not restrictive in their housing policy. No slave was to live in any house if a white or a free man of color was not living on the same lot to be responsible for the slave's actions. The penalty was the same as curfew violation. Landlords generally rented, however, to anyone who would pay, and slaves often lived without any supervision of their activities. The problem became so acute that in 1854 the law was amended. In addition to the night in jail, ten lashes, and a two-dollar fine, the new law provided for a ten- to twenty-five-dollar fine of the landlord and the slave's master for allowing such offenses.

The most scandalous of all housing-code violations was cohabitation. This subject of "extreme delicacy" horrified all "right thinking" Southerners. "Is there anything more revolting to our notions of morality," inquired the *Weekly Comet,* than the "white men in this community who are openly living in public places with ebony, colored members of a different race . . . ?" The standard practice was to "hire" the slave woman at eight to ten dollars per month and to "force her to become his wife" while the owner winked at the practice and acquired new wealth from the illegitimate children.

In an attempt to test the *Comet's* story, the single white men living with Negro women were tabulated from the 1850 and 1860 censuses. In the 1850 census, there are three cases of white men living with black or mulatto women, who had purely mulatto children. The 1860 census showed five such cases. In 1860, a Cecilia Barry was listed as a white woman from Italy. She had four mulatto children with her name. These cases are not conclusive. The Negro women could have been maids or could have been bought along with their children as a form of speculation. Cecilia Barry may have taken in four orphan children and given them her name. In any case, the practice apparently did exist, but it was extremely limited.

Although slavery was at times unjust and harsh, the town slave had many outlets for his spare time of which his country cousin could only dream. The availability of entertaining distractions did much to ameliorate the repressiveness of bondage, and to make town slavery more benign. Technically, the law forbade any assemblage of slaves, but as usual, law and practice were far apart.

One of the most common of Negro gatherings was the "frolic," or slave dance. The Black Code of 1806, as well as the town ordinances of 1831, prohibited slave dances. Not only did the slaves ignore the laws, but also their masters encouraged infractions, and brought pressure on the board of selectmen to change the law. Under the new city code in 1841, slave dances were permissible if the owner of the place in which the dance was to occur applied for a permit.

Dances, like any other slave gathering, opened up the possibility for slave fights. A town ordinance ordered the immediate flogging on the spot of any slave caught in a fight, and the town constable rigidly enforced the measure. Many fights began as gambling arguments; consequently to protect the slave owner's investment from harm (knives were the slaves' favorite weapons), and to deter the temptation of a slave to steal in order to cover debts, the town prohibited gambling. Whites who encouraged Negro "games" were liable to a fine not exceeding $1,000 and one year in jail. The betting fever only increased, however; and reports of card games and of the rolling of tenpins were common, especially near the steamboat landing.

In addition to dancing and gambling, a Baton Rouge slave enjoyed showing off on Sunday afternoons by racing his master's horse down Third Street at a fast gallop. Negroes could not ride without permits, but the masters freely gave permission. By 1846, the Sunday exercises had become common enough to cause danger to pedestrians on the boardwalks. The town government cracked down on violators with hearty floggings. In a short burst of morality, the Police Jury even abolished track races on the course outside of town in the fall of 1860.

Of all diversions available to the slave population of Baton Rouge, the one that was most popular and caused the most trouble was that of drinking. The cries of innocence raised by the merchants matched the complaints by slave owners; but the slaves were drunk on the streets, and often riotous, especially on weekends. One irate citizen reported that he saw a slave treat several Negroes at a local grog shop where the slave had a charge account. "It is really time to open our eyes to such abuses which ought not to be tolerated in an incorporated town," concluded another townsman. "Slaves are allowed here too much privilege." Two slaveholders offered ten dollars to anyone who would inform them where their slaves purchased liquor. The well-being of the chattels and the safety of their masters were said to be at stake.

Again the law was explicit in the matter of dispensing liquor to slaves. Ignorance of the law or of the sale was prima facie evidence of guilt. Slave owners had the right to sue in all cases; the state affixed penalties of up to eight hundred dollars for offenders. The strictness of the law and its high fine, however, caused juries not to convict. The parish Police Jury petitioned the legislature not only to lower the punishment, but also to dispense with jury trials.

Both the city government and certain slaves tried to set a good example in restricting the use of liquor. The jail suspended its liquor ration to slave prisoners in 1839, and slaves organized at least two temperance societies. Unfortunately, the first of these societies believed in experiencing the evils caused by drink firsthand before abstaining and had to be abolished posthaste. An attempt by the Police Jury to make East Baton Rouge Parish dry failed in 1855. The whites liked their liquor, too.

Naturally, after a weekend of gambling, hell-raising, and drinking, most slaves went to church on Sunday to expiate their sins. According to Wade, Negro churches were controversial in the South, for a separate church offered the slave another place to go free from direct white supervision. There was no record, however, of distrust by the whites of Negro churches in Baton Rouge. Both races enthusiastically supported religious services, whether held jointly or separately by race. A majority of Baton Rougeans felt churches and preaching made their slaves "contented and happy," and would "ameliorate the moral condition of the colored population. . . ." Slaves and free colored were invited to attend white churches, and encouraged to set up their own churches. In 1858 a colored church was established by the town government, on a petition from "many citizens."

They engaged a Methodist free colored preacher, George Menard, to preach. Although the townsmen condoned separate churches, they distrusted camp meetings, often led by Yankees, who slipped antislavery sentiments into their preaching.

The ease of establishing colored churches in Baton Rouge underlined an obvious aspect of the town's "peculiar institution." Slavery in Baton Rouge was an informal system of restraint of one part of the town's population. The Black Code and the city ordinances were harsh and strict, but the custom and tradition of nonenforcement informalized and ameliorated the letter of the law. The laws were, as Ulrich B. Phillips put it, like pistols kept for an emergency, but "out of sight and out of mind in the daily routine of peaceful industry."

In violation of the slave codes, Negroes roamed the streets, consumed large quantities of liquor, and lived away from their masters. When possible, masters exerted pressure to result in change of the laws. One example was the revision of the dancing laws. When the laws could not be changed, people conveniently ignored them, as when a storekeeper sold liquor to slaves or bought from them goods that they had possibly stolen. The merchant considered only the color of one's money, not the color of one's skin.

When the laws were violated, and the culprits were apprehended, the master was apt to administer discipline on the spot. The small number of court cases available involving slave crime for the period also suggests the possibility that the slaves were well behaved. The slave courts in Baton Rouge were not necessarily summary institutions of the quick whip, but were relatively fair in their application of the law. If slave courts decided on whim, they only reflected a problem brought on by the rise of the common man in the Jacksonian era, when any jury decision was liable to be "decided by a throw of the dice" by illiterate jurors.

One factor that may have been more than instrumental in assuring the slave a fair treatment in Baton Rouge was the lack of competition between skilled slaves and the white mechanics. Slaves and free men of color remained in the unskilled jobs classified as "nigger work." If a slave was skilled, he was an "apprentice" of a white mechanic. All of the free Negroes in Baton Rouge were unskilled day laborers, cigar-makers, barbers, or proprietors of colored rooming houses. The Negro thus provided needed services for the community by taking over occupations which whites did not want.

Baton Rouge, unlike larger southern cities, did not have a great discrepancy in the numbers of Negro males and females of working age. After 1840, the number of male slaves and female slaves became approximately the same. The probable reason was the demand for male slaves by artisans and industry. Foundry work and sawmilling employed nearly fifty slaves by 1860. Most of this increase came during the decade of the 1850's, and, in spite of the high prices for field hands in the countryside around Baton Rouge, the male slave population remained stable in the town.

The close ratio between male and female slaves also affected the amount of overt miscegenation. Contrary to the picture drawn by Wade, "amalgamation" was not more common in the city than on the plantation. Perhaps a small population that knew each other better was the explanation, or perhaps casual unions were kept secret from the prying newspapers. The increase in mulattoes in the 1850's was difficult to trace to miscegenation, and few open cases were apparent from the census or from editorial complaints.

While "amalgamation" was difficult to prove, so was its absolute counterpart, segregation. Surprisingly, there were few facilities in Baton Rouge for "whites only." Segregation was an informal, and never a total, situation. Baton Rouge really had few facilities, such as street cars or public parks, to segregate in antebellum times. However, the slave and free man of color were not "expected" in taverns, restaurants, and theaters. Although the slave could not attend the local theater, he could always find some store owner who would allow him and his Black friends to gather, play cards, drink, and enjoy themselves. Segregation was neither as absolute nor as extensive as that found by Wade in the larger southern cities. In the case of housing, segregation was desired by the slaves to avoid white control.

In Baton Rouge, the large slave owners were corporations and industries, a fact which conforms to Wade's findings for the South's larger cities. Unlike Wade's cities, however, in absolute numbers Louisiana's capital had no loss of slaves by 1860. Slavery in the small and medium-sized towns, if it resembled slavery in Baton Rouge, could be described merely as a viable economic institution, growing with the town, and continually involving a stable one-third of the city's white breadwinners.

FREE BLACKS IN ANTEBELLUM PHILADELPHIA
A Study of Ex-Slaves, Freeborn, and Socioeconomic Decline
THEODORE HERSHBERG

Afro-American history in general has received a great deal of attention from historians in the past decade. The same cannot be said about the history of Black Americans who were free before the Civil War. Studies published since Leon Litwack's *North of Slavery* have considered racial discrimination in the legal tradition, the relationship between race and politics, the establishment of Black utopian communities, and the role of Blacks in the abolitionist movement. With a few exceptions notable in the earlier studies of the free Negro by Luther P. Jackson and John Hope Franklin, the literature lacks a solid empirical base, a sophisticated methodological and theoretical approach, and a focus on the Black community itself. There exists an important need for new studies of the family and social structure, of the development of community institutions such as the church, school, and beneficial society, of migration and social mobility.

Antebellum Philadelphia offers the historian an important opportunity to study each of these topics. The free Black population of the city had its roots in the eighteenth century. Its free Black population in 1860, more than 22,000, was the largest outside of the slave South and second only to Baltimore. All-Black churches, schools, and voluntary societies

Reprinted with permission from the *Journal of Social History,* 5 (Winter 1971–1972), pp. 183–209. Footnotes and tables appearing in the original publication have been deleted in the present volume, and should be consulted for full documentation of the author's conclusions. The author wishes to acknowledge the financial support of the Center for Metropolitan Problems of the National Institute of Mental Health (2R01 MH16621), which made this research possible.

were numerous. The National Negro Convention Movement met for the first time in Philadelphia in 1830, and the city hosted such meetings frequently thereafter. Many of the leading Black abolitionists such as James Forten, Robert Purvis, and William Still were Philadelphians. Most significantly for the historian, the data describing all facets of this history are extant. The Black history collections and the papers of the Pennsylvania Abolition Society at the Historical Society of Pennsylvania and the Library Company of Philadelphia are even richer for the antebellum period than the Schomburg Collection of the New York Public Library.

In many ways this essay resembles a preliminary progress report. Despite the research and analysis which remain to be done, it is appropriate to discuss several important themes which emerge early in the study of nineteenth-century Black Philadelphians: the socioeconomic deterioration of the antebellum Black community, the condition of the ex-slaves in the population, and the value of understanding the urban experience for the study of Black history.

A CONTEXT OF DECLINE

The decision of the Pennsylvania Abolition Society in 1837 to take a census of Philadelphia's free Negro population was made for both a specific and a general purpose. The specific purpose was to defeat the move, already underway in Harrisburg, to write into the new state constitution the complete disfranchisement of Pennsylvania Blacks. The general purpose was "to repel" those who denounced "the whole of the free colored people as unworthy of any favor, asserting that they were nuisances in the community fit only to fill alms houses and jails."

The strategy employed to accomplish these ends reveals a good deal about the faith which the abolitionists had in hard fact and reasoned argument. The data from the census were presented to the delegates at Harrisburg and to the public at large in the form of a forty-page pamphlet summarizing the findings.

The pamphlet argued that disfranchisement should be defeated because the free Negro population made a worthy contribution to the well-being of the entire community. Blacks paid considerable taxes and rents, owned property, were not disproportionately paupers and criminals, cared for their own underprivileged, and, finally, put money as consumers into the income stream of the general economy. The facts contained in the published pamphlet, therefore, "gave great satisfaction affording the friends of the colored people strong and convincing arguments against those who were opposed to their enjoying the rights and privileges of freemen." Although unsuccessful in the specific purpose—Blacks were disfranchised in Pennsylvania until 1870 when the Fifteenth Amendment was adopted—the abolitionists and Quakers undertook further censuses in 1847 and 1856. As in 1838, these later censuses were followed with printed pamphlets which duly noted the discrimination and problems facing free Negroes and counseled patience to the "magnanimous sufferers," as they referred to their Negro brethren. The general tone of the pamphlets, however, was *optimistic* and pointed to important *gains* made in past decades. The overall optimism, however, proved unfounded when the actual manuscript censuses were submitted to computer analysis.

The "friends of the colored people," unfortunately, had been carried away by their admirable purpose. It was one thing to document that free Negroes were not worthless, that they could indeed survive outside of the structured environment of slavery, and even that they could create a community with their own churches, schools, and beneficial societies; but it was quite another thing to argue that the people and the institutions they created actually *prospered* in the face of overwhelming obstacles. It is not so much that the abolitionists and Quakers were wrong, as that they went too far. And in so doing, they obscured a remarkable deterioration in the socioeconomic condition of Blacks from 1830 to the Civil War.

Beginning in 1829 and continuing through the ensuing two decades, Philadelphia Negroes were the victims of half a dozen major anti-Black riots and many more minor mob actions. Negro churches, schools, homes, and even an orphanage were set on fire. Some Blacks were killed, many beaten, and others run out of town. Contemporaries attributed the small net loss in the Negro population between 1840 and 1850 in large part to riots. In the same decade, white population grew 63 percent. While it is important to maintain the perspective that the anti-Black violence occurred within a larger context of anti-Catholic violence, this knowledge must have been small comfort to Philadelphia Negroes.

A victimized minority, one reasons, should organize and bring *political* pressure on local government officials. But Black Philadelphians after 1838, as we have seen, were denied even this remedy. Disfranchisement of all Negroes, even those citizens who owned sufficient property to vote in all elections during the previous twenty-three years, was all the more tragic and ironic because, at the same time, all white males in Pennsylvania over the age of twenty-one were specifically given the right to vote.

In addition to the larger, less measurable forces such as race riots, population decline, and disfranchisement, after 1838 Black Philadelphians suffered a turn for the worse in wealth, residential segregation, family structure, and employment.

The antebellum Black community was extremely poor. The total wealth—that is, the combined value of real and personal property holdings—for three out of every five households in both 1838 and 1847 amounted to sixty dollars or less. This fact, it can be noted in passing, precludes the use of simple economic class analysis in determining social stratification in the Black community. The distribution of wealth itself, moreover, was strikingly unequal within the Black population. In both 1838 and 1847 the poorest half of the population owned only one-twentieth of the total wealth, while the wealthiest 10 percent of the population held 70 percent of the total wealth; at the very apex of the community, the wealthiest 1 percent accounted for fully 30 percent of the total wealth.

Between 1838 and 1847, there was a 10 percent decrease in per capita value of personal property and a slight decrease in per capita total wealth among Philadelphia Blacks. Although the number of households included in the 1847 census was 30 percent greater than in 1838, the number of real property holders fell from 294 to 280, and their respective percentages fell from 9 to 6 percent. There was, in other words, despite a considerable increase in the number of households, both absolute and percentage decrease in the number of real property holders.

Another way of highlighting the decline is to create roughly equal population groups, rank them by wealth, and determine at what point in the rank order Blacks ceased to include owners of real property. In 1838 owners of real property extended through the wealthiest 30 percent of the ranked population; in 1847 they extended less than half as far. In 1838, moreover, it required a total wealth holding of between two hundred and three hundred dollars in order to own real property; by 1847 an individual required a total wealth holding twice as high before he could purchase land or own a home.

This statistic is complemented by a measurable rise in residential segregation over the decade. Disfranchisement (perhaps as valuable to us as a symptom of contemporary feelings about Negroes as it was a cause), a decade of race riots, and a general backlash against abolitionist activities, all contributed to the creation of a social atmosphere in which it was considerably more difficult for even the wealthiest of Negroes to acquire real property. It is tempting to conclude quite simply that rising racism meant that a far higher price had to be paid in order to induce a white man to sell land to a Black man. Stating such a conclusion with complete confidence, however, requires further *comparative* research in order to determine if instead this phenomenon applied equally to all ethnic groups, i.e., a period of generally appreciating land values.

The actual measurement of residential segregation depends upon the use of a "grid square"—an area roughly one and one-quarter blocks square—and is a vast improvement over far larger geographical entities such as districts or wards. Each Negro household was located on detailed maps, and its precise grid square recorded. All variables about each household, then, are observable and measurable in small, uniquely defined units.

Residential segregation is measured in two dimensions: (1) the *distribution* of the household population—that is, the number of grid squares in which Negro households were located; and (2) the *density* of the population—that is, the number of Negro households per grid. Residential segregation was rising in the decade before 1838, and it increased steadily to 1860. Between 1838 and 1847 average density increased 13 percent in all grid squares inhabited by Blacks; more importantly, however, the percentage of households occupying the most dense grid squares (those with more than one hundred Black households) increased by almost 10 percent. Between 1850 and 1860 the average density changed very little, but the trend toward settlement in the more dense grids continued. By 1860 the number of households occupying the most dense grid squares reached more than one in four, an increase of 11 percent over the previous decade and the high point between 1838 and 1880. During the Civil War decade, residential segregation fell off but rose again from 1870 to 1880 as migration from the South swelled the Negro population of Philadelphia to 31,700, an increase of 43 percent over both the 1860 and 1870 totals.

Data from the abolitionist and Quaker censuses, the United States Census of 1880 and W. E. B. DuBois' study of the seventh ward in 1896-1897 indicate, in each instance, that two-parent households were characteristic of 78 percent of Black families. That statistical average, however, belies a grimmer reality for the poorest Blacks. There was a decline in the percentage of two-parent households for the poorest fifth of the population from 70 percent in 1838 to 63 percent ten years later; and for the poorest half of the Black population the decline was from 73 percent to 68 percent. In other words, among the poorest half of the community at mid-century, roughly one family in three was headed by a female.

An unequal female-male sex ratio no doubt indirectly affected family building and stability. Between 1838 and 1860 the number of Black females per 1,000 Black males increased from 1,326 to 1,417. For whites in 1860 the corresponding figure was 1,088. Between 1860 and 1890 the sex ratio for Blacks moved in the direction of parity: 1,360 in 1870, 1,263 in 1880, and 1,127 in 1890. The age and sex distribution throughout the period 1838 to 1890 indicates that the movement away from, and after 1860 back toward, equal distribution of the sexes was due to a change in the number of young Black males in the twenty-to-forty age bracket. Changes in this age bracket usually result from two related factors: occupational opportunities and in- and out-migration rates. The remarkably high excess of females over males throughout the period probably reflects poor employment opportunities for Black men (while the demand for Black female domestics remained high) accompanied by net out-migration of young Black males. The gradual improvement of industrial opportunities for young Black males after 1860, accompanied by net in-migration of increasing numbers of young Black men reduced the excess of Black females. The sociological consequences of such an imbalance in the sex ratios are familiar: illegitimacy, delinquency, broken homes, and such. In light of these statistics, it is surprising that the percentage of two-parent households was as high as it was.

More important for our purposes, however, is another measure of the condition of the entire Black population often obscured by the debate over the matrifocality of the Black family, focusing as it does on narrow statistical analysis of traditional household units. How many Blacks were living outside of Black households? How many were inmates of public institutions? How many were forced not only to delay beginning families, but to make lives for themselves *outside* the Black family unit, residing in boardinghouses as transients or living in white homes as domestic servants?

The data indicate that there was a slow but steady rise in the percentage of Black men and women who found themselves outside the Black family. Between 1850 and 1880 their numbers nearly doubled. By 1880, six thousand persons—slightly less than one-third of the adult population (inmates, transients, and servants combined) were living outside the normal family structures. One out of every five adults lived and worked in a white household as a domestic servant. That so many Negroes took positions outside their traditional family units is testimony to the strength and pervasiveness of the job discrimination which existed at large in the economy; that this occurred within a context of widening occupational opportunities for whites, a benefit of increasing industrialization and the factory system, makes it even more significant. In 1847 less than one-half of 1 percent of the Black male work force was employed in factories. And this came at a time, it should be remembered, when thousands of Irish immigrants were engaged in factory work.

Blacks were not only denied access to new jobs in the expanding factory system, but because of increasing job competition with the Irish they also lost their traditional predominance in many semiskilled and unskilled jobs. The 1847 census identified 5 percent of the Black male work force in the relatively well-paying occupations of hod carrier and stevedore. The following letter to a city newspaper written in 1849 by one "P. O." attests to the job displacement.

That there may be, and undoubtedly is, a direct competition between them (the blacks and Irish) as to labor we all know. The wharves and new buildings attest this fact, in the person of our stevedores and hod-carriers as does all places of labor; and when a few years ago we saw none but blacks, we now see nothing but Irish.

"P. O." proved perceptive indeed. According to the United States Census of 1850, the percentage of Black hod carriers and stevedores in the Black male work force fell in just three years from 5 percent to 1 percent. The 1850 census, moreover, reported occupations for the entire country and included 30 percent more Black male occupations than the 1847 census; nevertheless the absolute number of Black hod carriers fell sharply from ninety-eight to twenty-eight and stevedores from fifty-eight to twenty-seven.

A similar pattern of increasing discrimination affected the ranks of the skilled. Blacks complained not only that it was "difficult for them to find places for their sons as apprentices to learn mechanical trades," but also that those who had skills found it more difficult to practice them. The "Register of Trades of the Colored People," published in 1838 by the Pennsylvania Abolition Society to encourage white patronage of Black artisans, noted that 23 percent of 656 skilled artisans did not practice their skills because of "prejudice against them." The 1856 census recorded considerable deterioration among the ranks of the skilled. The percentage of skilled artisans not practicing their trades rose from 23 percent in 1838 to approximately 38 percent in 1856. Skilled Black craftsmen were "compelled to abandon their trades on account of the unrelenting prejudice against their color."

Job discrimination, then, was complete and growing: Blacks were excluded from new areas of the economy, uprooted from many of their traditional unskilled jobs, denied apprenticeships for their sons, and prevented from practicing the skills they already possessed. All social indicators—race riots, population decrease, disfranchisement, residential segregation, per capita wealth, ownership of real property, family structure, and occupational opportunities—pointed toward socioeconomic deterioration within Philadelphia's antebellum Black community.

EX-SLAVE AND FREEBORN

Among the 3,300 households and 12,000 persons included in the 1838 census, about one household in four contained at least one person who although free in 1838 had been born a slave. Living in these 806 households were some 1,141 ex-slaves or 9 percent of the entire population. What was the condition of the ex-slave relative to his freeborn brother? Were ex-slaves in any way responsible for the socioeconomic deterioration just described? Contemporaries perceived two very different effects of direct contact with slavery. "Upon feeble and common minds," according to one view, the slave experience was "withering" and induced "a listlessness and an indifference to the future." Even if the slave somehow managed to gain his freedom, "the vicious habits of slavery" remained, "worked into the very grain of his character." But for others "who resisted . . . and bought their freedom with the hard-earned fruits of their own industry," the struggle for "liberty" resulted in "a desire for improvement" which "invigorated all their powers and gave energy and dignity to their character as freemen." An analysis of the data permits us to determine whether both groups were found equally in antebellum Philadelphia or whether one was more representative of all ex-slaves than the other.

The richness of detail in the census schedules allows us to make several important distinctions in the data describing the ex-slave households: We know which of the 806 households were headed by ex-slaves themselves—314—and how these 40 percent of all ex-slave households were freed—if, for instance, they were "manumitted" or if, as they put it, they had "bought themselves."

We are dealing, then, with several ex-slave categories: (1) 493 households in which at least one ex-slave lived, but which had a freeborn household head; I shall refer to this group as free-headed, ex-slave households; (2) 314 households in which at least one ex-slave lived, but which had an ex-slave head; I shall refer to this group as ex-slave-headed households. In this second group of ex-slave-headed households, I have selected two subgroups for analysis: (a) 146 ex-slave household heads who were manumitted, and (b) 96 ex-slave household heads who bought their own freedom.

Cutting across all of these groups is the dimension of sex. The census identified household heads as males, females, and widows. There was a strong and direct relationship between family size, wealth, and male sex, so that the largest families had the most wealth and the greatest likelihood of being headed by a male. Because there was also a strong and direct relationship between sex and almost all other variables, with males enjoying by far the more fortunate circumstances, it is important to differentiate by sex in comparing the general condition of the ex-slave groups to that of the freeborn population. Ex-slaves differed from their freeborn neighbors in a variety of significant social indicators.

Family size: The family size of all ex-slave households was 10 percent larger than households all of whose members were freeborn: 4.27 persons as compared to 3.88. Families of ex-slave households headed by freeborn males and those families headed by males who bought their own freedom were 20 percent larger: 4.70. The instances in which freeborn families were larger occurred only where female and, to a lesser extent, widow ex-slave households were involved. (This, by the way, is the general pattern in most variables; in other words, ex-slave females and widows more closely resembled their freeborn counterparts than ex-slave males resembled freeborn males.)

Two-parent household: Two-parent households were generally more common among the ex-slaves. Taken together, two-parent households were found 80 percent of the time among ex-slaves, while the figure for the freeborn was 77 percent. A significant difference, however, was found in the case of ex-slave household heads who bought their own freedom. In this group 90 percent were two-parent households.

Church: For two basic reasons the all-Black church has long been recognized as the key institution of the Negro community: first, an oppressed and downtrodden people used religion for spiritual sustenance and for its promise of a better life in the next world; second, with the ability to participate in the political, social, and economic spheres of the larger white society in which they lived sharply curtailed, Negroes turned to the church for fulfillment of their secular needs.

Important in the twentieth century, the church was vital to Blacks in the nineteenth. Philadelphia Negroes were so closed off from the benefits of white society that church affiliation became a fundamental prerequisite to a decent and, indeed, bearable existence. For this reason, nonchurch affiliation, rather than poverty, was the distinguishing characteristic of the most disadvantaged group in the community. Nonchurchgoers must have enjoyed few of the benefits and services which accrued to those who were affiliated with a church in some manner. The socioeconomic profile of nonchurchgoers is depressing. They fared considerably less well than their churchgoing neighbors in all significant social indicators; they had smaller families, fewer two-parent households, high residential density levels, and they were disproportionately poor. Their ratios for membership in beneficial societies and for the number of school-age children in school was one-fourth and one-half, respectively, that of the larger community. Occupationally they were decidedly over-represented among the unskilled sectors of the work force.

In this sense, then, the percentage of households with no members attending church is a more valuable index of general social condition than any other. Eighteen percent of the freeborn households had no members attending church; for all ex-slave households the figure was half as great. Although ex-slave households were one in four in the community at large, they were less than one in ten among households with no members attending church. The ratios were even lower (one in twenty) for ex-slave-headed households and lowest (one in thirty) for ex-slaves who bought themselves.

About 150 households or 5 percent of the churchgoing population of the entire community attended 23 predominantly white churches. These churches had only "token" integration, allowing a few Negroes to worship in pews set apart from the rest of the congregation. Ex-slaves of all groups attended white churches in approximately the same ratio as did the freeborn, one household in twenty.

The churchgoing population of the entire community consisted of 2,776 households distributed among five religious denominations: Methodists (73 percent), Baptists (9 percent), Presbyterians (7 percent), Episcopalians (7 percent), and Catholics (3 percent). Methodists worshipped in eight and Baptists in four all-Black congregations scattered throughout the city and districts. Together they accounted for more than eight of every ten churchgoers. The various ex-slave groups were found an average of 11 percent more frequently among Methodists and 30 percent more frequently among Baptists.

In any case, Methodists and Baptists differed little from each other, and to describe them is to characterize the entire community: poor and unskilled. Within each denomination, however, a single church—Union Methodist and Union Baptist—served as the social base for their respective elites. And while ex-slaves attended all of the community's all-Black churches, it was in these two churches where the ex-slaves were most frequently found. The ex-slave members of these two churches shared the socioeconomic and cultural characteristics of the community's elite denominations, the Episcopalians and the Presbyterians; and it should not be surprising, therefore, to find ex-slaves of all groups underrepresented in each of these last two denominations.

Beneficial society: Next to the church in value to the community were the all-Black beneficial societies. These important institutions functioned as rudimentary insurance groups which provided their members with relief in sickness, aid during extreme poverty, and burial expenses at death.

There were over a hundred distinct societies in antebellum Philadelphia. They grew out of obvious need and were early manifestations of the philosophy of "self-help" which became so popular later in the nineteenth century. Almost always they were affiliated directly with one of the all-Black churches. The first beneficial society, known as the "Free African Society," was founded in 1787. A dozen societies existed by 1815, fifty by 1830, and 106 by 1847.

Slightly more than 50 percent of freeborn households were members of the various societies. Making good the philosophy of "self-help," half a century before Booker T. Washington, the societies found ex-slaves more eager to join their ranks than freeborn Blacks. Each group of ex-slaves had a higher percentage of members, especially ex-slave-headed households (61 percent), ex-slaves who purchased their own freedom (65 percent), and the males among the latter group (70 percent).

Membership in beneficial societies varied significantly by wealth and status. Ranking the entire household population in thirty distinct wealth categories revealed that, beginning with the poorest, the percentage of membership rose with increasing wealth until the wealthiest six categories. For this top 11 percent of the population, however, membership in beneficial societies declined from 92 to 81 percent. Among the wealthiest, and this applied equally to ex-slaves, there was less need for membership in beneficial societies.

Education: One household in four among the freeborn population sent children to school. For ex-slave households the corresponding figure was more than one in three. Ex-slaves households had slightly fewer children, but sent a considerably greater percentage of their children to school. For freeborn households the percentage was 55 percent; for all ex-slave households 67 percent; and for ex-slave-headed households the figure rose to 72 percent. To the extent that education was valuable to Blacks, the ex-slaves were better off.

Location and density: Small groups of ex-slaves clustered disproportionately in the outlying districts of Kensington, Northern Liberties, and Spring Garden. Twenty-five percent of the entire Black population of Philadelphia, they comprised about 35 percent of the Black population in these areas. Most ex-slaves, however, lived in the same proportions and in the same block as did the freeborn population.

More interesting than the pattern of their distribution throughout the city, however, was the level of population density in which they lived, i.e., the number of Black neighbors who lived close by. To calculate the number of Black households in a grid square of approximately one and one-fourth blocks, three density levels were used: 1–20, 21–100, and in excess of 100 households per grid square.

The less dense areas were characterized by larger families, greater presence of two-parent households, less imbalance between the sexes, and fewer families whose members were entirely nonnatives of Pennsylvania. In these areas lived a disproportionately greater number of wealthy families, and among them, a correspondingly overrepresented number of real property owners. Here white-collar and skilled workers lived in greater percentages than elsewhere in the city, and unskilled workers were decidedly few in both percentage and absolute number. The major exceptions to the distribution of wealth and skill came as the result of the necessity for shopkeepers and craftsmen to locate their homes and their businesses in the city's more densely populated sections.

Ex-slave households were more likely than freeborn households to be found in the least dense areas (one in four as compared with one in five). Conversely, ex-slave households were less likely to be found in those areas with the greatest density of Black population.

Wealth: The parameters of wealth for Negroes in antebellum Philadelphia have already been described. The community was impoverished. Poverty, nevertheless, did not touch all groups equally. In terms of average total wealth, including both real and personal property, free-headed ex-slave households differed little from the freeborn population. In considering the ex-slave-headed household, however, differences emerge. Average total wealth for this group was 20 percent greater; for males in this group 53 percent greater; and for males who freed themselves, 63 percent greater.

The most significant differences in wealth by far occurred in real property holding. One household in thirteen or slightly less than 8 percent among the freeborn owned real property. For all ex-slave households the corresponding ratio was one in eight; for ex-slave-headed households, one in five; for males who were in this group, one in four; and most dramatically, for males who purchased their own freedom, one in three owned real property. To these ex-slaves, owning their own home or a piece of land must have provided something (perhaps a stake in society) of peculiarly personal significance. Distribution of wealth, to view the matter from a different perspective, was less unequal for ex-slave households, particularly ex-slave household heads. The poorest half of the freeborn and ex-slave-headed households owned 5 and 7 percent respectively of the total wealth; for the wealthiest quarter of each group the corresponding figure was 86 and 73 percent; for the wealthiest tenth, 67 and 56 percent; and for the wealthiest one-hundredth, 30 and 21 percent. Overall wealth distribution, in other words, while still skewed toward pronounced inequality, was more equally distributed for ex-slave household heads in the middle and upper wealth categories.

Occupation: The final area of comparison between the ex-slaves and the freeborn is occupation. Analysis of the data using the same classification schema for Negroes as for white ethnic groups confirms an earlier suspicion that, although such schemata are necessary in order to compare the Negro to white ethnic groups, they are entirely unsatisfactory tools of analysis when social stratification in the Negro community is the concern. Despite the fact that the Negroes who comprised the labor force of antebellum Philadelphia described themselves as engaged in four hundred different occupations, a stark fact emerges from the analysis: there was almost no occupational differentiation!

Five occupations accounted for 70 percent of the entire male work force: laborers (38 percent), porters (11.5 percent), waiters (11.5 percent), seamen (5 percent), and carters (4 percent): another 10 percent were employed in miscellaneous laboring capacities. Taken together, eight out of every ten working men were unskilled laborers. Another 16 percent worked as skilled artisans, but fully one-half of this fortunate group were barbers and shoemakers; the other skilled craftsmen were scattered among the building-construction (3.2 percent), home-furnishing (1.3 percent), leather-goods (1.2 percent), and metalwork (1.2 percent) trades. Less than one-half of 1 percent of Negroes, as pointed out in another context, found employment in the developing factory system. The remaining 4 percent of the labor force were engaged in white-collar professions. They were largely proprietors who sold food or secondhand clothing from vending carts, and should not be considered as "storeowners."

The occupational structure for females was even less differentiated than for males. More than eight out of every ten women were employed in day-work capacities (as opposed to those who lived and worked in white households) as domestic servants: "washers" (52 percent), "day workers" (22 percent), and miscellaneous domestics (6 percent). Fourteen percent worked as seamstresses, and they accounted for all the skilled workers among the female labor force. Finally, about 5 percent were engaged in white-collar work, which, like the males, meant vending capacities in clothing- and food-selling categories.

It should come, then, as no surprise that there were few distinctions of significance in the occupational structure of the ex-slaves and freeborn work forces. The differences in vertical occupational categories find male ex-slave household heads more likely to be in white-collar positions (7 percent as opposed to 4 percent for the freeborn), equally distributed in the skilled trades, and slightly less represented in the unskilled occupations (75 percent as opposed to 78 percent). Within the horizontal categories there were few important differences. Male ex-slave household heads were more likely than the freeborn to be employed as porters, carpenters, blacksmiths, preachers, and clothes dealers.

In summary, then, we find the ex-slaves with larger families, greater likelihood of two-parent households, higher affiliation rates in church and beneficial societies, sending more of their children to school, living more frequently in the least dense areas of the county, generally wealthier, owning considerably more real property, and being slightly more fortunate in occupational differentiation. By almost every socioeconomic measure the ex-slave fared better than his freeborn brother. While ex-slaves were distributed throughout the socioeconomic scale, they were more likely to be part of the community's small middle class which reached into both the lower and upper strata, characterized more by their hard-working, conscientious, and God-fearing life style than by a concentration of wealth and power.

AN URBAN PERSPECTIVE

On the basis of the data presented, it is possible to state two conclusions, offer a working hypothesis, and argue for the necessity of an urban perspective. First, the relatively better condition of the ex-slave, especially the ex-slave who was both a male and who bought his own freedom, confirms the speculations of a few historians that the slave-born Negro freed before the Civil War was exceptional: a uniquely gifted individual who succeeded in internalizing the ethic of deferred gratification in the face of enormous difficulties. More striking was the fact that the socioeconomic condition of the great majority of ex-slaves was not markedly inferior to that of the freeborn. That ex-slaves were generally better off than freeborn Blacks, however, should not suggest anything more than relative superiority; it does not imply prosperity and should not obscure the generally impoverished and deteriorating condition of the Black community. Second, because the remaining 91 percent of Philadelphia's antebellum Black population was freeborn, the dismal and declining socioeconomic circumstances of that population cannot be attributed to direct contact with the "slave experience." Direct contact with slavery was undoubtedly a *sufficient* cause of low status and decay; it most certainly was not a *necessary* cause.

In a very important sense the first conclusion has little to do with the second. The latter is not arrived at because those who had direct contact with slavery fared better in the city than those who were born free. The second conclusion is not based upon a recognition that slavery was less destructive or benign (although in some aspects it certainly could have been so), but rather that the antebellum northern city was destructive as well. It is significant to understand that slavery and the discrimination faced by free Negroes in the urban environment were both forms of racism which pervaded the institutions and informed the values of the larger white society.

The comparison of the freeborn and the ex-slave was undertaken in an effort to learn more about the question which students of the Black experience want answered: What was the effect of slavery on the slaves? In the case of antebellum Philadelphia the ex-slaves may not be representative of the slave experience. If they were, however, our insight would necessarily be limited to the effect of the mildest slavery system as it was practiced in Maryland, Delaware, and Virginia.

Deemphasizing direct contact with slavery does not imply that the institution of slavery, and the debasement and prejudice it generated, did not condition the larger context. The indirect effect of slavery cannot be underestimated. The proslavery propaganda provided the justification not only for the institution, but for the widespread discriminatory treatment of the free Negro both before and long after emancipation.

Yet, on the other hand, one must not allow this understanding, or an often overwhelming sense of moral outrage, to lead to a monolithic interpretation of the effects of the slave experience. Stanley Elkins' treatment of slavery may be in error, but few historians doubt that his urging of scholars to end the morality debate and to employ new methods and different disciplines in the study of slavery was correct and long overdue.

There is no historically valid reason to treat the slave experience as entirely destructive or entirely benign; nor, for that matter, does historical reality necessarily fall midway between the two. It may be more useful to study the problems which Blacks faced at different times and in different places in their history and make the attempt to trace their historical origins rather than to begin with slavery and assume that it represented in all instances the historical root. Some of the problems faced by Blacks may more accurately be traced to the processes of urbanization, industrialization, and immigration, occurring in a setting of racial inequality, rather than to slavery.

One of the most significant contributions to Black history and sociology in recent years presents data which suggest the postslavery, possibly urban, origins of the matrifocal Black family. In ground-breaking essays on the Negro family after the Civil War, Herbert Gutman has demonstrated convincingly that traditional interpretations of slavery and its effect on the Black family are seriously misleading. Examining "the family patterns of those Negroes closest in time to actual chattel slavery," Gutman did not find "instability," "chaos," or "disorder." Instead, in fourteen varied southern cities and counties between 1865 and 1880, he found viable two-parent households ranging from 70 to 90 percent.

It is significant to note that of the areas studied by Gutman the four lowest percentages of two-parent households were found in cities: Natchez and Beaufort, 70 percent; Richmond, 73 percent; and Mobile, 74 percent. The urban experience was in some way responsible for the weaker family structure, and for a whole set of other negative socioeconomic consequences all of which are found in the Philadelphia data.

Yet the city is more than a locale. Slavery itself underwent major transformations in the urban setting. Sustained advances in technology, transportation, and communication made the city the context for innovation; and the innovation, in turn, generated countless opportunities for upward mobility for those who could take advantage of them. And here was the rub. Blacks, alone among city dwellers, were excluded not only from their fair share, but from almost any chance for improvement generated by the dynamics of the urban milieu. That the exclusion was not systematic, but, by and large, incidental, did not make it any less effective. The city provided an existence at once superior to and inferior to that of the countryside: for those who were free to pursue their fortunes, the city provided infinitely more opportunities and far greater rewards; for those who were denied access altogether (or for those who failed), the city provided scant advantages and comforts. There were few interstices.

The data presented in this essay point to the destructiveness of the urban experience for Blacks in nineteenth-century Philadelphia. To proceed, data comparing the Black experience to that of other ethnic groups are necessary, and they are forthcoming. Although much research remains, it is possible to offer a hypothesis. The forces which shaped modern America—urbanization, industrialization and immigration—operated for Blacks within a framework of institutional racism and structural inequality. In the antebellum context, Blacks were unable to compete on equal terms with either the native-white American worker or the thousands of newly arrived Irish and German immigrants. Philadelphia Negroes suffered in the competition with the Irish and Germans and recovered somewhat during the Civil War and Reconstruction decades, only to suffer again, in much the same circumstances, in competition with the "new" immigrant groups, this time the Italians, Jews, Poles, and Slavs who began arriving in the 1880's. Best characterized as a low-status economic group early in the century, Philadelphia's Blacks found themselves a deprived and degraded caste at its close.

Students of Black history have not adequately appreciated the impact of the urban experience. In part this is due to several general problems: to the larger neglect of urban history; to unequal educational opportunities which prevented many potential Black scholars from study and other students from publication; to difficulties inherent in writing history "from-the-bottom-up"; and to present reward mechanisms which place a high premium on quickly publishable materials involving either no new research or shoddy and careless efforts.

There are, however, other and more important considerations, with no little sense of irony. The moral revulsion to slavery prevented development of alternative explanations of low status and decay. In the immediate postslavery decades and throughout the twentieth century, Blacks and then white allies took refuge in an explanation used by many abolitionists before them, namely, that slavery and not racial inferiority was responsible for the Black condition. They were, of course, not wrong; it was rather that they did not go far enough. It was, and still is, much easier to lament the sins of one's forefathers than it is to confront the injustices in more contemporary socioeconomic systems.

Although August Meier and Elliot Rudwick titled their well-known and widely used text, *From Plantation to Ghetto,* and, with the little data available to them, subtly but suggestively wove the theme of the impact of urban environment through their pages, scholars have been slow to develop it in monographic studies.

The Philadelphia data from 1838 to 1880 enable one to examine this theme in minute detail. Although 90 percent of the nation's Black population in 1880 was southern and overwhelmingly rural, the key to the twentieth century lies in understanding the consequences of the migration from the farm to the city. The experience of Philadelphia Negroes in the nineteenth century foreshadowed the fate of millions of Black migrants who, seeking a better life, found different miseries in what E. Franklin Frazier called the "cities of destruction."

If we are to succeed in understanding the urban experience, we must dismiss simplistic explanations which attribute all present-day failings to "the legacy of slavery" or to "the problems of unacculturated rural migrants lacking the skills necessary to compete in an advanced technology." We must understand, instead, the social dynamics and consequences of competition and accommodation among different racial, ethnic, and religious groups, taking place in an urban context of racial discrimination and structural inequality.

4

SOUTHERN CITIES
AFTER THE CIVIL WAR

A large majority of Southerners, both Blacks and whites, continued to live in rural areas and be occupied with agricultural pursuits after the Civil War. As late as 1890, only about 15 percent of the region's Blacks lived in cities. But for these persons, the city was a much more dynamic location than the countryside could ever be. Urban areas were centers of culture, education, transportation, trade, and, to a lesser degree, industry. Perhaps most important, the cities displayed much greater ethnic and social diversity than the homogeneous countryside. If there was a place for southern Blacks to grow and progress, in economic, social, or political terms, such possibilities were much more likely in the large towns and cities than on the farm and plantation.

Even before the end of the Civil War, Blacks began migrating to southern cities in increasing numbers, at first largely as refugees. Throughout the remainder of the 1860's the Black urban population grew as dislocations from the war continued to be felt, particularly as persons were involuntarily pushed off their old plantations. Others, hoping to forestall starvation, came to the city seeking government relief, although federal policy was to return such refugees, forcibly at times, to the countryside. Many Blacks who migrated to the cities came, however, for more positive reasons. Disillusioned with the specter of sharecropping and peonage, seeing that prospects for owning land were largely illusory, ambitious Blacks came seeking a new life away from the reminders of slavery and plantation agriculture. These migrants were part of the American mainstream, lured from rural backgrounds by the image, if not always the reality, of wider opportunities and a more varied, faster-paced life in the city. Unfortunately, where genuine opportunities existed, racial folkways often defined them as for "white only." Consequently, Black migration was a two-way pattern, as disillusioned and jobless urban residents returned to the soil. What were the realities of economic opportunity in the urban South? Many cities were war-torn, and considerable rebuilding took place, although a return to prosperity was no overnight phenomenon. Blacks found jobs in municipal reconstruction, clearing harbors and rivers and rebuilding railroads, but in general there was not sufficient new employment to meet all the expectations of the migrants. The South as a whole generated only a small proportion of the nation's industrial output, and even where factories were common, Blacks had to struggle for employment opportunities. In some industries Blacks continued to fill the same positions that slaves held before the Civil War. But elsewhere, particularly as mechanization was introduced, as in the cigarette industry, Blacks found themselves frozen out of factory work. Before the Civil War many skilled craft jobs were performed by slave craftsmen. With the advent of freedom many of these individuals continued practicing their skills, and their number may even have swelled with migrants from the countryside. But as the century drew to a close, increasing immigration of skilled or semiskilled foreigners plus trade-union pressures, restricting Black apprentices and denying protection to Black artisans, eroded the position of all skilled Black workers. When white laborers began to organize, race solidarity tended to prevail at the expense of class solidarity. Although there were significant cases of interracial unionism, as in New Orleans, no permanent tradition was established.

The Black middle class expanded in postbellum southern cities as ambitious or skilled former slaves made their way up the class ladder and shared social status with the small prewar elite. But this middle class, composed of small businessmen, skilled workers, and a tiny handful of professionals, was severely hampered by the inability of the Black masses adequately to support it and of the white middle class to recognize it. In some cities, like Raleigh, North Carolina, social and political divisions within the Black community may have contributed to weak mass support for its middle class. But the more fundamental reasons had to do with the general poverty of the Black urban masses. For most of them, buying a Black newspaper (and thus supporting the editor) was a distinct luxury. Purchasing groceries or other merchandise from the small "mom-and-pop" store was often a few cents more expensive than buying at the better capitalized, more established white business. Appeals to "Buy Black" could rarely be persuasive to a population that had to count every penny to survive. And with a generally unequal administration of justice, many urban Blacks either did without the services of an attorney or concluded that only a white lawyer could gain them sympathy from the court. This is not to deny that there were prosperous, even well-to-do members of the upper echelons of Black society, particularly in cities with a long heritage of free Black social development like Charleston and New Orleans. But for most, the struggle for prosperity was painfully slow, and entrance to the middle class was no guarantee of permanent social progress. Schoolteachers, for example, enjoyed considerable social status, but their pay was meager and often had to be supplemented by other employment, even agricultural or domestic work. Ministers experienced a similar discrepancy between status and income. Advances in housing, too, were likely to be impermanent. In 1865 most cities lacked a tradition of strict housing segregation, and Blacks could be found living in all sections of the cities. Not infrequently, well-to-do Blacks located in the same neighborhoods where prosperous whites resided. But by the 1880's, municipalities were placing increasing pressure on Black housing mobility, and the beginnings of more strict geographical segregation can be dated from this period.

The foregoing catalogue of restrictions and disabilities should not obscure the real communal and social opportunities which opened up for Blacks in southern cities after the Civil War. A more educated leadership began to make its influence felt. The city provided the economic wherewithal to support a much broader range of racial organization than even before, including churches, schools, and literally hundreds of different social clubs, literary and musical societies, militias, business groups, and benevolent and fraternal organizations. Furthermore, the concentrated urban population for at least thirty years after the war made rigid racial relations impossible. Up through the 1880's, the color line was often fluid in southern cities, although a rapid hardening was to take place in the next decade. Protest activities flourished in many southern cities during Reconstruction and even after. In Charleston, New Orleans, Richmond, Louisville, and Savannah, Black communities mounted vigorous and successful boycotts against segregated streetcars; not until the turn of the century was Jim Crow seating again officially imposed. In addition, southern cities provided a base for meaningful political organization and progress, although heavily Black rural areas also returned their share of Afro-American elected public officials. In assessing the political and social possibilities in the cities, the legislative record does not reveal the complete picture. Even after Reconstruction, as discriminatory laws were again passed, considerable flexibility existed in the color line. In more cosmopolitan cities like New Orleans, interracial fraternizing on many levels—at theaters, sporting events, houses of prostitution, and in residential neighborhoods—was not uncommon; for years municipal laws to prohibit such mixing was as often as not ineffective. Yet in other cities, rigid race relations came much sooner after the Civil War. There was no single pattern for southern urban race relations.

By the 1890's, race relations were deteriorating throughout the South, in the cities as well as the countryside. As whites began to pass comprehensive new discriminatory codes, and invented poll taxes, literacy tests, and grandfather clauses to eliminate Black political participation, urban Black populations found themselves under increasing white suspicion. Some urban leaders, following Booker T. Washington, advocated a strategic retreat away from the political and social arenas to the safer ground of economic progress, although others refused to adopt such an accommodating stance. How well a particular Black community survived new assaults from the aggressive white community depended upon twin factors of leadership and community solidarity. Some city populations managed to perpetuate the solidarity, and perhaps the best evidence of this is the recurrence of boycotts in the early years of the twentieth century protesting newly imposed streetcar segregation. That these boycotts were not successful in preventing the imposition of rigid caste restrictions is not the important point here; rather, these Black communities still mustered the internal cohesion and courage to protest in the face of militant white opposition. Some thirty southern cities saw such protests—an impressive number indeed. Other urban communities, like Raleigh, failed to muster the unity and sense of solidarity necessary to protest rapidly deteriorating conditions, and their populations became increasingly helpless in the face of a Jim Crow world. Before we pass too harsh judgment on Blacks in cities like Raleigh, however, it would be well to question the risks involved in militant protest. In Wilmington, North Carolina, whites went on a rampage against the Black community in 1898, angered by the persistence of Blacks in asserting their voting rights. Eight years later, Atlanta whites rioted, focusing their hatred particularly on middle-class Blacks. Atlanta had perhaps the highest percentage of well-educated Blacks, as it was the home of several colleges serving the race. But it was precisely their culture and progress that whites feared and determined to blunt. The Atlanta riot told all southern Blacks, especially those in urban areas, that they could not expect economic progress and self-improvement to lead to a lessening of racism.

BEFORE THE GHETTO
The Making of the Black Community in Savannah, Georgia, 1865-1880

JOHN W. BLASSINGAME

The urbanization of American Blacks has been second only to slavery in the impact it has had on their lives. Urbanization created the preconditions for the emergence of an intelligent leadership class, a sense of unity, and the will and the economic means to fight against white oppression. The city's diverse occupations gave urbanites an independence unmatched by Black ruralites trapped in an unending cycle of poverty, crop liens, and tenantry. The concentration of numbers in the city freed urban Blacks more quickly from the antebellum customs perpetuated in the countryside and gave them a large arena to develop a variety of social, intellectual, and creative talents and to build the community infrastructure denied to them as slaves and as quasi-free men. Although historians have obscured many of these factors by emphasizing the pathology of the "enduring ghetto," they were clearly present in many nineteenth-century southern cities. In few places was this more apparent than in the old city of Savannah, located in Chatham County on the Georgia seacoast.

While the city of Savannah itself was old, the Black community did not emerge with its full complement of social institutions and articulate leaders until after General W. T. Sherman's troops marched into the city and liberated the slaves on December 21, 1864. Emancipation

Reprinted with permission from the *Journal of Social History,* 6 (Summer 1973), pp. 463-488. Footnotes and tables appearing in the original publication have been deleted in the present volume, and should be consulted for full documentation of the author's conclusions.

led immediately to an increase in the Black population. Thousands of slaves from the interior of Georgia and South Carolina, attracted by the rations issued by the army and the charms of city life, or repelled by masters who refused to accept the abolition of slavery, flocked to Savannah in the winter of 1865. Later, in the 1870's, a series of crop failures, the poverty of white plantation owners, and the freedmen's ignorance, improvidence, indolence, and inability to purchase land led hundreds of other Blacks to flee from the disappointments of the plantation to the city. As a result of the postwar migration, the Black population of Savannah increased from 8,417 in 1860 to 15,654 in 1880, in other words, 51 percent of the total population of the city.

The addition of more than 7,000 migrants to the city's population in less than twenty years heightened racial tensions and initially increased the economic problems confronting Blacks. Feeling that they were being engulfed by a Black horde, Savannah whites viewed the rapid influx of the freedmen with apprehension. Reluctantly accepting the abolition of slavery, whites vowed never to accept Blacks on equal terms. The specter of social equality was omnipresent in the minds of whites. One young white asserted in 1865 that he would leave the country before he would "live in a city where I have got to mix with free niggers." A white woman declared: "My old mama who nursed me is just like a mother to me; but there is one thing that I will never submit to, that the Negro is our equal. He belongs to an inferior race." Acting on the premise of Black inferiority, white officials of Savannah repeatedly excluded Blacks from the jury box and for several years from the schoolhouse. Since whites regarded Negroes as children, they punished them severely in order, they said, to teach them respect for the law. For example, in 1876 a county court sentenced a Black woman to ten years in the penitentiary for allegedly stealing five dollars.

Given the extent of white prejudices, the Blacks crowding into Savannah faced an uphill struggle to achieve economic self-sufficiency. Fortunately, however, native Savannah Blacks had built a relatively strong economic foundation during the antebellum period. For example, many Blacks were skilled artisans in 1865 because of the training they had received as slaves. Before the war, owners taught their slaves skilled trades to make it easier and more profitable to hire them out. Many Savannah slaves worked for drayage firms, in rice mills, on construction sites, and at various municipal tasks. Slaves were members of four Negro fire companies in the city. Some of the slaves also gained business experience while working as butchers, fishmongers, and vendors of fruits, vegetables, candy, and flowers in the Savannah market. The free Negroes of the city, although few in number (705 in 1860), contributed to the Black man's business acumen and occupational skills.

Generally, Blacks maintained their corner on the Savannah labor market when slavery ended. At the same time, there was a greater occupational differentiation in the Negro labor force. While Black men were working at fifty-eight different occupations in 1870, they were working at ninety-two different occupations in 1880. And, although Negroes made up only 50 percent of the population, more than 50 percent of all draymen, porters, bricklayers, coopers, and cotton samplers in Savannah from 1870 to 1880 were Black. The apprenticeship of young Negroes to skilled Black artisans led to an increase in the percentage of Negroes in the total number of shoemakers (38 to 66 percent), butchers (38 to 66 percent), barbers, (43 to 82 percent) and blacksmiths (17 to 31 percent) from 1870 to 1880. At the same time, however, the organization of large construction companies led to a decline in the percentage of black carpenters (40 to 32 percent), plasterers (73 to 44 percent), and painters (32 to 23 percent).

While the percentage of the Negro labor force engaged in manufacturing, mechanical and building trades declined in the 1870's, the number of Blacks working as common laborers, firemen, and engineers, on the railroads, boats, and in the factories increased. Many artisans, earning from $1.81 to $3.50 per day, refused to allow their wives to work. Even so, about 70 percent of the Negro women in 1870, and 60 percent in 1880, were gainfully employed. Generally, Black women worked less than twenty different occupations, most of them being laundresses, domestic workers, and cooks. During epidemics in Savannah many of them, although untrained, worked as nurses.

Prejudice and white competition forced a larger percentage of the Black men to become common laborers (33 to 43 percent) and domestic workers (10 to 18 percent) by 1880 than had been the case in 1870. Condemnation to such casual labor had important consequences for Black men. For example, the Black unemployment rate was much higher than that of whites. Although unemployed for a shorter period (4.7 months for Negroes, 4.8 months for whites) than whites in 1880, Blacks constituted 75 percent of the male unemployed. Of the 767 Black unemployed, 57 percent were common laborers, 13 percent were servants, and 4 percent were porters. Thus, 74 percent of the Black unemployed were concentrated in those occupations containing 61 percent of the Negro labor force. To protect themselves from white prejudice, rapacious employers, and to provide mutual aid and a richer social life, Black working men organized twenty-one protective and benevolent associations and quasi unions. The only strikes on record are those of the Negro stevedores of 1869 and 1880.

Negro businesses followed the same general path of growth and differentiation as the Black labor force. In 1870, sixty-six Negroes operated twenty-seven different kinds of businesses. Two hundred and fifty-three Blacks operated forty-one different kinds of businesses in 1880. Some of them owned small manufacturing concerns. As the Negro population became more concentrated in the 1870's, the number of Black businesses increased rapidly. Capitalizing on racial pride, Black businessmen opened lunch counters, saloons, groceries, barber shops, hair-dressing shops, and one mortuary. Others invested small amounts of capital and became petty traders. Concentrated in service industries, Negro businesses were usually small, one-owner, marginal concerns. Only one Black businessman, livery stable owner Daniel Button, had as much as $15,000 in property in 1870.

Many Black businessmen and artisans in Chatham County accumulated property in the fifteen years following the Civil War. A few of them had acquired property before the war: in 1860, the free Negroes had $92,280 in property and a per capita wealth of $130.89. Although the wealth of the leading Blacks of Savannah in 1865 surprised some Northern observers, an overwhelming majority of the freedmen were penniless.

Encouraged in the next few years by their success as artisans and businessmen, the freedmen began opening savings accounts, buying land, and accumulating personal property. By 1870, they had acquired more than $400,000 in property. From 1866 to 1874, thousands of Negroes deposited $153,000 in the Savannah branch of the Freedmen's Saving Bank. The number of Negro landholders increased steadily; while there were only 96 Black landholders in Savannah in 1870, the number had increased to 648 by 1880. Although the value of property held by Negroes in Chatham County declined more than 50 percent in the 1870's, the amount of land they owned more than doubled (from 1,055 acres in 1874 to 2,687 acres in 1880). Primarily as a result of the general decline in property values, the aggregate value of land owned by Negroes decreased from $192,000 in 1870 to $79,000 in 1880. Similarly, the per capita wealth of Blacks declined from $17.79 in 1870 to $7.31 in 1880.

The low per capita wealth of Savannah Blacks exacerbated two serious social problems facing them: high dependency and mortality rates. In the first two years after the war the rate of dependency (swelled by the emigrants) of Blacks was much higher than that of whites. From

September 1865 to September 1867, the Freedmen's Bureau issued rations to an average of 529 Negroes and 159 whites per month in Savannah. As Negro and white refugees began to find work, the monthly average declined; from March 1867 to September 1868, the Bureau issued rations to an average of sixty-nine Negroes. Although no statistics are available before September 1865, undoubtedly the number of Blacks and whites depending on Bureau rations for their subsistence early in 1865 was much higher than the record indicates. For instance, there were 2,470 Negroes and 359 whites receiving rations from the Bureau in September 1865. On the other hand, the average for 1867 and 1868 appears to be a close approximation of dependency in the Black community for most of this period.

The Black migrants not only added to the number of dependents, but increased the morbidity and mortality rates among Blacks. Unaccustomed to city living, the Black migrants crowded into ill-ventilated huts on the outskirts of the city of Savannah or lived in unhealthy basements in the badly drained areas of the city. As a result of these conditions and ignorance of hygiene, proper childcare, and diets (which included an insufficient supply of milk and vegetables), fatal diseases took a heavy toll in the Black community. Between 1865 and 1880 the Black death rate fluctuated between 33 and 75 per thousand. Because Blacks were less likely to go to doctors until diseases had advanced too far to be checked, were less able to afford proper medical attention, and believed more in untrained "medicine men" than whites, the death rate for Negroes was generally .05 to 38.0 per thousand higher than that of whites from 1865 to 1880.

White prejudices, economic dislocation, large-scale migration, high dependency and mortality rates, and the accumulation of wealth and property all affected the development of a viable community among Blacks in Savannah. One of the first, and most enduring, problems Blacks encountered in trying to build a community infrastructure was that they were an overwhelmingly illiterate group living among whites who were highly literate. Although a few of the Savannah slaves and free Negroes had been educated before the war, they were almost inundated by the sea of Black migrants who rushed into the city. The first prerequisite, then, for building a viable community was to diffuse knowledge more widely among the Blacks. Savannah Blacks were anxious to lift the veil of ignorance clouding their future. John W. Alvord, secretary of the American Tract Society, for instance, wrote on January 11, 1865, that the Negroes in Savannah had "a passionate desire for education." On March 25, 1865, the Savannah *Republican* noted the "earnestness and avidity [with which] these liberated people seek information. All manifest a desire to learn." Similarly, war correspondent Charles Coffin wrote that freedmen in Savannah were "eager to obtain knowledge." Various Black groups in the city moved quickly to translate their desire into action and made strenuous efforts to educate Black youths. These efforts were all the more important because the Chatham County Board of Education refused to establish schools for Blacks until 1872. The Blacks could not wait; a few days after their liberation, the Negroes organized the Savannah Educational Association. In January 1865, Alvord, James Lynch, agent of the American Missionary Association and later Mississippi secretary of state, and Reverend Mansfield French examined dozens of applicants and found ten Negroes competent to instruct students in the Association's schools. Acquiring the use of Bryan's slave mart and Oglethorpe Hospital from General John W. Geary, the Association opened two schools on January 10, 1865, with about five hundred students. Supported entirely by the freedmen, the Association collected and expended $900 for educational purposes in its first year of operation.

Confronted by white indifference from 1865 to 1872, the freedmen maintained their schools with difficulty. There was a chronic shortage of books, supplies, schoolrooms, and funds. In addition to obtaining supplies for the schools, the freedmen had to pay monthly salaries ranging from $15 to $35 to thirty-eight teachers in 1865, twenty-one in 1868, and seventeen in 1870. The monthly tuition ($1.00 to $2.50) charged by most of the schools placed a heavy financial burden on Negro parents. For example, in 1868 the freedmen paid from $275 to $550 per month to educate fourteen hundred students for nine months. Because of the expense, the educational campaign would probably have failed or been sharply curtailed if sympathetic northern whites had not supported it. Answering appeals from Lynch and Alvord, northern aid societies sent teachers and supplies to Savannah. The American Tract Society sent a supply of books, and by the end of 1865 the American Missionary Association was financing five schools; the New York Society of Friends and the National Freedmen's Aid Society, two; and the New England Freedmen's Aid Society, one school in Chatham County. More importantly, in 1867 the American Missionary Association built a $13,000 secondary school, Beach Institute, on a bequest left by Alfred E. Beach, prolific inventor and editor of the *Scientific American.*

Unfortunately, northern financial support of the Black schools quickly decreased: by 1871 the only societies which maintained schools in Chatham County were the American Missionary Association and the St. Joseph's Sisters. As a result of the financial problems, the number of Negro schools in Chatham County declined from thirteen in 1865 to five in 1870. Similarly, the number of Black students declined from

1,877 in 1865 to 672 in 1870. More than 8,000 Negroes over ten years of age were illiterate in 1870.

With the decline in northern support for their private schools, Blacks began to put political pressure on the Chatham County Board of Education to organize public schools. Complaining that they received nothing for poll taxes they paid ($5,225 in 1874), early in the 1870's Blacks held several mass meetings and vowed not to vote for candidates for city office who opposed public schooling for Negroes. Coincidentally, there was a change in the opinion of whites toward the education of Blacks. One reason for the development of a more favorable attitude toward the education of Negroes was the fact that throughout the 1870's Blacks paid more poll taxes (used to support schools) than whites—$212 more in 1874 and $901 more in 1880.

As a result of the political pressure and the change in public opinion, in 1872 the Board of Education began to consider the establishment of public schools for Blacks. On August 15, 1872, Board members met with prominent Savannah Blacks and decided to try to convince the American Missionary Association to transfer Beach Institute to the Board. Because of the Association's reluctance to allow the Board to control the hiring of its teachers, it did not transfer the Institute until 1875. After failing to obtain Beach Institute, the Board of Education opened two schools for Negroes in December 1872. By 1875, there were 2,070 Black and 2,502 white students in the public schools. In the same year, there were more than 3,600 Negroes and 1,800 whites of school age who were not attending public schools. While most of these white children were in private schools, most of the Black children had no school to attend. Consequently, Blacks continued to petition the Board to establish more schools for Negro children.

Although the Board of Education was unsuccessful in supplying all of the schools needed in Savannah, the shift to publicly supported schools improved the chances of Black children being educated. Financial support, although small in amount, was consistent. The schools were better equipped and more efficiently operated than they had been from 1865 to 1872. On the other hand, the teachers were only a little more competent.

The campaign to stamp out illiteracy, despite its limited success, contributed significantly to the growing sense of community among Blacks. For the first time Blacks worked in concert to solve common problems: organizing their own schools, opening churches to Black scholars, and attending mass meetings to obtain public schools. Such actions created among Blacks the feeling that they were in some way independent and had some control over their destiny.

The movement for independence reached its apogee in the churches. Almost from the beginning of slavery, Negroes in the city had received some religious instruction either in the churches of their masters or in separate congregations. By 1865 whites and Blacks had established five Negro churches with about four thousand members and an aggregate value of $63,000. Whites, however, controlled all of these churches: they served as trustees and frequently as Sunday School teachers. After the abolition of slavery, the freedmen fled from the churches of their former masters and rapidly established their own churches. Between 1865 and 1880, Negroes organized ten new churches and began to join new denominations. In 1865, Negroes were attending three Baptist churches, one Methodist, and one Episcopal church. Fifteen years later, they communed at five Baptist and five Methodist churches, one Presbyterian, one Catholic, one Congregational, and one Episcopal church.

While the increase in Negro churches expanded the number of institutions solely controlled by Blacks, they also helped to uplift them and create a sense of solidarity among diverse groups in a variety of ways. The ministers sought to make Negroes more religious through their Sunday sermons, Sabbath schools, and week-night lecture and prayer meetings. Some of the larger churches tried to keep in contact with members who could not attend regularly by establishing "prayer-houses" in different areas of Savannah and the county. Most of the ministers stressed the importance of education, racial pride, living a Christian life, and having self-respect. In this regard, the churches were important agents of social control. They consistently expelled members who did not abide by the rules of the church and castigated them for drunkenness, lawlessness, and immorality.

The churches were also important centers of communal recreation. They frequently gave fairs, suppers, concerts, picnics, spelling bees, and Sunday-school programs. Perhaps the most notable church event of this period was the memorial service for Charles Sumner at St. Phillips A. M. E. Church in 1874 which was attended by four thousand Negroes. The highlight of the service came when the audience heard songs by Elizabeth Greenfield, the Negro Quaker from Philadelphia who had sung in London in 1853 and was known as the "Black Swan."

Outside the church, there were several organized social activities which both contributed to and reflected the development of a sense of unity among Blacks. Antebellum proscriptions had so restricted Blacks from acting in concert that they had only established a small number of social organizations. After the war, however, centripetal forces outweighed the centrifugal ones: the general tendency was toward organized social activities. In fact, by 1880 Savannah Blacks had organized more than

193 clubs and mutual-aid societies. The Skidmore Club String Band and the Braham String Band furnished music for the balls given by the Social Club of Savannah, the Union Coterie, the Ladies and Gents Social Club, and the Committee of Nine. The eight militia companies (one official) frequently drilled to the music of the Washington Cornet Band and held shooting matches and riding contests in the Forsyth Park parade grounds. The four Masonic and three Odd Fellow lodges had frequent meetings and suppers and paraded in full regalia through the streets of Savannah. During the summer, Blacks went to picnics and to games between Negro baseball teams or on railroad and steamboat rides (excursions) to the resorts in Chatham County and to various places in Georgia and South Carolina. They also celebrated several special days: Liberian Independence, Emancipation Day, Lincoln's birthday, and anniversaries of the adoption of the Fifteenth Amendment. Those Blacks who enjoyed serious or light intellectual exercises attended the meetings of the Young Beginners' Literary and Social Society or the Young Men's Bible and Literary Association.

As Blacks gained a greater sense of unity, they began to grapple with the many serious social problems undermining their community. One of the most difficult of these problems was the weak family structure. There had been no legal marriage in slavery. Of necessity, fathers had little authority over or responsibility to their "families." Any connection between slaves had little permanence. There was no "illegitimacy." Their children cared for in plantation nurseries, many mothers learned little about childcare. However, in spite of the legacy of slavery, Blacks had a strong sense of the sanctity of the family. Many of the Blacks, seeking another badge of freedom, flocked to the Freedmen's Bureau offices in 1865 to obtain marriage certificates. Others went in search of loved ones from whom they had been separated by the vicissitudes of slavery.

The desire of the freedmen for regularized family relations was encouraged by Black ministers and newspaper editors. Partially as a result of this campaign the family had become relatively stable by 1880: males headed 75 percent of the families, and the number of nonworking wives and one-family dwellings was relatively high.

Blacks responded to the specters of dependency and death by organizing several benevolent and mutual-aid societies to aid the poor and sick, and by paying the burial expenses of indigent members. Practically all of the Black churches did the same things on an informal basis, sometimes established burial associations and often raised money to support the short-lived Lincoln Freedmen's Hospital.

The degree to which Blacks were able to solve community social problems depended to a large extent on the quality of their leaders. The quality of the leaders and the way they emerged was in turn significantly affected by the low per capita wealth and high rate of illiteracy of Blacks. Perhaps more important, however, was the fact that few of the Black people had had an opportunity to act as leaders before the war. Although the ministers provided some leadership functions, they were so completely under the thumb of whites that they could rarely speak for their followers. For the most part, antebellum "leaders" had little influence and less power because there were few formal procedures for legitimizing their positions.

The abolition of slavery created several bases for the emergence of a new leadership class. First, the relative scarcity of influential men guaranteed that many relatively young Blacks would rise to leadership positions. Second, the formation of many community organizations created several power bases for those Blacks ready to take advantage of them. Numerically, the most important of these bases were the 193 clubs and societies Blacks established. From 1865 to 1880, more than 922 persons served as officers in these clubs. Seventy-two percent of these officers were men; 64 percent were born and raised in Savannah; 96 percent had been slaves, and their average age was thirty-seven. An overwhelming majority of the leaders were skilled artisans and included twenty-eight draymen, twenty-four porters, twenty-two carpenters, fifteen laundresses, and eight bricklayers.

Forty-six prominent families were the social leaders of the Black community. These families held 234 of the offices in clubs organized during this period. At the apex of the social pyramid were fifteen families whose members held one hundred of the offices. The socially prominent families had several characteristics in common. Generally they were stable, literate, and relatively well-off. Ninety percent of the women in these families did not have to work, and the children were either at home, in school, or serving as apprentices. The eighty-four socially prominent families listed as property holders in the 1870 census had a per capita wealth of $783. Still, only a small percentage of the 922 social leaders held property. Apparently literacy and a pleasing personality were surer guarantees of social prominence than wealth. The same was true of the color factor. Whatever was true of the relationship between mulattoes and Blacks in other cities, in Savannah neither group was able to garner a disproportionate share of the leadership posts; whenever they did, education, and not color, appeared to be the deciding factor.

There was an intimate relationship between the officers of social organizations and institutions and political leaders. In fact, the two groups were often interchangeable. Building on a solid base of influence and power in community institutions, many Blacks were able to translate social preferment into political power. For example, 90 percent of all the Negroes who served as clerks, justices of the peace, magistrates, or constables in the county, as officers in the county and state Republican party or delegates to the national conventions, or who held patronage jobs in the U.S. Customs House or Post Office were also officers in several of the Black social clubs in Savannah. Similarly, all of the Savannah Blacks who served in the Georgia legislature in 1870 and 1872, except Aaron Bradley, were officers in the clubs or prominent church officials. Ulysses L. Houston, representative of Bryan County, served as pastor of the First Bryan Baptist Church from 1861 to 1880. James M. Simms, representative of Chatham County, was an ordained minister who served as clerk and deacon of the First African Baptist Church from 1858 until he went to Boston in 1863. He returned to Savannah in 1865, ran successfully for the legislature in 1868, and received an appointment as state district judge from Governor Bullock in 1871. (The legislature abolished the court before Simms ever held a session.) James Porter, representative of Chatham County, was president of the board of wardens and vestry of St. Stephen's Episcopal church.

Ideologically, the Black leaders ranged from the far right (where such ministers as William J. Campbell adjured political participation and took an extremely obsequious attitude toward whites) to the far left (where Henry McNeal Turner, James M. Simms, and the peripatetic Aaron Alpeoria Bradley frequently advocated violent attacks on whites). Men such as John H. Deveaux, editor of the Savannah *Tribune* and member of the legislature in 1872, and most of the ministers were centrists, insisting on the necessity for racial pride, uplift, constant struggle to obtain civil rights and racial cooperation. Most of the attention, however, was focused on the far left.

Aaron Bradley, an irrepressible and fiery orator, won the undying hatred of most whites in Georgia and wholehearted support from the Blacks in Chatham, Bryan, and Effingham counties who elected him as a senator to the Georgia legislature in 1868. Escaping from slavery in Georgia when he was nineteen, Bradley went north and later became a lawyer. Returning to Savannah in 1865, he promptly began urging Blacks in the area to seize abandoned plantations and to fight if the Freedmen's Bureau or the U.S. Army tried to dispossess them. Arrested and imprisoned by military officials for his "insurrectionary language," Bradley was soon released and began organizing Blacks in Chatham County into political cadres and incipient labor unions, and gathering petitions demanding the right to vote. Usually armed with a derringer and a bowie knife, Bradley often appeared at political rallies with an armed escort, led riots against white citizens and police, and was probably arrested more times than any other politician in the nineteenth century. An advocate of what is today known as "Black power," Bradley insisted that Blacks should hold all of the offices in any district in which they were in a majority and often bolted the regular Republican party when a few Blacks were nominated for important offices. Although mendacious and arrogant, Bradley won the support of Savannah Negroes with his showmanship, fearless attacks on whites, advocacy of an eight-hour day, an end to convict leases and chain gangs, the inclusion of Negroes in the state militia, his belief in women's suffrage and integration of public carriers, and his laudation of Negroes as the greatest of races.

While no leader could match Bradley in his aggressiveness or physical assaults on whites, Henry McNeal Turner was a more honest, constructive, and dependable man. The most influential Negro minister in Savannah, Turner was pastor of St. James A. M. E. Church. Born to free parents in South Carolina, in 1863 he was appointed chaplain of the First United States Colored Troops. After the war, Turner settled in Macon, Georgia, and represented Bibb County in the Georgia legislature in 1868. The University of Pennsylvania (1872) and Wilberforce University (1873) conferred, respectively, the honorary degrees of Doctor of Laws and Doctor of Divinity upon him. In 1872, Turner became a customs inspector in Savannah. One of the leading Republicans in Georgia, Turner served on the party's state central committee and was one of the delegates to the Republican National Convention in 1876.

A shrewd man, Turner was initially much more conservative and conciliatory toward whites than Bradley. But after one of his cohorts was murdered and all Blacks were illegally expelled from the Georgia legislature in 1868, Turner became increasingly more radical. He immediately organized a State Civil and Political Rights Association and later led strikes of agricultural workers in middle Georgia, organized labor conventions, and promised to kill whites who threatened him. By the time he arrived in Savannah in 1872, Turner was beginning to advocate emigration from the South. Eventually he reached the point where he called the flag of the United States "a dirty contemptible rag" and asserted that he wished his native land nothing but ill fortune.

Although Turner, Bradley, Deveaux, and Porter fought valiantly for equal justice, an untrameled ballot box, fair wages for the laborer, and integrated transportation, they did not have a strong enough power base to achieve all of their objectives. Outnumbered by whites in the state, Black voters had no consistent friends among the motley crew of racist white Republican officeholders. Blacks had little voice in governing the city of Savannah because they were a minority of the voters. The quick "restoration" of Georgia had ended whatever effective political power Blacks had by 1872. Consequently, the correspondent Edward King could report in 1873 that in Savannah "the Negroes no longer have any voice whatever in political matters, and are not represented in the City Government." Because they had a majority of the voters in rural areas of Chatham County, however, Blacks continued to win county offices until the late 1870's. But even this power was sharply curtailed by the machinations of Savannah's white officials bent on disfranchising Blacks.

Although there were severe limits on their power, the emergence of Black leaders was crucial in the fight Savannah Negroes waged against white proscriptions and prejudices. In spite of white fears of social equality, the white press's frequent use of "darkey" and "coon" to describe Blacks it considered obnoxious, and physical altercations between the races, Negroes fought against any obvious efforts to discriminate against them. Black leaders complained consistently against the exclusion of Negroes from the jury box and the harsh penalties meted out to them. On April 1, 1876, for example, the Savannah *Tribune* asserted that white officials in Georgia displayed "the most wanton disregard for any rights of the Negro, human, or divine." Because of the inequities in law enforcement, James Simms and Porter introduced several bills in the legislature in 1870 to reform the prison system and to change the manner of selecting jurors.

Porter was also one of the leaders in the campaign against Jim Crow in Georgia. A bill he introduced in the legislature led to the passage of an act on August 24, 1870, which provided that "all common carriers of passengers for hire in the State of Georgia shall furnish like and equal accommodations for all persons without distinction of race, color or previous conditions." The law, however, remained a dead letter in Savannah until 1872 when Blacks started "sitting in" streetcars reserved for whites and fighting with the white passengers when they were pushed off the cars. On several occasions disgruntled Blacks shot into the all-white passenger cars and had officials of the line arrested for refusing them seats.

Negroes also fought discrimination on other fronts. When one of the express companies placed an "Exclusively for White People" sign over a water cooler, the *Tribune* declared on August 19, 1876: "Pshaw! boys, to the pump." The rush of Negroes to the pump caused the company to take the sign down. Apparently there was no standing rule about segregation in the theaters. When the all-Negro Braham Musical Club gave a concert in the Savannah theater where the manager had forced

Negroes to sit in the balcony, the *Tribune* was indignant. The performance of the club under these restrictions was all the more regrettable, the editor declared on April 29, 1876, because Negroes and whites sat in the same sections on streetcars (until 1906) and because there was "no well bred gentleman in the city of Savannah who hesitates to ask a colored man to take a seat in his parlor, if he is decent in his person and respectful in his manner."

Although the *Tribune* obviously exaggerated the extent of racial harmony, there were many indications of cordial relations between Blacks and whites. There was, for example, occasional fraternizing between white and Negro communicants. Whites invited Blacks to attend the dedication of new churches and often visited Negro churches. Because of its central location, many white Catholics attended Mass with Negroes at St. Joseph's Catholic Church. Similarly, Negroes often attended white churches. For instance, when the First African Baptist Church expelled Deacon John H. Brown, he "spent his time visiting the white churches" in the city from 1875 to 1877. While it is practically impossible to determine the extent of miscegenation, at least three interracial marriages had occurred by 1880. Two white men had married Negro women, and one Negro man had a white wife.

The most important factor in promoting interracial contacts in the city was the continuation of the relatively integrated antebellum housing pattern. Before the war, Negroes had lived all over the city in the small cabins behind the residences or in the homes of their masters. In 1860, from 28 to 48 percent of the inhabitants in each of Savannah's four militia districts were Black. Ten years later, they made up from 34 to 53 percent of the population in each district. The residential pattern in 1870 reflected the large number of Negroes who lived in the homes of their employers, a significant number of Black and white laborers inhabiting the same houses and the large number of Blacks and whites who lived next to each other on practically all of the streets of Savannah. On few of these streets did Negroes constitute more than 50 percent of the inhabitants. Even when these streets appeared, they were rarely contiguous to each other.

In the late 1870's the color line became somewhat more rigid: Three areas where more than 50 percent of the inhabitants were Negroes had developed by 1880. The heaviest concentrations were in "Yamacraw" and the areas bounded by Broughton, Price, and Liberty streets. Blacks, however, were not restricted to these areas. While the concentration of Negroes on the periphery of the city had increased, Blacks continued to reside on practically every street in Savannah. In fact, throughout the 1860's and 1870's Black and white laborers tended to reside in the same areas, and more prosperous Negroes and whites tended to live in the same areas. The relatively open housing pattern is reflected in the fact that even in 1880 nine of the fifteen Negro churches and nineteen of the thirty-six Negro businesses which appeared in the city directory were located outside the areas with the heaviest concentration of Blacks. Residential segregation during this period appears to have been based as much on class and economic status as on race.

When the general ignorance, widespread improvidence, confusion, immorality, poverty, and the weak and limited number of social organizations and institutions of Savannah Negroes in 1865 is compared with their situation in 1880, it is obvious that they had made great strides in building their community. Still, the profile of Savannah Blacks does not emerge in a clear outline. While housing was relatively open, justice was not color blind. Coincidental with riots between Black and white voters, Negro and white church members enjoyed cordial relations. Integrated streetcars and parks coexisted with Jim Crow theaters. The number of landholders increased steadily; but the Freedmen's Bank failed; property values and total wealth declined; and in 1880 the Black 51 percent of Chatham County's population owned only 9.7 percent of the county's total wealth and had only 12 percent of the per capita wealth of whites. With the largest Negro population in the state, Chatham County Negroes ranked seventy-fifth in per capita and fourth in total wealth of the Blacks in Georgia's 137 counties. Although there was an increase in occupational skills, Negroes were concentrated in unskilled, low-paying, casual jobs. While education became more widespread, about three thousand Black children did not attend school. Even so, with native leaders, a rich social life, close cooperation, strong churches, and a militant newspaper to sustain and defend them, during this period Savannah Blacks built the foundation of a viable community.

Perhaps if scholars take the blinders off and resist the temptation to read allegations of the all-pervasive present-day pathology of a Newark or Harlem back into the nineteenth century, we may find that Savannah was a typical Black community. Although few cities have been analyzed, this examination of Savannah Blacks should cause scholars to ponder anew the meaning of the Black urban experience. Even when we concede the existence of endemic social problems, increasing political powerlessness, and widespread illiteracy, the "enduring ghetto" of twentieth-century northern cities does not appear in Savannah. This suggests that the theoretical framework applied by Alan Spear to Chicago and Gilbert Osofsky to New York may be inapplicable to nineteenth-century southern cities.

Given what we know (admittedly limited) of the experience of Blacks in many nineteenth-century southern cities, it may be fruitful for scholars to formulate new theoretical models to study Black communities. This is especially necessary because contemporary theories are based, it seems to me, on several questionable assumptions: (1) that certain economic, social, political, and psychological benefits accrue to Blacks from integrated housing patterns which automatically outweigh those benefits that come from living with persons of similar culture and identical racial origin; (2) that there was an inexorable retrogression of Blacks from the halcyon days of integrated housing immediately after the Civil War to the pathology of ghettoes made in the 1890's; and (3) that Black intellectual, social, and economic developments are tied so closely to the actions of whites that we learn more about Blacks from the migration patterns of whites and the machinations of white and Black realtors than we do from studying the internal dynamics of the Black community.

Such assumptions seem entirely unwarranted when considering southern cities. Whatever problems nineteenth-century urban Blacks encountered in the South, they apparently had little to do with either emerging or enduring ghettoes. In fact, contemporary segregated housing patterns in southern cities are the result of twentieth-century legislation. Beginning in 1910 with Baltimore, dozens of southern cities passed a bizarre series of segregation ordinances to reverse traditional integrated housing patterns. In spite of integrated residential patterns in nineteenth-century Savannah and other cities, southern Blacks faced many of the same problems plaguing Blacks locked in ghettoes. The common problems and features of urban living begin to emerge, paradoxically, when one recognizes the regional, economic, and cultural diversity of new and old, manufacturing and commercial, inland and port, northern and southern cities. There is, for instance, both a world of difference and many similarities in the Black community in postbellum, war-ravaged Atlanta peopled mainly by new migrants (Black and white) and the New Orleans community with its large antebellum Black population. Rebuilt quickly after the war, Atlanta immediately segregated Blacks while New Orleans continued its traditional pattern of integrated housing. Yet, as different as housing patterns were, there were many similarities in occupational trends, racial ideology, institutional developments, and mortality rates among Blacks in the two cities.

It is obvious that the character of Black-white housing patterns does not determine the nature of the Black urban experience. Housing patterns may be, in fact, ancillary rather than central to that experience. When, however, scholars attempt to study the Black community from the inside, focus on people rather than solely on real estate, analyze Black hopes as well as Black frustrations, and the solutions Blacks proposed as well as the problems they faced, we will begin to understand the impact of urbanization on Blacks. We need to know as much about Black dreams as we do about white fears of Blacks, as much about Black institutions as housing patterns, Black occupations as unemployment, and Black successes as Black failures. Viewing the Blacks in Savannah from this perspective suggests that nineteenth-century urban Blacks had visions of the future which included self-determination, solving their social problems, educating their children, and working and playing in ways which had little to do with later historians spinning fanciful theories (based on the European experience of Jews) about them being locked in "enduring ghettoes." They were building "enduring communities."

5

THE URBAN NORTH
BEFORE
THE GREAT MIGRATION

Northern cities experienced great growth from the end of the Civil War to the beginning of World War I, fueled by an increasing rural-to-urban trend within the country and continued immigration from abroad. Not only did city populations expand, but with new developments in mass transit—electric trolleys, elevated railways, subways, and cable cars—geographical boundaries also grew. The beginnings of urban sprawl appeared as new suburbs opened for the rich. Even some middle- and working-class neighborhoods developed on the outskirts of cities where growing industries were taking advantage of large plots of land with good railroad connections. Geographical expansion brought new and improved city services—lighting, heat, power, water, sewage disposal—in addition to municipal transit. This fueled growth in the electrical, iron, steel, lead-pipe, and streetcar industries, as well as expansion of residential, office, and factory construction. New demands for construction machinery, building materials, and metals also resulted. The expanding urban population also created a vast new market for consumer goods, from typewriters to telephones, from sewing machines to soda pop, from bicycles to Buicks. In short, the pre-Civil War commercial cities were being transformed, by the late nineteenth century, into manufacturing cities. These growing metropolises now provided the principal market for both industrial and consumer goods, having displaced the countryside. America was no longer primarily a rural, agricultural country; industrialization and urbanization, working in tandem, were creating a nation of cities which became the magnet for millions of foreign immigrants. But what prospects did they hold for Blacks?

Northern cities symbolized, for rural Blacks, places to which one might escape the imprisonment of sharecropping and agricultural peonage, or perhaps find greater prospects for political and social expression. Acting on these hopes, a steady although modest trickle of migrants left the South between 1870 and 1890. The volume picked up somewhat between 1890 and 1915, although it did not approach the massive numbers who would relocate after the latter date. These migrants chose eastern and midwestern cities as their destination. But despite the images of urban promise, the economic reality was otherwise. Blacks were systematically barred from industrial jobs except as strikebreakers. Readily available employment was found only in low-paying service occupations or occasional unskilled labor where few prospects for advancement or security existed. In other words, Blacks were not permitted to participate in and gain from the dramatic industrial expansion of the economy. Studies of a number of northern cities demonstrate this. Blacks found themselves suffering under a job ceiling in which entrance into some professions and skilled trades was being increasingly curtailed, and sometimes blocked entirely, while opportunities for employment and subsequent upward mobility were being accorded non-English-speaking immigrants. Occupational eviction was a second economic handicap. In trades where Blacks had traditionally enjoyed good employment opportunities, like longshoring and construction, and sometimes near monopolies, like barbering, catering, and waitering, they found themselves faced with organized and often successful attempts to force employers to discharge Blacks and hire only whites. The result was that by the turn of the century, in city after city of the North, the proportion of Blacks in unskilled or service occupations numbered 80 percent or more.

The search for decent housing in northern cities presented corollary problems. Concentrated in low-paying occupations, Blacks naturally had to commit a greater proportion of their earnings to the bare essentials of food and shelter. But here, again, they faced a handicap not borne by foreign immigrants. Not only did Blacks frequently have to dwell in some of the city's worst housing—dilapidated and lacking in sanitary conveniences, much less comfort—they usually had to pay more for equivalent slum housing than did white immigrant groups. Often paying the highest rents in relation to quality, many Black families had to resort to one of two solutions: either make use of multiple breadwinners to meet the rent, or sacrifice space and privacy by taking in lodgers, sometimes relatives but frequently total strangers. Historians dispute the alleged effects of the presence of unrelated lodgers on family morality and stability, but it seems likely that in most cases a supplementary income was the only benefit. In an era when much lower-class urban housing was by modern American standards unspeakably crowded and unsanitary, it is no wonder that the death rate, as well as the infant mortality rate, was alarmingly high. That the majority of urban Black households supported two-parent intact families in the face of severe economic and housing pressures, is a testament to the sense of kinship and family unity nurtured, if not fully realized, during slavery.

It should not be assumed, however, that distinct ghettoes, defined as large majority-Black concentrations of population, existed in late nineteenth-century northern cities. First, there were simply too few Blacks to form such ghettoes. Of the eight northern cities with the largest Black population in 1900, only in Indianapolis did the proportion of Blacks in the total population approach 10 percent; six of the remaining seven had fewer than 5 percent. Typically the Afro-American population was scattered throughout the city, with a tendency for modest and sometimes only tiny enclaves of Blacks to exist. These concentrations might be only one tenement building, elsewhere several apartment buildings on a "mixed" block. But to find a whole block inhabited solely by members of the race, much less a section larger than that, would have been rare before 1915. The areas where Blacks lived were ethnically quite diverse, with lower-status immigrants sometimes the majority population, sometimes a sizeable minority. In some cities competition for jobs was the major source of racial friction, but in others clashes over housing were the most important factors in generating interracial ill will. Such was the case in Chicago. White unwillingness to allow Blacks to move into new areas as their numbers increased led to the gradual creation of a physical Black ghetto with more or less defined boundaries. The density of such geographically restricted areas then began to increase. The "Black Belt" in Chicago, and similar concentrations elsewhere were thus born. They would mature as ghettoes after 1915.

Black community life in northern urban areas became both more diversified and more socially complex between the Civil War and World War I. A pronounced and broad class structure was one such development. The old elite, which had attained its preeminent position before the Civil War, still remained, but a new, commercially based middle class began to develop by the turn of the century. Its criteria for social acceptance were different. The old elite emphasized lineage, inherited wealth, culture, education, and long-standing ties to the "better whites." In contrast, the emerging middle class was business oriented, including as it did successful entrepreneurs and younger professionals and measuring success almost exclusively in terms of monetary gain, no matter what one's background or educational attainments were. The northern

Black Bourgeoisie was coming into existence. This growing social differentiation between old and new elites often divided communities more than it united them, as was the case in Detroit and Chicago. No longer was there one homogeneous class above the masses; no longer did single organizations, other than political parties, have such community-wide membership that they cut across all class lines and included participants from all levels of society. The proliferation of urban churches illustrates this phenomenon. Upper-status Blacks tended to join Episcopal, Congregational, and Catholic churches, although in most large cities there was at least one upper-status Methodist and Baptist church. The various Methodist denominations drew heavily from the middle class. Baptist churches were the most numerous, and they had a primarily lower-class membership. Fraternal and benevolent or insurance societies also tended to mirror class differences. Other social clubs reflected and emphasized social distinctions and provided, especially for middle- and upper-class men and women, a distinct social niche. For example, in the late 1800's the Black women's club movement began, and this became a significant social outlet for members of the middle class. There was, unfortunately, much less organized activity among the Black working masses.

The most significant communal trend in the late nineteenth- and early twentieth-century northern cities was the birth of Black social service agencies. Their importance lies in their pioneering efforts to identify and meet the daily needs of the urban masses, as well as the assumption that Blacks could not afford to wait for either government or white charities to remedy pressing social ills. The White Rose Mission, which later became known as the Association for the Protection of Colored Women, undertook to aid young women, recruited in the South to work as domestics in northern urban areas, who found themselves friendless, penniless, and often duped into prostitution by unscrupulous employment agents. The Committee for Improving the Industrial Condition of Negroes in New York attempted the formidable task of encouraging white employers to hire more skilled Black workers, while at the same time compiling lists of individuals with such craft skills and acting as an employment bureau. The Committee also promoted night schools for adults and kindergartens for the children of working mothers. These goals soon spread to other cities. Again in New York, the Committee on Urban Conditions Among Negroes, responding to the absence of sympathetic and helpful social work among the poor of the race, began a program of graduate training in urban social work for Blacks, providing them with community internships in the process. These organizations, founded by socially aware members of the Black middle and upper classes, merged in 1911 and became the National Urban League, the first countrywide organization focused on problems of urban adjustment and employment. Although its top leadership and financial support drew on both races, its community-level activities were staffed by Blacks.

This development of a social program to deal with urban challenges of unemployment, poor housing, exploitation of female labor, and a lack of modern skills and training opportunities, should be put into the context of the Progressive Era. During the early twentieth century long overdue social reforms were enacted, especially in the cities of America. But many white progressives were oblivious to the needs of the Black community; these urban social activists concentrated their solicitude on foreign immigrants. As was the case among free Blacks in the North before the Civil War, the main energy for reform and improvement in the emerging Black ghettoes would have to come from within the community itself. Local government too frequently turned a blind eye to overcrowded Black tenements. Prostitution and other vices, often catering to a white clientele, were tolerated, even protected, in Black neighborhoods. Labor unions were more interested in keeping Black workers out of their locals than helping them gain industrial protection. So a familiar pattern was reenacted: the Black community had to turn to its own resources. And it was none too soon, for in the late teens and the twenties, a million and a half Blacks would crowd into the cities of the North and Midwest in the Great Migration.

THE TWO-PARENT HOUSEHOLD
Black Family Structure
in Late Nineteenth-Century Boston
ELIZABETH H. PLECK

Once the most rural of American ethnic groups, Afro-Americans are now the most urban. Slavery, migration to the city, and the adaptation to urban culture have had major effects on Black life, yet we know little about the ways in which the most basic unit of Black life, the family, was affected by these changes. Through research in the manuscript census schedules of the federal census for 1880 and other largely quantitative materials, I looked for answers to the following questions. What was the effect of migration on the Black family? What was the occupational situation of Black heads of household? How did urban and rural families differ in their adaptation to life in the city? How did literate and illiterate families differ? What family forms predominated? How frequent was "family disorganization," as reflected in an imbalanced sex ratio, frequent desertions by the head of household and large numbers of female-headed households?

We can learn a great deal about Black family life from an examination of Boston in the late nineteenth century. The Hub was a major northern metropolis, with a large and diversified economy, which should have offered opportunities for unskilled but willing Black workers. As a result of the long efforts of Blacks and whites in the abolitionist movement, the city had no segregated institutions and a widely respected system of

---

Reprinted with permission from the *Journal of Social History,* 6 (Fall 1972), pp. 3-31. Footnotes and tables appearing in the original publication have been deleted in the present volume, and should be consulted for full documentation of the author's conclusions.

free public schools. Boston had acquired a reputation among Blacks as "the paradise of the Negro," a city of unparalleled freedom and opportunity. Since the Black population was so small a percentage of the inhabitants of the city, the racial fears and animosities of the white population appeared, surfaced, but did not explode into major race riots like those in New York and Philadelphia during the Civil War. The large Irish and small Black populations lived in an uneasy truce, with the two groups dwelling in close proximity in the west and south ends of the city. Unique in some ways, representative of major northern cities in others, Boston is an interesting city in which to study many facets of Black family life.

The most typical Black household in late nineteenth-century Boston included the husband and wife, or husband, wife, and children. This predominant household form prevailed among all occupational levels and among families of both urban and rural origins. By enlarging the household to include boarders, families from all occupational strata augmented the family income and provided homes for the large numbers of migrants in the population. This evidence from the manuscript census contradicts the commonly held association between "the tangle of pathology," "family disorganization," and the Black family.

Before examining the composition of the Black household, I will indicate how inferences were made about the origins and literacy of heads of household, and I will discuss three aspects of social life in Boston—the transiency of the population, the depressing occupational position of Black heads of household, and the physical circumstances of life—which severely constrained family survival.

COMPARISON OF RURAL AND URBAN, LITERATE AND ILLITERATE HEADS OF HOUSEHOLD

In the analysis of one- and two-parent households which follows, the foreign-born heads of household were excluded since they offer too few cases for valid comparisons. Comparing the northern- and southern-born heads of household, I looked for possible differences in urban and rural family adaptation to life in Boston. Since the manuscript census schedules indicate the state of birth of an individual, but not the city or area where the individual was born or raised, the comparison is imperfect. Although a majority of northern-born Blacks lived most of their lives in urban areas, the northern-born category also included farmers from New England, townspeople from western Massachusetts, and settlers from the free Black communities of Ohio. By further separating those born in Massachusetts (mostly natives of Boston) from the rest of the northern-born, I was able to discern differences between that part of the population which was born in Boston and that portion of the population which migrated into the city.

While most southern-born Blacks were rural folk, that category also includes city dwellers from Richmond, Baltimore, or Washington, D.C. Even more difficult to distinguish are those southern-born Blacks who were urban in experience, if not in place of birth. But despite these qualifications, it seems useful to perceive the northern-born as essentially an urban group, and the southern-born as a rural group.

The distinction between literacy and illiteracy may have been as important as the difference between urban and rural families. Seven out of ten Black adults could read a few words and sign their names, the nineteenth-century standard of literacy. Even this minimal knowledge reflected a variety of skills which facilitated successful adaptation to urban life. Those without such skills—the illiterates—were more at a disadvantage than they were on the farm and more noticeable for their deficiency as well. Whole families headed by illiterates faced far greater difficulties in cities than those headed by literate parents.

In the South, illiterates tended to be ex-slaves. (The equation of illiteracy and slave status would have been unnecessary had the Boston census takers directly enumerated the number of freedmen in the Black population.) Under slavery, most Blacks were not taught to read or write or were prevented from even learning. While there were exceptions, self-educated slaves (Frederick Douglass is the best-known example), the opportunities for literacy were much greater for free Blacks than for slaves. But before equating southern-born illiterates with ex-slaves, two important qualifications must be added. First, even the majority of free Blacks, like the slaves, was untutored. Second, the number of illiterates was very low, far below any estimate we might make of the number of ex-slaves in the population. Thus, while illiteracy appeared in both northern- and southern-born families, its presence among the southern-born, in addition, reflected the existence of ex-slaves in the population.

GEOGRAPHIC MOBILITY

From the 3,496 Blacks living in Boston in 1870, the population grew ten years later to include 5,873 persons. By 1910, the population had expanded three times to 13,654. In the same forty-year period, the white population grew over two and one-half times, and the foreign-born white population tripled. The metropolis was growing rapidly, and within the city the Black population, although small in absolute number and in size relative to the white population—never more than 2 percent of the total population throughout the period—was growing at a rate faster than that of the foreign-born immigrants.

In the late nineteenth century the Black population absorbed a large number of migrants. While a minority, 42 percent of Boston's Blacks in 1880, had been born in the North, a majority were strangers to northern life; 49 percent of the population was born in the South, while another 9 percent were born in foreign countries. Of the northern-born population, especially those born in Massachusetts, the majority probably were natives of Boston. Other northern-born Blacks came from neighboring cities in the Northeast, and a few were from rural areas in New England. For the foreign-born, their life in Boston was the culmination of the long journey from Nova Scotia, New Brunswick, or other parts of Canada, or the end of a long sea voyage from the West Indies. The largest group in the population, the southern-born, included migrants from the upper South, especially Virginia.

These southern newcomers seem to contradict prevailing theories of migration to cities. Rather than traveling short distances and settling at the first stop along the way, these migrants moved as much as five hundred miles from home, often passing through other urban centers. Why did these men and women make the long journey? The usual explanation of Black migration to the North refers to Jim Crow segregation, racism, and declining economic opportunities in the South, combined with the expanding economy and promise of a freer life in the North. Pushed out by southern conditions, pulled to the North, the land of golden streets and busy factories, the combination of push and pull factors explains the Great Migration, the period during and after World War I. The earlier movement, described by Carter Woodson as the migration of the Talented Tenth, represented a period when Blacks were more pulled to the North than pushed from the South. The absence of two factors—widespread agricultural depression and active recruitment of Blacks by northern employment agents—further distinguished the earlier migration from the Great Migration of World War I. Despite the propaganda of some of their brethren and the appeals of some southern whites, the Black emigrant was above all looking for a better life in the northern city. One migrant was Ella Beam, a young woman who left the South Carolina Sea Islands for Boston:

She stated that she did not leave home on account of hard times. When she left, her father was doing well on the farm. There were several boys in the family, so she was rarely called upon to go into the fields. She felt, however, that she was not especially needed at home. The fact that she manifested sufficient initiative to take the course at the training school [domestic science] is perhaps indicative of the courage and energy of a young woman who wanted to better her condition. She had been in Boston only one year when she received a simple job caring for children in the home of a Melrose family.

For the most part, the migrants included young adults above the age of twenty, very few of whom came with their families. In households headed by a southern-born parent, 72.1 percent of the oldest children in the family were born in the North. Among the oldest children of a Canadian parent, 60.7 percent had been born in the North. Six out of seven of the oldest children in West Indian families had been born in the North. Thus the migration from the South and from foreign countries included single individuals or couples, but in very few cases did the whole family make the move.

The story of migration does not end with the arrival of the newcomer in Boston. Instead of settling down, the transient frequently packed up and left. Evidence from several nineteenth-century cities in the Northeast indicates a high rate of Black migration, generally higher than that of other groups. But in the South and West the rate of Black out-migration was about the same or a little lower than among other groups. Assuming this pattern is substantiated in further research, it indicates the absence of job opportunities for Black workers in nearby southern areas, in contrast to the proximity of many cities in the urban Northeast where the transient could find employment.

An examination of Boston city directories reveals that only 25 percent of adult Black males listed in the 1880 census were enumerated in the 1890 city directory, while 64 percent of a representative sample of adult white males in 1880 remained in the city ten years later. The rate of persistence for Blacks was very similar among all occupational levels while the rate of persistence among white males decreased for lower-status workers.

Among Blacks heading households, the rate of persistence was 31 percent, compared with the 25 percent overall figure. Adult sons residing at home, although few in number, were more transient than their fathers, since only 21 percent of them remained in the city for the decade 1880–1890.

High rates of turnover were common in other northeastern cities. In the depression years of the 1870's Black out-migration occurred frequently among Poughkeepsie and Buffalo residents. Only one-third of the Black workers in Poughkeepsie in 1870 remained in the city ten years later. In a twenty-year trace of Black adult males in Buffalo from 1855 to 1875, only 12 percent could be found. The northern pattern of high Black out-migration and much lower out-migration for other groups is reversed in the South and West. In Atlanta, for example, Blacks were much more likely to remain in the city than either foreign-born whites or native whites. Even more remarkable, within all occupational categories, the Black departure rate was lower than that of native white and foreign-born immigrants. For Birmingham, Alabama, the much higher rate of Black persistence was the result of fewer opportunities elsewhere for Black workers. During the depression decade 1870–1880, in San Antonio, Blacks, European immigrants, and native whites had very similar rates of persistence— 36 percent for Blacks, 36 percent for European immigrants, and 35 percent for native whites—while the Chicano population was the most transient, with only 25 percent of the male population remaining there ten years later. The question remains whether this pattern of southern Black geographic stability was also reflected in long-lasting marriages and continuity of parental care for Black children.

OCCUPATIONAL STRUCTURE

The occupational position of Black heads of household placed a great strain on the Black family. While the children of white immigrants moved up the occupational ladder, the Black child, like his parents, remained fixed in a world of menial and temporary jobs. Eight occupations— waiter, servant, cook, barber, laborer, porter, laundress, and seamstress— accounted for 74 percent of all Blacks at work in Boston in 1880. The largest group by far were the 858 servants who worked in white homes, hotels, and institutions. Two occupations, laundress and seamstress, were largely the preserve of single women and women heading households. The last hired and the first fired, Blacks in late nineteenth-century Boston formed a surplus labor force at the bottom of society. Overall, 86.7 percent of the total Black work force consisted of unskilled and service workers; 7.2 percent of Black workers held skilled positions; 2.9 percent performed clerical jobs or owned small shops; and 3.2 percent were professionals. The Boston Irish, an immigrant group of peasant origins, were the white ethnic group which ranked lowest in the Boston social order. Except at the top of the occupational structure, where there was a slightly higher percentage of professionals among the Black work force than among the Irish, Irish workers had much larger percentages of white-collar and skilled workers and much smaller percentages of unskilled and service workers than the Black labor force. While 68.9 percent of the Irish were laborers, teamsters, hostlers, and other unskilled and service workers, 86.7 percent of Blacks performed this low-status work. The classification of menial labor, moreover, tends to obscure the wage differences between the two groups. The Black waiter and the Irish cotton-mill operative both worked long hours at low pay, but the rewards were somewhat greater for the Irish worker than for his Black counterpart.

Of all wage earners, 7.2 percent of the Blacks and 19.8 percent of the Irish were skilled workers. Such work, particularly in the building trades, required apprenticeship training which was generally closed to Blacks; even buying tools could be an expensive proposition for a Black worker. The white-collar group, over three times as large among the Irish as among Blacks, owed their jobs to the expansion of recordkeeping, paper work, and sales in an industrial society. The new jobs in the Boston labor market—office personnel, sales clerks, even telephone and telegraph operators—employed some of the children of Irish parents, while job discrimination and lack of the proper educational qualifications closed this employment to the aspiring Black worker. The figures for the white-collar group also reflected the larger proportion of petty proprietors among the Irish than among Blacks.

For the Black professionals, Boston deserved its reputation as the city of the "Talented Tenth." The relatively large number of Black lawyers, doctors, and other professionals, compared with the somewhat smaller Irish percentage, was the result of the attractiveness of the city to educated Blacks from the South and other parts of the North, as well as the educational opportunities for the Black elite in the New England area.

Even so, the Black child and the Black parent clearly faced more limited job opportunities than even the proletarian Boston Irish. How did the occupational situation of heads of household compare with that of the Black worker with no family responsibilities? Although the head of household, in order to support dependents, needed to earn more money than the unattached Black worker, there were virtually no differences in occupational situation between Blacks heading households and those not heading households. Among unskilled and service workers, one finds 86.8 percent of Black heads of household and 87.9 percent of the unattached Black workers. Providing for a family was even more difficult for the widowed or deserted wife. Female-headed households included 22 women with no occupations and 105 women at work, most of them in unskilled and service jobs.

Black workers, including male heads of household, female heads of household, and workers with no family responsibilities were concentrated in the lowest ranks of the occupational structure. While there were slight differences in occupational level for heads of household as compared with all other workers, heads of household, in general, were no more occupationally diverse than other Black workers.

CONDITIONS OF LIFE

In the vast new areas of Boston, large frame houses with plenty of rooms, indoor plumbing, and spacious backyards were being built for the middle class. But the streetcar suburbs of late nineteenth-century Boston were restricted to whites. In 1880, about 42 percent of the Black population lived in the West End (sometimes referred to as Nigger Hill), a conglomeration of tiny alleyways and side streets on the seamy side of Beacon Hill. Tenement commissioners visiting the area described filthy streets, polluted air, overcrowded housing, dirty cellars, unsanitary water closets, poor drainage, and unsafe buildings.

At No.– Anderson Street is a little court. Here a single water closet in a small shed, the bowl filled and in abominable condition, was the only accommodation in this line for eight or ten families of colored people, besides the hands in a stable and a couple of little shops.

Since the tenement rooms were crowded, poorly heated and ventilated, children played in the streets. Playing stickball in the summer and using Anderson and Phillips streets as ski slopes in the winter, Black children made the most of their urban environment. But street play also resulted in children being crushed under the wheels of fast-moving teams of horses.

The poor physical conditions and the inability of parents to provide an adequate family income resulted in sickness and sometimes death for Black children. Mission workers from a settlement in the West End found "a young girl, whose only bed was two broken chairs placed between the cooking stove and the door. She was dying with consumption and was left all day with the care of a two-year-old child, tied into a chair beside her, while its mother was at work." In the same neighborhood, they found a poor Black child "who shared the floor with the rats and mice on a cold winter's night." These cases were probably the most dramatic, not the typical, circumstances of Black poverty in the West End. The mission workers, no doubt, chose examples which would underline the importance of their work and the need for hospital care for their clients.

Individual human tragedies like the deaths of these two children are hidden in the high death rates in the Boston Black community. Although the birth rate for Blacks was higher than for whites, the number of deaths was so great that deaths generally exceeded births. In fact, 1905-1910 was the first five-year period since the Civil War when the Black birth rate was higher than the death rate. Year after year, the city registrar reported more Black deaths than births. In 1884, the registrar speculated that "there can be no question that, so far as the limited field furnished by this city affords the means of judging, were accessions from without to cease, the colored population would, in time, disappear from our community." Arguing that the "colored" race was unsuited to northern climates, he concluded:

In short, it would not be too much to say, that were all opposing obstacles of every kind, and in every direction, to the entire liberty of the colored race removed, and they were allowed to seek and occupy any position they were qualified to fill, they would instinctively and inevitably gravitate to southern and congenial latitudes as naturally as water seeks its own level.

As a result of poor diet, extremely high rates of infant mortality and deaths for mothers in childbirth, and the frequent incidence of tuberculosis and contagious diseases, the mortality rate for the Black population in 1886 was 41 per 1,000, almost twice the white rate. A Black person who grew up in the West End recalled that on Sundays after church his family discussed the number of deaths in the neighborhood and which of the neighbors were dying of consumption. Diseases connected with childbirth accounted for the slightly higher death rate among Black females than among Black males. In 1890 the death rate per 1,000 for white males in Boston was 15.86, for Black males, 32. Among white females the mortality rate was 24 out of 1,000, while Black females died at the rate of 35 for every 1,000.

The death rate was highest among children under one year of age, and higher still among male children. But significant reductions in infant mortality for both whites and Blacks led to a sharp decline in the death rate in the first decade of the twentieth century. From 1900 to 1910, the white death rate for children under one year of age fell from 189 per 1,000 to 185, while the Black death rate dropped from 322 to 294. These figures were comparable to the mortality rates in other northern and western cities.

The high death rate among adults created a large number of widowed persons. About one-third of women aged 41–50 and a little less than half of women aged 51–60 lost their husbands. Either as a result of migration or in consequence of a higher rate of remarriage, the census takers found only about one-third as many widowers as widows. Some of the widows remarried; others went to live with relatives; and the remaining women made up the bulk of one-parent households in the Black community. The death of both parents left about 17 percent of Black children homeless in Boston in 1880. These orphans were a much larger part of the population in late nineteenth-century cities than were the one out of ten Black youngsters in 1968 who were not living with one or both parents. Homeless Black children, in most cases, lived with relatives or friends, for few such children found their way into asylums and homes for foundling children. Discrimination by public institutions combined with the desire of Black families to adopt Black children meant that few Black children without parents became wards of the state.

FAMILY STRUCTURE

The high death rate and overcrowded, unsanitary tenements, the transiency of the population, and the low occupational position constitute the kinds of pressures often cited as the causes of family disorganization. But several quantitative indicators—the sex ratio, the small number of one-parent households, the infrequency of desertion, and the adaptation of the household to include large numbers of migrants—suggest that the Black family structure maintained its organization despite the many depressing aspects of life in Boston.

Several statistics are useful gauges of the nature of family life. One such statistic is the sex ratio, the number of males per one hundred females in the population. A western frontier area, with a ratio of males to females of ten to one, or even higher, would have little family life. For everyone who chose to marry, a stable ratio of males to females would theoretically insure the selection of a mate. Another arrangement of sex ratio, a small male population and a large female population, is said to produce a society with few stable marriages and high rates of illegitimacy, desertion, delinquency, and female-headed households. These theoretical possibilities, reasonable in the abstract, have less meaning in concrete historical situations. Even in societies with quite similar sex ratios, great deviations can occur in patterns of sexuality, marriage, and family life. Still, for a population on the move, such as the Black population over the last one hundred years, the possibility of imbalanced sex ratios due to large numbers of migrants is an important consideration in assessing the framework of family life.

In fact, among Blacks in late nineteenth-century Boston, parity of the sexes existed. The overall sex ratio in 1880 was 102.9 though much higher—121—for the marriageable age group of those 25 to 44. In two other age groups, the very young and the very old, there were more females than males, reflecting the differential mortality of the sexes. The preponderance of males in the 25 to 44 age group stems from the relatively greater economic opportunities drawing adult migrants to the city. Many of these males were "beachhead" migrants, husbands who sent for their wives after they had established themselves in Boston.

When the Black sex ratio is contrasted with the sex ratio of the foreign-born and native white populations, we find greater imbalances in the two white groups. For all native whites in 1880 the sex ratio was 95.7, while it was much lower—79.4—for foreign-born whites. Among young adults, there were 96 native white males for every 100 females, and 83.8 foreign-born white males for every 100 females. The large number of adult females in the foreign-born white group reflects the presence of adult working women, usually employed as domestic servants and factory workers, some of whom were earning enough money to finance their dowries.

Throughout the last decades of the nineteenth century, there were slightly more males than females in the Black population of Boston. Only in 1910 did the census takers find the reverse. Many young adult females, migrants to Boston, created this surplus of females in the population.

The second important statistic for assessing the possibilities of family life is the number of married persons deserted by their spouses. Even though parity in the sex ratio suggests the necessary environment for stable family life, it is still quite possible that a high number of desertions would modify this conclusion. The number of desertions was determined by tabulating all those married persons in the census record who were not living with their spouses. Of those deserted by their spouses, there were 157 females, about 11 percent of all married women, and 167 males, about 13 percent of all married men in this category. The figures for males, as we noted earlier, were probably increased by the large number of men awaiting the arrival of their wives. In a middle-class district of late nineteenth-century Chicago, where few of the desertions could be explained as the result of large numbers of migrants, about 11 percent of households included a deserted wife or husband.

What seems impressive in these figures for Blacks in Boston is the low rate of desertion and separation, given the extremely high rate of out-migration, even among heads of household, and the dismal occupational prospect that Blacks faced. W. E. B. DuBois discussed some of the causes of desertion and separation among Blacks in Philadelphia.

The economic difficulties arise continually among young waiters and servant girls; away from home and oppressed by the peculiar lonesomeness of a great city, they form chance acquaintances here and there, thoughtlessly marry and soon find that the husband's income cannot alone support a family, then comes a struggle which generally results in desertion or voluntary separation.

As a result of death, desertion, or voluntary separation, 18 percent of Black households came to be headed by one parent. In nine out of ten instances the one parent was a female. In assessing one- and two-parent households, I included households in which there were no children present as well as those with children. If childless couples were excluded, we would be unable to examine households of young couples, that is, future parents, as well as those households where grown offspring had moved away.

How did one- and two-parent households differ? Without substantial historical evidence it would be foolhardy to apply present-day, widely questioned theories about the "tangle of pathology" associated with one-parent households. Regretably, I have found no qualitative evidence which bears on the issue of how members of the Black community viewed the one-parent household.

Nevertheless, there was an important economic difference between the one- and two-parent household. Although precise income figures are not available for Black households, Black males enjoyed higher wages than Black females. In consequence, a family dependent on a woman's wages almost always lived in poverty. The yearly wage among female domestic servants, for example, was half the wage of male domestic servants. Moreover, given the concentration of female heads of household in the most poorly remunerated occupations, overall income levels between male- and female-headed households were even more disparate. In many two-parent households, the husband's wage was supplemented by his wife's earnings from domestic service or laundry work and the rent money from the boarder. Without these several income sources, the one-parent household was at an even greater disadvantage. Lacking the wages or unpaid labor of a wife, even the one-parent household headed by a male suffered economically.

From an analysis of the manuscript census schedules, three important distinctions emerged among two-parent households in the Black community. First, there were proportionately more two-parent households among migrants to Boston than among native Bostonians. Second, the proportion of two-parent households among rural Blacks was greater than among urban Blacks. Finally, literate Blacks headed two-parent households more often than illiterate Blacks.

As we observed above, the early movement of Blacks to Boston brought persons especially attracted to the advantages of the northern city. Both those heads of household from the rural South and those northern heads of household from outside of Massachusetts revealed large and almost identical proportions of two-parent households, 83.3 percent and 83.4 percent respectively, while native Bostonians contributed fewer two-parent households. Given the many theories about the disruptive nature of migration, we might expect a higher percentage of one-parent households among the newcomers to the city than among the long-established urban Blacks. But, in fact, the percentage of two-parent households among these migrant groups was much higher than among Black natives of Boston. Thus, the stereotype of disruptive migration does not fit the situation of Blacks in late nineteenth-century Boston.

The combined effects of rural origins and long-distance movement away from family and friends made southern-born rural migrants to Boston a distinctive group. We can compare the effect of rural origins on the household by contrasting rural heads of household (the southern-born) with urban heads of household (the northern-born). Slightly more two-parent households occurred among rural than among urban heads of household, 83.3 percent as opposed to 78.7 percent. If we assume that a majority of the southern-born Blacks were freedmen, the large number of two-parent households among them is even more remarkable. The common argument, that the abrupt transition from rural to urban life created indelible strains on the Black family, does not hold for late nineteenth-century Boston. If anything, we find the reverse of this common proposition. Households in which both parents were present were more frequent among rural-born than among urban-born Black heads of household.

Even greater than variations between urban and rural households were variations within these two types of households. For both urban and rural heads of household, a literate Black was more likely to head a two-parent household than an illiterate. The percentage of two-parent households dropped from 86.5 percent of southern-born literates to 75.7 percent among illiterates from the same region, and from 80.1 percent among northern-born literates to only 68.6 percent among illiterates born in the North. Although these northern-born illiterate heads of household were a very small group, only eleven persons, nevertheless it is striking that a larger percentage of one-parent households was found among them than among any other group in the population.

If slavery permanently weakened family ties among Blacks, one would expect to find greater numbers of one-parent households among the ex-slaves. To be sure, there were fewer two-parent households among ex-slaves (southern-born illiterates) than among southern-born literates, but the freedmen had two-parent households more often than northern-born heads of household who were also illiterate. Thus, among both northern- and southern-born heads of household, illiteracy was associated with higher proportions of one-parent households.

It is possible that the relationship between illiteracy and one-parent, generally female-headed households, is only a statistical artifact, the consequence of a higher rate of illiteracy among females than males. In order to preclude a spurious relationship, I compared the number of illiterates among two groups of women, female heads of household and those females living with their husbands in two-parent households. If higher rates of illiteracy among one-parent households in both the North and the South were merely the result of the fact that one-parent households were mostly female, we would expect to find roughly similar proportions of illiterates among married women living with their spouses as among females heading households. Instead, female heads of household were much more commonly illiterate than women living with their husbands. Significantly more female heads of household than married females were illiterate; about one-fourth of married women were illiterate, while more than a third of females heading households could not read or write. Among the southern-born women, most of whom were born into slavery, the rate of illiteracy was much higher. However, the general pattern remained the same; while about one-third of married women were illiterate, almost half of the females heading households were illiterate.

Whether or not illiterates thought less of themselves than Blacks who learned to read or write, the numbers will never tell us. What is clear, however, is that for both urban and rural heads of household there were significantly more one-parent households among the illiterates. Speculation might lead us to conclude that illiteracy was both a real handicap in an urban society and, in addition, a characteristic found among the most disadvantaged adults in the Black community.

Migrants and native Bostonians, rural and urban adults, illiterate and literate persons, differed significantly in the number of two-parent households they formed. Did differences appear as well in the composition of the household? A single individual, or that person and boarders, lived in one out of seven Black households in Boston. These solitary adults were excluded from the analysis of household composition. The great majority of Black households consisted of nuclear families—usually husband and wife, or a husband, wife and children, but occasionally a single parent and child. Families which added other relatives to the nuclear family, in what is termed an extended household, were 9.7 percent of all Black households. Finally, about one out of three Black households included boarders, and in a few cases, boarders and relatives, in addition to parents and children. DuBois discovered roughly the same number of augmented households—that is, households with boarders—in late nineteenth-century Philadelphia.

Virtually the same patterns of family composition existed among rural and urban Blacks. In both cases the majority of households were nuclear, although a significant minority—about one-third—included boarders. Only when native Bostonians are separated from the rest of the northern-born do differences appear in the composition of the household. The household headed by a Black person born in Boston was somewhat more likely to mix relatives or boarders in the home than a household headed by a migrant. However, the differences in household composition between Blacks born in Massachusetts, other northern states, and the South are not striking. What is important, in fact, is the uniformity of household composition among migrant and stable, urban and rural, heads of household.

It might be thought that relatives were more frequent among the poorest families, huddling together because they could not afford to live by themselves. This was not the case. Controlling for the occupational level of the head of household, the proportion of relatives increased among higher-status heads of household, while the proportion decreased among lower-status households. Relatives may have been more welcome to join the family in higher-status households which could afford to sustain additional members. The George Ruffins (he was lawyer and judge; she, a prominent clubwoman and suffragist) absorbed into their homes Mrs. Ruffin's niece, Daisy Nahar. In other cases, the presence of additional adult family members may have financed the education or supported the family business, which, in turn, resulted in the higher status of the head of household.

Relatives were more common in higher-status households, but lodgers appeared more often in lower-status households. The number of augmented households shows that about one-third of blue-collar households included a boarder, while slightly fewer boarders resided in professional and white-collar homes. Among households headed by unskilled and skilled workers, just as in the female-headed household, the lodger's rent money was often an essential part of the family budget. In response to the influx of southern migrants, the Black family accommodated these lodgers, generally single women and men who worked as servants and waiters. The augmented household was a product of necessity, but it met the housing needs of the lodgers, as well as additional income requirements of Black families.

Nineteenth-century observers often described the "demoralizing" influence of lodgers on the household. DuBois exemplified this attitude, fearing that "the privacy and intimacy of home life is destroyed, and elements of danger and demoralization admitted" when the lodger entered the Black home. Given the desperate economic circumstances of most Black families, the boarder's rent money may have insured family survival rather than destroyed it. Moreover, boarders were common additions to higher-status households. The boarder, in many cases, became a "relative" of the family, in function, if not in kinship. Richard Wright recalled that as a boarder he easily became a part of a Memphis home—more so than he liked, since a matchmaking mother was eager for the boarder to marry her daughter.

CONCLUSION

This study of the Black family in late nineteenth-century Boston views the Black family structure at one point in time. Subsequent studies must trace the family over the years in order fully to comprehend changes in the household. If we want to learn about the acculturation of children in the Black family, it is particularly important to employ a dynamic perspective. For example, while we know that about seven out of ten Black children in Boston in 1880 lived in two-parent households, we do not know how many of these children spent their early years in such a household. Nor, for that matter do we know how the family situation of the minority of children in 1880 who were missing both parents affected their futures, for better or worse. This kind of analysis can only be pursued through the tracing of individuals, a method extremely arduous to undertake, given the mobility of the population.

Any study of Black family life largely employing quantitative informa-tion represents only a point of departure for further analysis of Black families. While the high number of two-parent households, 82 percent of all Black households in Boston, indicates the existence of much greater family organization than has been generally assumed, we need evidence about the cultural context in which the urban Black family operated. How were one- and two-parent households viewed? Were different values placed on marriage, the family, even desertion in the

Black community than in other groups? Did the addition of boarders and relatives endanger the intimacy of the home or create additional adult models for Black children? Except in the few instances of family diaries and personal accounts, these questions may prove difficult, if not impossible, to answer through literary materials.

While there are limitations to numerical analysis, it does allow for comparisons across time and space. How then did Boston compare with other cities? Perhaps one could argue that, despite the poverty-stricken condition of Blacks in Boston, there was still some way in which Boston was, indeed, "the paradise of the Negro," if only because the situation of Blacks in the South was so much worse. Although more studies need to be undertaken, overall figures from southern urban, southern rural, and northern urban centers in the late nineteenth century demonstrate a striking similarity in the percentages of two-parent households. Theodore Hershberg reports that in both 1880 and 1896 the two-parent household comprised 76 percent of all households among Blacks in Philadelphia. He found roughly similar proportions of two-parent households in ante-bellum Philadelphia, where 77 percent of all Black households were two-parent. Among a special group of about eighty-seven slaves who had bought their freedom, 91 percent formed two-parent households. From the major work of Herbert Gutman on the Black family, the two-parent household in 1880 appeared among 81 percent of Adams County, Mississippi, Black households and 77 percent of Mobile, Alabama, Black households. In three urban areas in 1896, Atlanta, Nashville, and Cambridge, Massachusetts, Gutman found respectively, 77 percent, 85 percent, and 90 percent two-parent households. It would be tempting here to contrast the relative effects on the Black household of southern urban, southern rural, and northern urban environments. But what we find in the few areas studied is greater variation within a single locale than between locales. All in all, the two-parent household was the prevailing family form in southern rural, southern urban, and northern urban areas.

The figures cited above, except in the case of antebellum Philadelphia, do not distinguish between native-born city dwellers and rural migrants to the city. Such an analytic strategy is vital to the study of the effects of city and country origins and the migration from one area to another on the Black household.

How did migration to the city affect the Black family? The standard texts on Black history scarcely mention the migration of Blacks to northern cities before the Great Migration of World War I. On the whole, the northward migration was a movement of single individuals or couples; in few cases did the whole family move north. After the migrants from the South or other parts of the North reached Boston, an incredible number of single individuals and families left the city. This movement out of Boston in some cases left behind deserted wives and husbands, but the rate of desertion was rather low given the lack of occupational opportunity for Blacks in Boston and the general rootlessness of the Black population.

In the work of DuBois and E. Franklin Frazier, migration to the city is viewed as a disruptive factor which weakened the family and produced large numbers of one-parent households. DuBois wrote that "as a whole, it is true that the average of culture and wealth is far lower among immigrants than natives, and that this gives rise to the gravest of the Negro problems." What these writers generally meant by migration was the transition from rural to urban culture among southern migrants to the city. This disruptive *transition* was said to have been the source of desertion, delinquency, and female-headed households. Frazier, in his discussion of the "city of destruction," noted: "Family desertion among Negroes in cities, appears, then, to be one of the inevitable consequences of the impact of urban life on the simple family organization and folk culture which the Negro has evolved in the rural South."

At least for late nineteenth-century Boston, quantitative evidence calls Frazier's thesis into question. Two-parent households were more frequent among both migrant *and* rural Black heads of household. Such evidence can be interpreted in two ways. One explanation would reverse the Frazier argument: instead of migration and the transition from rural to urban culture weakening the Black family, these influences strengthened it. Persons who had invested so much effort to leave family, friends, and familiar ways had a greater stake in establishing households once they were settled in the city. Also, the limited expectations of rural Blacks may have meant that city life in the North was, indeed, a significant improvement over life in the rural South. Finally, the special character of this early migration might have distinguished the early newcomers to the city (both in antebellum Philadelphia and in Boston about fifty years later) from more recent city-bound Blacks.

A second explanation of the differences in the number of two-parent households, offered by Theodore Hershberg, is that neither slavery nor migration but the urban environment produced greater numbers of one-parent households. Tremendous differences in wealth, poor health conditions for Blacks in cities, the destructiveness of urban culture—all these are cited as the causes of "family disorganization" among Blacks. Without more knowledge of the internal workings of Black culture, of the values Blacks placed on different family forms, it is impossible to know whether the one-parent, female-headed household was viewed by Blacks as "family disorganization." The use of this value-loaded term generally presupposes a hierarchy of family types, with the male-present, nuclear, and patriarchal household representing the most-valued family form.

Another danger in substituting one grand interpretation of "family disorganization" in place of another is that it may tend to obscure other important differences in family type and composition which do not appear between rural and urban, ex-slaves and free-born Blacks. Important differences between city dwellers and rural Blacks must be noted. But in late nineteenth-century Boston the composition of the Black household was similar for both rural and urban Black heads of household. Moreover, significantly more one-parent households occurred among illiterate Blacks from both rural and urban origins. The social meaning of illiteracy for Blacks in the city remains enigmatic, but the discovery that the illiteracy of the head of household significantly altered the proportions of two-parent households hints at the existence of other fundamental social characteristics differentiating Black households.

While variations in household composition and percentage of two-parent households which are associated with place of birth, illiteracy, and migration should be noted and considered, the similarities in two-parent households among diverse groups in the Black population are even more striking. The evidence suggests a family pattern of nuclear, two-parent households which prevailed among migrant and rural Black heads of household as well as among stable and urban Black heads of household. Despite the existence of Blacks at the lowest rung of the occupational ladder, most Black children lived in homes where both parents were present, and Black families generally included husband, wife, and children.

The presentation of these raw statistics forces us to challenge and revise previous conceptions about the Black family. More lies hidden behind a high death rate, a transient population, and a poverty-stricken Black community than the phrases like "culture of poverty" or "family disorganization" convey. Our vision of the family as an institution which reacts to and reflects changes is oversimplified, while there seems little understanding of the family as an institution which itself produces changes in individuals and institutions. If the Black family were merely the image of the social conditions of urban Blacks, we would find a rootless, disorganized mosaic of families. Notions of "Black matriarchy" and "the tangle of pathology" of the Black family have captivated sociologists and historians alike, but now the task before us is to tell the rather different story of the complex organization and continuity of the Black household.

6

FROM GREAT MIGRATION
TO GREAT DEPRESSION

The pace of migration out of the South increased dramatically after 1916. Between that date and the onset of the Great Depression in 1929, nearly a million and a half Blacks left their homeland, a half million alone in the late 'teens. They located overwhelmingly in the Northeast and Midwest; relatively few made the longer journey to the Far West. And the migrants went into the cities, because there was little rural opportunity for them outside the South. Besides, they were fleeing agricultural distress, and most ex-sharecroppers hoped to construct new lives in some nonagricultural occupation.

This movement has been called the Great Migration. It was more than the sum of its participants, and more than a population shift: it was a folk movement. Individuals migrated but so, too, did families, multigenerational families, church congregations, lodge chapters, and in some cases, whole rural communities. For many migrants the motive was more than economic or political. Some felt they were taking part in a biblical Exodus in which crossing the Ohio River into the North was like crossing the River Jordan. Beyond such religious and psychological aspects, we can separate causes of the migration into push and pull factors. Push factors are forces that encourage persons to leave a particular locality. Primary among these during the Great Migration were economic pressures: devastation of the southern cotton crop by the boll weevil; low cotton prices; and general disillusionment with sharecropping and debt peonage. Social and political push factors included disfranchisement, segregation, and racial violence; poor or nonexistent educational opportunities; bad treatment at the hands of police and the courts;

and the inability of younger Blacks to accommodate themselves as easily as their parents did to second-class citizenship.

All these push factors had existed, to varying degrees, prior to 1916. What made possible the Great Migration was a unique set of pull factors, forces that particularly encouraged Blacks to set northern cities as their destination. Before 1916, there had been very few opportunities for Blacks in northern industry, except in cases of strikebreaking, which usually resulted only in temporary employment. But World War I created a significant labor shortage by first drying up the stream of foreign immigration on which industry had traditionally relied for supplying its growing labor needs. Then, as manufacturing expanded rapidly to supply war materials to the European Allies, and later for American troops, large numbers of additional workers were required in basic industry (iron, steel), munitions (tanks, airplanes, warships), textiles, and food processing. Jobs went begging, and Blacks moved into positions readily, although primarily in the lowest-paying and least-skilled categories. Finally, when war came to America, and whites and Blacks were drafted, still more job opportunities opened up for southern migrants, including Black women. Once the momentum of migration was generated, even the decline in industrial output at the end of the war did not significantly slow the flood of migrants. Social and political pull factors should also be added, although they were probably secondary. Many southern Blacks perceived that life in the northern cities would be more fast paced, varied, and exciting than in the southern rural environment, and that overt racial indignities would be absent. In addition, the possibilities for better-quality educations and meaningful political participation were thought to be much greater.

The Great Migration was above all a rural-to-urban phenomenon. It was not confined to the North, for significant numbers of rural Blacks went into southern cities. This movement, however, depended heavily on expanding war-related industries, and in the 1920's some southern Black urban populations declined. The most dramatic and permanent increases were in northern industrial cities like Gary, Cleveland, Akron, Toledo, and Detroit; more modest proportional increases were registered in commercial cities like New York and Philadelphia. But wherever they went, the effects of the Great Migration were dramatic. One of the most visible was a heightened competition for residential space. Housing construction all but came to a halt during World War I, and as more and more Blacks crowded into neighborhoods where members of the race already resided, greater population density resulted as families doubled and tripled up in deteriorating apartments and flats. Where there had been no obvious ghetto before, often a ghetto now became visible. Where the population had already been confined by race, significant deterioration resulted as absentee owners split apartments into "kitchenettes" and jacked up rents while neglecting maintenance and long-term improvements. Like every other immigrant group to the cities, Blacks had little choice but to move into the worst neighborhoods, but unlike previous white ethnics, they were not afforded the chance for significant mobility upward and out from the ghetto. Even though no areas became 100 percent Black, the density increased dramatically.

Competition with the white population for housing led to an increase in racial friction, especially in 1919 and 1920. Racial tensions had been at a comparatively modest level before the Great Migration, because the number of Blacks, and their attitudes, had posed relatively few threats to whites. But the growing number of clashes, as whites attempted to prevent Blacks from spilling out of the overcrowded ghettoes into neighboring "white" areas, as well as dramatic large-scale race riots in Chicago, Washington, D.C., Omaha, and other cities in 1919, mirrored the increasing animosities between the races. Competition for jobs also fueled racial distrust. During the wartime labor shortage, employment friction had remained at a low level, but when hostilities ended, industry cut back, and as hundreds of thousands of whites returned from service and demanded their jobs back, they came into direct competition with Blacks, many of whom were bumped from their recently gained positions. A wave of labor strikes in the postwar months also fueled racial antagonisms, as Blacks found themselves caught in the middle, courted as strikebreakers by employers and simultaneously urged by unions not to undercut labor solidarity, although they were not at the same time sincerely offered a fair shake by the unions.

Finally there were more general social frictions arising from the war and the Great Migration which kept the level of tension high between whites and Blacks in the growing northern cities. A new militancy had been born during World War I, as Blacks gained self-confidence and a sense of national participation through war service overseas. A "New Crowd Negro" arose out of the ashes of the war, a young city-bred militant, impatient with both older Black leaders and white domination. Whites perceived this new militance and, fearing cracks in the status quo or even "race war," initiated new attempts to segregate schools and recreational facilities, contain Blacks within the urban ghettoes, and reduce their political influence. At the same time the Ku Klux Klan enjoyed a rebirth, this time not only in the South but in rural and suburban areas of the North and Midwest as well.

The Great Migration also had far-reaching effects on Black communities in the northern cities. The family faced new challenges.

Employment in the city brought better pay on an hourly basis than agricultural work in the South, but it was often more erratic. In general, steadier job opportunities existed for females than for males in the northern cities, although usually in low-paying domestic service. With male incomes more precarious than female incomes, this led, in some cases, to family breakup and female-headed families, although the intact nuclear family was still the most common pattern. As in previous periods, it was the poorest members of the race whose families were hardest hit. Other signs of strains can be seen in marriage patterns. Blacks in the northern cities married at a slower rate, and at a later age, than their peers in the rural South. Many young couples felt compelled by financial insecurities to postpone having children. In addition, high death rates—particularly infant mortality rates—appeared in the statistics of every city with a ghettoized Black population.

On the more positive side, the Great Migration created a new market for businessmen and professionals. With large populations concentrated in small geographical areas, it was easier than before for a storekeeper to hope to capture a clientele. But the obstacles that had always hampered Black business continued to plague merchants. A lack of capital, caused in good part by the refusal of white-owned banks to lend to Blacks, made it difficult to finance expansion and modernization. Black entrepreneurs faced stiff competition from more advantaged white businesses, often chains, that entered the ghetto market. Small Black stores had higher fixed costs and were forced to sell goods more expensively. And the average Black consumer, whatever his inclination, generally had no choice but to buy from the white merchant who charged a few pennies less. Some significant business successes were registered, but usually in fields like cosmetics manufacturing, journalism, and banking where whites chose not to compete for the Black trade. On the whole, the Black share of the business and commercial market did not expand during the Great Migration at a rate to meet expectations.

Intraracial strains were another consequence of the Great Migration. "Old settlers"—residents who had lived in the cities earlier in the century—tended to idealize premigration race relations as harmonious. Consequently, they blamed newcomers for the visible hardening of northern white racial attitudes. As the old settlers saw it, the migrants' allegedly uncouth behavior caused whites to turn to segregation and discrimination so as to isolate themselves from unwanted associations with lower-class elements. Naturally, the newcomers resented this attitude on the part of those Blacks who had resided longer in the cities. Relations between West Indians and native-born Blacks were also less than harmonious. Blacks from the West Indies migrated to Atlantic seaboard cities in sizeable numbers in the 1920's, and their striving for upward mobility, hard work, and pride in British traditions often grated on their new neighbors. Native-born Blacks stereotyped West Indians as clannish, overly sharp in business dealings, and haughty; West Indians, for their part, often looked down on American Blacks as hopelessly timid and passive. Such invidious distinctions were often perpetuated by members of Marcus Garvey's Universal Negro Improvement Association (UNIA) as well as by those who opposed Garvey. These instances of intraracial friction illustrate the painful creation of a more complex Black social structure in the cities.

Increasing urbanization as a result of the Great Migration also provided new opportunities for formal race organization. The Urban League idea spread to most major cities of the North and Midwest, and was helpful in promoting social work among the Black population. Another major Urban League goal—that of expanding employment opportunities— was much less successful; the modest gains achieved in the twenties were wiped out in the depression that followed. The National Association for the Advancement of Colored People (NAACP) was founded in 1909 and within a decade had a network of chapters, primarily in urban areas, some in the South. With its concentration on fighting for civil rights and eliminating lynching and segregation, it provided one avenue for expression of urban militancy by the time of the Great Migration. But the NAACP had to compete with Marcus Garvey's UNIA, which offered the vision of a Black nationalist, nonintegrated future, with an eventual destiny in Africa. Garvey's followers were primarily working-class folk in northern and midwestern cities, and his success would only have been possible in an urban environment, where parades, rallies, and mass meetings could attract large throngs. A master orator, Garvey struck a responsive chord in the minds of ex-Southerners and West Indians who had found that the promised land did not lie in Harlem or any other Black Belt. Garvey's organization declined by the late 1920's, but urban militancy continued during the depression years. "Don't Buy Where You Can't Work" committees used picketing and boycotts to put pressure on white businesses to hire Black employees in those stores operating in Black neighborhoods. Modest gains resulted from these campaigns, but they could not begin to solve the massive urban Black unemployment of the depression decade.

The Great Migration transformed the northern urban landscape. On the positive side can be listed increased racial militancy and self-confidence. The Harlem Renaissance encompassed a creative explosion in all the arts, and centers of culture were to be found in New York, Boston, Philadelphia, Washington, D.C., and Chicago. New business and employment possibilities appeared for both the masses and a growing middle class, albeit below expectations. But the debit column proved far longer. High death rates resulted from overcrowded housing and poor sanitation, for both of which the cities themselves were largely responsible. Wide-open prostitution, gambling, and bootlegging were tolerated by city authorities in Black neighborhoods. Juvenile delinquency, overcrowded schools, and a constantly shifting population went hand in hand. Black social agencies did their best to meet the needs of their communities, but could aid no more than a few. In fact, to deal with problems piecemeal was to ensure futility: unless vice, drugs, poor health, inadequate housing, and low salaries were simultaneously attacked, little progress could be expected. So by the late 1920's, the sociological and geographical boundaries of today's Black ghettoes had been established in many cities. It should be stressed that social pathology did not characterize entire Black areas; while there were slums aplenty, each community had its more prosperous and stable areas, where single family homes or well-built apartments existed as middle-class islands. Harlem and the Chicago South Side were not all slum, and in a strict sense they weren't all ghetto; sizeable minorities of non-Blacks still lived there. But the major concentrations were densely enough populated so that they comprised genuine Black cities.

American cities were struck hard by the Great Depression which burst upon the nation in 1929 and lasted until the outbreak of World War II. Economic hardship was the most pressing problem. Those urban dwellers most effected were the unskilled, the young, and those who belonged to an ethnic minority. Blacks fitted into all three categories; many recent migrants were young and, whether possessing crafts or not, had found only unskilled positions. The foothold gained in northern industry during the twenties was an insecure one. Although in a few fields, Blacks moved up the occupational ladder and managed to preserve some of these gains in the depression years, in general the familiar formula of "last hired, first fired" accurately described both male and female Black labor. Consequently, in the majority of cities, Black unemployment was consistently above the white rate. In some southern cities traditional "Negro jobs" in street maintenance and trash collection were redefined as "white jobs" so as to reduce unemployment among the privileged caste.

The Roosevelt administration introduced a wide variety of federal programs in attempting to end the depression. Several of these New Deal initiatives directly affected urban Blacks. Federal housing construction was designed both to provide better shelter and to increase employment. But although a high proportion of urban Blacks, both North and South, were inadequately housed, the new projects were only a mixed blessing. Most were designated solely for whites or Blacks; very few were integrated. Worse, the sites for Black housing developments were usually located within existing Black ghettoes, almost no effort being made to provide housing in new areas. So the government contributed both to continued high densities and to residential segregation. Certainly many persons benefited from the modern apartments that were constructed—in fact, Blacks got a higher proportion of units than their proportion in the total population—but still the new apartments did not come close to meeting the needs of ill-housed Blacks in inner cities. The second federal goal—to stimulate employment—depended on massive public-works projects. To a degree, Blacks gained from these programs, but too often they were employed below their qualified level. Foremen and others responsible for hiring and firing commonly practiced discrimination by clustering Black workers, regardless of skills, in common labor categories.

The disillusionment, bitterness, and anger of hundreds of thousands of Black urban dwellers could not be assuaged by New Deal economic programs. Nor could "Don't Buy Where You Can't Work" campaigns, even when successful, begin to meet the need for new employment opportunities. Many city residents became more and more alienated as the depression worsened, and the Harlem Riot of 1935 revealed the cancer festering in America's cities. Unlike previous riots which were initiated by whites and devolved into hand-to-hand combat, Harlem exploded on Black initiative, and residents engaged in wholesale looting of both white- and Black-owned businesses. The only Black-white fighting was between rioters and police. The underlying causes of this ghetto uprising were unemployment, discrimination, and police maltreatment. These conditions were not unique to New York City, but in fact common to all metropolitan areas with a significant Black population. The Harlem riot in historical retrospect is not surprising; the surprise is that other cities did not erupt. Only a small proportion of Harlem's residents joined in the riot, but on another level this minority represented far more than themselves. Theirs was a voice of alienation and desperation crying out from the nation's Black ghettoes. The New Deal could not provide sufficient employment, housing, or hope. Not until the economy was revived by World War II would anything approximating prosperity return to America's Black urban colonies. And by then a new generation of southern migrants would be headed for the cities.

AN ECONOMIC PROFILE OF BLACK LIFE
IN THE TWENTIES

THEODORE KORNWEIBEL, JR.

Migration of Black peasants from the farms to the cities was no new phenomenon in the early twentieth century. Such population movements had been taking place ever since emancipation, when for the first time the illusion of urban opportunities, combined with wartime dislocation and discontent, drew many Black families away from their rural occupations and roots. During the decade of the 1860's the Black population doubled in southern cities like Atlanta, Memphis, and New Orleans. Beginning in the 1880's, the direction of migration changed significantly, and Blacks took to the cities of the North and Midwest. What has become known as the Great Migration—the mass movement of folk from the South seeking industrial opportunity and a freer, more dignified life in the North—took place during the second decade of the twentieth century, particularly in the war years of 1916-1918. In 1910 a little over a quarter of the Black population was urbanized; by 1920 the proportion was one-third; and at the end of the twenties more than two-fifths lived in city environments. At that same time 88 percent of northern Blacks found their homes in urban areas.

The Great Migration during World War I witnessed half a million southern Blacks forsaking their rural homes for the cities. During the twenties, nearly a million more (and, as was the case with the Great

---

Reprinted from the *Journal of Black Studies,* 6 (June 1976), pp. 307-320, by permission of the publisher, Sage Publications, Inc. Footnotes and tables appearing in the original publication have been deleted but should be consulted for full documentation of the author's conclusions.

Migration, thousands of whites as well) came out of the South. The newcomers did not all flock to the old Northeast; they spread themselves far across the country. But their concentration was in urban, industrialized centers.

The greatest wave of migration into the North in the twenties took place in the years 1921 through 1924 as the industrial economy slowly picked up from the postwar depression and as agricultural conditions in the South, particularly in cotton, grew worse. But the North did not prove to be the land of opportunity of which many had dreamed. The newcomers often found residential segregation, high rents, social ostracism, and racial discrimination. Frequently the migrations provoked deep intraracial antagonisms through competition both with other newcomers and with older northern residents for jobs, for housing, for a share of the good life. The twenties may have been "roaring" for some, but as James Weldon Johnson has pointed out, the vast majority of Black citizens of a metropolis like Harlem were too busy scraping out a living and keeping a step ahead of the rent collector to be drinking and dancing all night in cabarets. Life had been a struggle on the farm; it was still a struggle in the city, albeit in many ways a different one.

For Black Americans the "perils of prosperity" were real and not metaphorical. The twenties for them were not times of jazz and gin, Babbitts and a lost generation, stock-market speculation and a Ford in every garage. Prosperity was an elusive thing: *if* one had the good fortune to possess a skilled trade *and* gain entrance to the union controlling the craft, *if* one could open the only Black funeral parlor in the neighborhood, then, perhaps prosperity could be a reality. But for many, good times must have been the great illusion—it was what the white eastern papers talked about, what the ticker tape spelled out to gawkers on Times Square.

Statistics on unemployment are few in number and frequently of questionable reliability for the 1920's. One of the best measures of the federal government's unconcern for unemployment is the fact that it expended almost no effort to assemble data on the jobless before 1930. What we know about unemployment is more relative than actual, more in percentages and estimates than in "hard" statistics. But it is clear that there were wide fluctuations in urban and industrial employment, not to speak of agricultural employment, throughout the twenties. Indeed, several years in this period can justly be labeled as "depression" or "recession" years, particularly for Black people. One academic study, dealing with only the years 1919 through 1924, found that industrial-business fluctuations were of the following pattern: in 1919, industry revived from the postwar depression with extraordinary activity by midyear, and immigration again picked up. Prosperity continued into 1920 until late spring when stagnation set in; unemployment became severe at the year's end and was exacerbated by large numbers of foreign immigrants. Depression characterized nearly all of 1921 with many industries stagnant and unemployment worst in the summer; fortunately, immigration slacked off. By 1922 gradual recovery was taking place with rapid improvement in employment, and by early 1923 production records were being set in some sectors, although activity receded mildly in the summer and a recession began thereafter. Nineteen twenty-four again saw depression, although not as severe as in 1921, but the economy began to revive with some vigor in the third quarter of the year.

If one can assume that for the rest of the decade the economy (and peoples' lives) suffered similar, if not identical, fluctuations, it is clear that the welfare of a population as precariously attached to the industrial order as was that of Black America would be affected by every rise or fall of the industrial indices. It may be true, as Spero and Harris claim, that the aphorism "last hired, first fired" is not entirely borne out by the facts of employment in the twenties, but they point out that Blacks suffered more than any other group because of their lack of seniority and their concentration in the unskilled and semiskilled categories. A recent inquiry into the operation of the Chicago branch of the Urban League has found that unemployment was prevalent in Black Chicago throughout the latter part of the 1920's. There was less and less demand for Black labor in industry despite general prosperity in the area. The Urban League could hardly build a viable industrial program around the few hundred jobs a year it found for domestics. Even if, as Cayton and Mitchell claim, Chicago's Black metropolis knew prosperity from 1924 to 1929, it was not so much the unskilled and semiskilled who enjoyed it but the professional and business types who found an ever-expanding race market on which to capitalize.

The twenties were not prosperous for farmers, either. The Black landsman in particular suffered almost continually throughout the decade. A declining foreign market for cotton and devastation by the boll weevil explain a good deal of distress in the southern Black Belt. Troubles in cotton were a "push" factor of great importance to the migrations, but even the exodus of thousands of Blacks from southern farms did not significantly improve the conditions of those who remained behind. The same poverty, the same labor and land exploitation, which the New South had vainly tried to eradicate, still prevailed.

Speaking exclusively of northern industry, unskilled Black workers got their first really substantial foothold during World War I, particularly in the urbanized metalworking, automobile, and meat-packing industries.

Far too many of these jobs were in the lowest-paid categories, even though it was a significant advance for more than five thousand Blacks to be employed in Henry Ford's plants by 1923. Many unskilled workers also found places in road and other construction projects, and their women folk secured employment in commercial laundries, food industries, and the less skilled branches of the needle trades. But far out of proportion to their actual numbers, Black workers were crowded into the lower end of the industrial scale. Within a given industry, Blacks were likely to be assigned the least remunerative tasks on a piecework basis. New jobs might still be had through strikebreaking, but the repercussions in racial violence were coming to seem more alarming even to conservatives. Furthermore, American industry appeared to be heading toward equilibrium after 1924, and the demand for cheap, unskilled workers slacked off as the labor shortage disappeared. Any downturn in the economy could have serious results for the Black laboring population, and hard times came to many a Dark Ghetto before the Great Depression.

The gains in industry secured by Black workers in the early 1900's should not be ignored. Despite the precariousness of many positions, the industrial gain was certainly the race's greatest step forward since a dubious emancipation fifty years earlier. But in key respects the progress of Black workers by the twenties was out of step with that of the rest of the labor force. Labor historians have pointed to the twenties as signaling a shift from manual to nonmanual employment, from blue-collar to white-collar work. But Blacks did not share in much of the upward mobility taking place in such fields as public services, trade, clerical work, and the professions. The number of Black persons in white-collar occupations grew in the 1920's but not nearly as rapidly as in the previous decade. In 1910, 2.8 percent of all Black gainful workers held white-collar jobs (professionals, proprietors exclusive of farmers, managers, officials, and clericals); in 1920, this percentage was 3.8 percent, and by 1930, 4.6 percent. However, the rate of increase was slowing down precipitously—while the rate of increase from 1910 to 1920 was 35.7 percent, it decreased during the twenties to only 21.5 percent. The white-collar problem was an acute one: colleges and high schools were graduating an increasing number of educated and trained young persons who had aspirations to lead middle-class lives supported by white-collar occupations. But job possibilities within the segregated race market were meager indeed, and the trend in the 1920's was to continue the restriction of Black employment by the federal government. The Black community of Washington, D.C., was particularly hard hit in this regard, starting in the war years, and the policy of the Republican administrations in the 1920's was not one to open up new employment or even restore that curtailed under Wilson.

A second labor trend in the 1920's was the beginning of the phenomenon of technological unemployment. One statistician estimates that between 1920 and 1929, in the fields of manufacturing, coal mining, and railroads, machines displaced 3,272,000 workers, of whom only 2,269,000 were reabsorbed in the same industry. If Black workers in general lacked seniority and were clustered in the nonskilled or semi-skilled categories, this would indicate that Blacks suffered proportionally more from technological unemployment than did other groups. Certainly Blacks were heavily represented in the unskilled positions in the three industries used as examples. Gunnar Myrdal has underscored the point:

In most cases changes in the economic process seem to involve a tendency which works against the Negroes. When modern techniques transform old handicrafts into machine production, Negroes lose jobs in the former but usually do not get into the new factories, at least not at the machines. Mechanization seems generally to displace Negro labor. When mechanized commercial laundries replace home laundries, Negro workers lose jobs. The same process occurs in tobacco manufacture, in the lumber industry, and in the turpentine industry.

An additional piece of evidence may well be applicable to this problem. The total percentage of Blacks in the labor force of the country was declining, while that of native whites was steadily growing. Part of this growth was due to the decrease in foreign-born employment; as immigration all but ceased in the later 1920's, native whites took up the slack, not Blacks.

What is perhaps the most graphic evidence of the continuing position of Blacks as an "industrial reserve," to use Spero and Harris' term, is the relative proportions of Blacks and whites in the major occupational categories of the work force. Even in 1930, over two-thirds of all Black workers were still unskilled. Also, since the skilled, semiskilled, and the unskilled are all manual workers, this means that in 1930 four-fifths of all Black nonagricultural workers were in manual labor of some sort. It is probable that most of the Blacks listed in the federal census as proprietors were in fact farm tenants and owners, and thus also manual laborers. If this is so, then over 95 percent of all Black workers in 1930 were manual workers. Furthermore, if the category of farm owners and tenants is broken down into actual owners and sharecroppers, and if the croppers may be considered unskilled, then fully three-fourths of all Black workers in 1930 were unskilled.

A high percentage of Black workers were in unskilled—and lowest-paid—categories in the seven manufacturing and mechanical industries employing large numbers of Blacks. Despite some increases in total employment in the 1920's, a smaller proportion of Blacks in the urban North was in manufacturing and mechanical industries and trade and transportation in 1930 than in previous years; considerable numbers had gone back into the general field of domestic and personal service, while many Black women who had given up outside employment were forced back to work to help support their families.

The problems of Black workers in the skilled trades were without satisfactory solution in the 1920's. Two investigators found that although there were more skilled Black workers in the building trades (carpenters, bricklayers, and plasterers) in the North after the war than before, this was not an increase in skilled labor as such but merely a migration of skilled tradesmen out of the South. In the South the remaining skilled Black building tradesmen were losing ground. One major cause was the inability to adjust to the accelerated industrial tempo demanded by an advancing and modernizing South, but a rising class and racial consciousness among poor white workers was also of significance. Whatever gains there were by Black skilled workers were probably not as encouraging as they seemed, for the number of Black apprentices in these trades was decreasing as a result of increasing union control of the trades North and South. The problem of union hostility to Black skilled labor cannot be divorced from the general question of opportunities for Black tradesmen.

Were the chances for success and a secure future any better for the urban Black business entrepreneur than for the Black workingman? Census data for the year 1929 indicate that by the end of the decade Black retail business had only a precarious hold on the Black population and was certainly an insignificant part of the country's retail business structure—1.67 percent of the total. In that year there were 25,701 Black-operated retail stores, primarily groceries, filling stations, restaurants and lunchrooms, cigar stores and stands, and drug stores (excluded were wholly service establishments like laundries, barber shops, and undertaking parlors). The aggregate sales for these retail establishments in 1929 was $101,000,000, or an average of slightly more than $4,000 in sales per establishment, representing only .21 percent of national retail sales. This was hardly a foundation on which to build either substantial wealth or substantial employment for persons other than the proprietors. A comparison with white retail establishments shows that the Black enterprises were not nearly as diversified as were those in the white community. While 57.5 percent of Black retail sales were in the grocery and restaurant line, only 26.4 percent of white receipts came from these businesses.

Two facts stand out in the social history of American workers, Black and white, in the decade of the twenties: the labor movement was on the defensive, if not actually declining, and the general attitude of business and government was one of apathy toward economic distress. Dealing with the former problem, several studies have noted that the urban North was not only not the promised land of full and remunerative employment, but it also was often a place of deep and mutual racial antagonisms between Black and white workers; this did not help the cause of labor at a time of aggressiveness from the business sector. Black-white labor divisions proved useful to the growing antiunion crusade. Organized labor in general faced the difficulties of the postwar years by attempting to check deteriorating conditions by maintaining short hours and wages at a high level. This gave rise to a strike wave that was often violent and always bitter. Blacks were not the invariable strikebreakers, but they contributed their share. Some strikes the unions won, particularly in the needle trades and textile industries, but more were lost than gained. Meanwhile, company unions and open shops—the "American Plan"—gained headway across the country. From the point of view of organized labor it was an exceedingly poor time for Blacks, allegedly ignorant of union traditions and philosophy, to enter the work force. Organized labor, as a generalization, continued to be hostile to Black workers, despite the strong efforts of Black labor radicals like A. Philip Randolph and Chandler Owen, editors of the *Messenger*.

Labor was on the defensive in another respect; the nonlaboring part of the country seemed to evince no great concern for the economic problems of any workers in a decade of on-again-off-again depression and recession. As thousands of urban workers, particularly Blacks, lost jobs in industry when recessions set in, many considered them unfortunate but unavoidable casualties of a new industrial age in which it was to be expected that there would always be several million persons unemployed. As a political issue, unemployment was low on the interest scale; in the election of 1928, when even a conservative estimate puts the figure at more than two million out of work (6.4 percent of the nonfarm labor force), there was no more than passing attention to the problem in campaigning. During the twenties the federal government was presumed to have no obligation, moral or legal, to do anything about unemployment relief—the prevailing constitutional interpretation on the issue dated from a veto by President Franklin Pierce in 1854! In 1921 and 1922, efforts had been made to secure some form of federal unemployment relief, but a conference staged by Secretary of Commerce Herbert Hoover, the hero of postwar European relief, reaffirmed the responsibility of local governments to provide amelioration through compensatory programs like public works. And there the matter rested for the decade.

The fruits of a decade of uncertain economic progress are plainly seen in the 1930 census. The unemployment figures for the country as a whole showed that there was in fact a smaller percentage of Blacks (5.1 percent) unemployed than whites (5.4 percent), but these figures, including as they do rural southern "employment" on farms, obscure the degree of differential between Black and white urban unemployment. In the urbanized North, Black male unemployment reached 14.3 percent, while the white male rate rose to only 8.2 percent. Given such economic conditions in the twenties, the significance of the urban migrations in the early 1900's may well be demographic rather than economic. True prosperity for the mass of the Black population would have to wait.

THE EVOLUTION OF RACISM
IN AN INDUSTRIAL CITY, 1906-1940
A Case Study of Gary, Indiana
NEIL BETTEN and RAYMOND A. MOHL

Gary was similar in many ways to other northern industrial towns. Although Blacks voted, discrimination and segregation persisted well past mid-century. While an Urban League study of 1944 discovered some examples of "liberal attitudes and practices" in Gary, it also found that "attitudes and practices are exhibited which are evident in a typical community in the deep South." The latter seemed more prevalent. Gary's segregation did not develop accidentally out of housing patterns. As in other northern cities with large Black populations, Gary's discrimination and segregation in education, housing, employment, public services, and recreation were established and carried out by business and government.

Moreover, traditions, especially pride in nationality, could easily be transformed into a form of white superiority; anti-Semitism, particularly among East Europeans, could evolve into racism. In Europe the immigrants had lived in a world of class antagonism and ethnic conflict, but the peculiar brand of American racism which taught Black inferiority and sublimation had to be learned. The Gary establishment did the teaching. At the same time, sharply varying responses from the Black community prevented the establishment of a united front against white racism. The NAACP opposed segregation but rejected militance, while the Garvey movement, though brief, supported segregated institutions as a means

Reprinted with permission from the *Journal of Negro History*, 59 (January 1974), pp. 51–64. Footnotes appearing in the original publication have been deleted in the present volume, and should be consulted for full documentation of the authors' conclusions.

of building racial pride. Obviously, these divisions among Black organizations served the interests of the city's white elite.

Founded in 1906 by the United States Steel Corporation, Gary quickly became a city of East and South European immigrants. Within a decade, the city also attracted substantial numbers of Black newcomers from the American South. Although the Black population did not increase significantly until the outbreak of World War I in Europe, some Black railroad and construction workers had come to Gary at the city's very beginning. The turmoil of war, however, gradually disrupted European migration to the United States, forcing steel companies, along with much of American industry, to turn from immigrants to the neglected reservoir of southern Black labor. This pattern became prevalent after the United States entered the war. As in all wars, the common people did the fighting; thus Gary lost a considerable portion of its labor force, as almost one-fourth of the city's white mill workers entered the armed forces.

Although retired workers replaced some lost to the battlefield, Blacks and Mexicans provided a significant portion of the new labor. Many Black rural workers came to Gary responding to job opportunities advertised in the Black newspapers freely distributed in the South in order to draw workers North. Steel representatives also recruited workers in the South, shipping them to northern industrial cities by railroad, especially during the AFL Steel Strike of 1919. William Z. Foster, who directed the national AFL strike, estimated that steel companies imported between thirty thousand and forty thousand Black strikebreakers to Gary, Cleveland, and other steel centers.

After an initial period in which the steel companies housed Gary's Black laborers in barracks, the workers moved to the city's southern fringe—"the unlovely south side," as one social worker described it. The city, laid out and built by U. S. Steel, included no permanent provisions for housing Blacks; nor were most unskilled immigrant workers provided for either. Thus, Blacks were forced into the unplanned area south of the city originally called "the Patch," where they found space among already overcrowded eastern and southern European ethnic groups. The immigrants at first seemed to consider Blacks just another ethnic group. This is not to say that social interaction existed, but significant social contact did not occur among white ethnic groups either. A later Urban League study noted that the "clannishness of these ethnic groups and language differences were early barriers to the Negroes against establishing satisfactory community relations with their neighbors." It should also be pointed out that national cohesiveness kept immigrant groups from interacting with each other. Even groups from similar European homelands, such as Serbs and Croatians or Bulgarians, Macedonians, and Greeks, had little social contact in Gary.

Although they lived in the same neighborhoods, Blacks and other ethnics did not join the same organizations, churches, or social groupings. Nevertheless, there is no evidence of significant conflict between white working-class immigrants and their Black neighbors on the south side until the mid-1920's. And even then few reported incidents occurred. In 1922 the Neighborhood House, a Presbyterian settlement, did report a conflict between Italians and Blacks which erupted into street fights. In 1927 students at the white Emerson High School demonstrated against token integration of Blacks, but Emerson served mainly the children of the middle class and elite skilled workers; few were southern and eastern Europeans.

By contrast, many developments indicate a degree of harmony between other ethnics and Blacks before the late 1920's. For example, Greeks held their first church services in a small building they shared with a Black family. More importantly, Black city councilmen were elected from central wards where other ethnics and Blacks both lived. At one point in the late 1920's there were three Black councilmen from mixed wards, yet campaign literature and press reports do not suggest that racism played a part in election campaigns. Gary was also spared the race rioting so common in industrial cities during 1919. Even as late as 1925, after some racial tension became evident, Hampton Institute's journal, the *Southern Workman,* could still report that "while there are occasional interracial conflicts in this section, yet the lines of color are not very rigidly drawn." It pointed out that Blacks, Mexicans, and Europeans lived in the same buildings, "the Negroes perhaps being the only ones conscious that there is anything unusual in such an arrangement." Even Gary's Ku Klux Klan activities were not directed at Blacks, but at Catholics. Finally in interviews held by the authors, older Blacks and ethnics categorically denied that racial conflict existed between the two groups before the mid-twenties and that it remained insignificant during these years. Yet by World War II, Gary had become a fully segregated city with staunch racist elements, and many people of the ethnic communities adopted such attitudes.

Racism did not appear suddenly during an industrial strike, nor did it emerge from conflict over housing. In Gary's earliest years, elements of white racism emerged by way of the city's elite—realtors, professionals, businessmen, officials of U.S. Steel—the most established and Americanized segment of the community. The *Gary Evening Post* reported in 1909 that the community's leadership was sponsoring a "clean out the Negro" campaign aimed at ridding the city of Black construction workers remaining after U.S. Steel completed its initial building project. Two years later, the *Evening Post* again announced that Gary's leading white citizens were determined to rid the city of its "bad Negroes." "Worthless Negroes Being Driven Out of City by the Police" was one of the headlines. The *Post* warned that "any Negro in Gary who hasn't got a job had better lose no time in getting one." After pointing out that fifty Blacks had been run out of the city within two days, the paper reported that Police "Chief Martin is determined that the city shall be cleared of the worthless Negro who refuses to work and has issued strict orders that every member of this race who is without work be driven out of the city."

In the same summer, some residents of Tolleston, a separate town that preceded the establishment of Gary but later incorporated into the city, attempted to bar Blacks. This section consisted mainly of German-Americans, small businessmen, and American-born skilled workers. The Germans had come well before the more recent eastern and southern European migrations, and Tolleston was one of the more Americanized sections in the city. Tolleston real-estate men panicked at the thought that a boardinghouse would be built for Black workers. Nine local realtors petitioned the city to exclude Blacks from the area, in effect preventing the establishment of the boardinghouse. Although Gary building commissioners denied the petition, white spokesmen pledged to continue to fight. "Every conceivable plan will be resorted to," stated Frank Bormann, president of the Sixth Ward Improvement Club, "before the citizens of the district will permit the erection of the boardinghouse on Fourth Avenue, which is to be the opening wedge for the colored settlement." Although officially losing this battle, the real-estate interests managed to keep Tolleston white until after World War II.

The city's elite nurtured the introduction of racism by setting examples illustrating that "true Americanism" meant Black subordination. Although Gary's Black and foreign-born working class lived in the same areas, the school board, headed by U.S. Steel Superintendent William Gleason and Superintendent of Schools William Wirt, quickly established a segregated system. As early as 1908, when housing patterns were racially integrated, the Gary school board rented a church to serve as a separate school for Black children. Superintendent Wirt rationalized the move by stating that "we believe that it is only in justice to the Negro children that they be segregated." Robert Wynn Johnson, editor of a local Black newspaper, unsuccessfully opposed the move, stating that "we do not endorse the separation, but if it goes through we want capable teachers for the colored school." In 1922, legislation was passed on the state level officially recognizing and accepting racial segregation of schools in the state of Indiana. From 1908 to 1947, a complicated system of partial segregation emerged in Gary. On the elementary level, almost all Blacks attended segregated schools; only one or two "white" schools had some Black students. On the secondary level, one high school remained white, while some Black students attended another high school, Froebel, but faced continuous discrimination and segregation within that school.

In 1928, school segregation was intensified after white protests over integrated education. Eighteen Black students who attended the Virginia Street School—an antiquated Black primary school with poor facilities—were transferred to Emerson School, a prestigious institution on the "north side," the part of the city originally designed for families of U.S. Steel management, skilled workers, and foremen. On September 26, 1927, six hundred students walked out of Emerson and paraded along Broadway protesting the admission of Black students. Their banner read, "We won't go back until Emerson is white." Four hundred did return, but the next day the number of student strikers increased to 880; on the third day of the strike, 1,357 refused to attend classes out of 2,800 students in the combined primary and secondary school. On September 30, the city council met, and the idea of a totally segregated high school for Blacks emerged. Construction started immediately on the all-Black Roosevelt High School. In the meantime, the eighteen students were forced back to the Virginia Street School, which had no athletic facilities, library, or other necessary school equipment.

In Froebel, the racially mixed secondary school, Black students clearly had a second-class position. Black seniors attended a separate prom, and their pictures were excluded from the school yearbook. The school administration refused to permit Black students to join extracurricular activities, such as the band, athletic teams, or ROTC; they could only use the swimming pool the day before it was cleaned. For many years classes were segregated, and there were no Black teachers.

Although Black students faced virtual segregation at Froebel, whites later became concerned that Blacks might acquire influence within the school. In 1943, white parents organized a parent-teacher association which excluded parents of Black children. The state PTA body, however, refused to accept the Froebel charter until the local branch omitted the discriminatory clauses. As late as 1945, white students struck at Froebel in order to keep the school from being, as one student leader put it, "overrun" by Blacks.

Segregation in the schools was paralleled by the development of discrimination in Gary's city services. The original plan of the city provided for two parks, both on the north side in the heart of U.S. Steel's original property. Since Blacks (and eastern and southern

Europeans) lived on the other side of town, they did not use these parks, which later became known as "traditionally" white parks. From the origin of the city until the mid-1930's, city parks remained inaccessible to Blacks. During the depression years Gary expanded its park system with the help of federal programs. U.S. Steel provided the city with a lakefront area east of Gary which the WPA shaped into a large park with beach, picnic area, and pavilion. The new Marquette Park was segregated from the beginning, with the beach integrated only after an uproar during the late 1950's. The city, again with WPA and FERA doing the work, also built a large park in the southern part of the city along the Little Calumet River. Actually there were two parks—one white, one Black. The white area, South Gleason Park, had 310 acres of grass and trees, an eighteen-hole golf course, a playground, and a wading pool. The immediately adjacent Black park, North Gleason, had 48 acres of grass and trees, a playground, a golf course—in this case, nine holes—and a small swimming pool, theoretically to compensate for Black exclusion from Marquette Beach. But the *Gary American,* a local newspaper, viewed the city's park compromise unfavorably.

The nearby Dunes State Park also segregated the few Blacks that used its facilities, but not until 1934 did this discrimination draw the attention of the news media. In that year fifty Black teachers and their friends used the park's recently improved picnic grounds, but only over the vigorous protest of John S. Fishback, park superintendent. The officials did manage to keep the Blacks from the main beach area. In a letter to Indiana governor Paul V. McNutt, A. Theodore Tatum, the Black principal of Roosevelt High School, protested that "there is no law preventing colored people from enjoying the privileges of a state park." William Hamilton of the Gary Public Library also complained to the governor, who replied that the Department of Conservation would "make a thorough investigation of the matter." However, nothing came of the investigation: park officials continued the discrimination and harassment of Blacks. "Is this Indiana or Alabama?" asked a member of another Black group picnicking at the Dunes three years later. He complained that after Blacks paid the admission fee, the lifeguard ordered them to swim on the extreme west end of the beach unprotected by a lifeguard.

Racial discrimination occurred in other public services as well. Segregation of concerts financed by the Gary schools ended in 1928, but only after Tatum vigorously protested anti-Black discrimination to School Superintendent Wirt. Other public-service problems were not so easily resolved. Most Black municipal employees cleaned streets and collected garbage, while those few in police and fire positions served on a segregated basis. During the 1930's federal agencies, as in other cities, acquiesced in Gary's racist practices. Although local public relief agencies provided minority groups with assistance, they still discriminated against them. The township trustees' office harassed unemployed Mexicans to return to Mexico or face exclusion from the relief rolls; the city ran a shelter to house and feed some of the unemployed, but on a whites-only basis. Even when World War II broke out in Europe, and Gary's citizens patriotically organized for civil defense, Blacks were forced into a separate unit.

Government agencies, U.S. Steel, and local realtors eventually imposed ghettoization on Gary's Black people, who for many years had lived alongside white working-class immigrants. With no open-housing legislation to inhibit discrimination, Gary realtors refused to sell houses outside of the central district (the old "south side") to Black buyers. When whites bought homes outside of midtown, their deeds often contained restrictive covenants preventing resale to Blacks. U.S. Steel policies supplemented those of small realtors. In building houses for its workers, the giant corporation established a segregated pattern as early as 1910. It did not permit Blacks to occupy company-built homes during the city's first decade. Later, in 1917, when U.S. Steel did build some housing for Blacks, it was segregated—for Blacks only. The *Gary Evening Post* defended U.S. Steel's real-estate subsidiary, the Gary Land Company, contending that "colored people everywhere prefer to live together." The paper noted approvingly that "the Gary Land Company is going to permit them to live in the same neighborhood decently and well."

During the 1930's, the federal government built two separate housing projects in Gary, perpetuating racial segregation. The Gary Housing Authority continued to segregate residents by placing Blacks in the central-district structures while locating whites outside of midtown. Often the white project had apartments vacant for some time, while applicants waited for available residences in the black project. The city kept Blacks waiting, for it did not begin integrating public-housing projects until ordered to do so by the courts in 1957.

Blacks were thus confined to the central district, whose borders expanded too slowly to compensate for Black population increases. As midtown became more congested, whites raised in the area left the city or established homes in adjacent areas. Likewise, new white immigrants also settled in lower-cost, less-congested areas. Over several years, owing to attrition through death and the steady out-migration of the original white population, the area became almost completely Black. White-owned businesses, ethnic churches (which sometimes remained after the foreign-born population left), and some white municipal employees constituted the remnants of the district's white presence.

As the Black population increased and as absentee landlords responded to supply-and-demand conditions, rents rose, and investment in building repairs decreased. A Gary housing survey conducted during the early 1920's found that Blacks paid 20 percent higher rents than native-born whites for substantially poorer accommodations; Black rentals also exceeded those paid by foreign-born whites, although by a lesser margin. Thus, like many immigrants, one-third of Gary's Black families sacrificed privacy and took in boarders to meet high rent costs. Other families doubled up, sometimes in basements with primitive living conditions. In one case, fifteen families from one tenement house used a single outside toilet and one outside water faucet.

These conditions continued into the 1930's. A property inventory made in 1934 by two federal agencies (CWA and FERA) found Gary housing substantially overcrowded, with many homes requiring repairs. In one area, of the 1,446 homes examined, 290 required major repair problems and 59 homes were declared unfit for use. In only 655 cases did one family reside in a single home. Six years later, the housing crisis for Blacks remained unimproved, as both the census and a Gary Housing Authority report indicate. The authority examined the 305 families admitted to the all-Black Delaney Housing project, finding that previously 212 had no bathroom facilities, 271 had no hot water, and 147 no gas (the standard fuel in Gary at that time) for cooking. In this city of small houses, the 1940 census found that only 30 percent of the Black families lived in one-family homes. The remainder resided in apartment houses or, more typically, in small homes converted into apartments. Black residencies were significantly deficient compared to those of whites.

Ghettoization led to congestion, intensifying the living problems of low-paid, unskilled industrial workers. It was not surprising that Blacks had much higher mortality rates than whites. Racism, in the form of discriminatory hospital policies was partly to blame. Gary's two major hospitals, Mercy and Methodist, at first prohibited admission of Black patients. In the mid-twenties, Mercy set aside a small number of beds for Blacks in a segregated ward attended only by white doctors. Methodist later followed Mercy in also establishing a segregated ward. Both hospitals excluded Black nurses as well as Black physicians from their staffs for some time. In response to the policies of Gary's main hospitals, small private clinics emerged in the midtown area to serve Blacks. But neither Patients Hospital nor St. John's had modern facilities, and both closed after Mercy and Methodist relaxed their exclusion policies.

Like any city of the deep South, discrimination and segregation permeated all aspects of Gary society. Local theaters at first refused admittance to Blacks and later limited them to balconies; but by 1940, segregated seating had been largely ended through court action. The YMCA and YWCA operated segregated facilities as well; neither became integrated until after World War II. Gary's First Baptist Church, Black, organized a separated Black Y in response to the restrictions. Until 1956, Gary's transit system fostered a subtle form of discrimination. Buses leaving the steel mills often passed through Black areas without stopping, thus effectively excluding Black passengers. Discrimination continued even in death, for the cemeteries also segregated by race. As late as 1963, Ridge Lawn Mount Mercy Cemetery refused to bury the body of a Black soldier killed in Vietnam.

Blacks faced overt discrimination in Gary's economic sector. Until 1931, merchants in the Black central district refused to employ Black women as sales clerks. At that time a campaign, by the NAACP, using the slogan "Don't spend your money where you can't clerk," successfully integrated midtown's labor force. The Gary street railway also refused to hire Blacks until the 1940's; so did stores in the white shopping district on the north side. The *Gary American* protested that "chain stores start up next door to our homes, get our trade, and refuse to hire even one Negro clerk. Downtown stores want Negro dollars but not Negro workers." Some white businesses turned away Black customers. A local restaurant displayed a sign saying, "We cater to white trade only." The *Gary American* protested that such notices were not unusual in Gary, but that this sign, located in the public bus station, constituted a greater insult. "Spend your money where you are not subject to insults," the *American* urged, "even if you have to go to Michigan City or Chicago." "For whites only" signs in rest rooms of gas stations also continued for many years.

The steel mills employed more Black workers than any other local business. Nevertheless, U.S. Steel discriminated. Black women could not work in the mills until 1940. After that date, U.S. Steel hired some Black women, but they worked mainly in janitorial jobs. Before World War II the company employed Black men primarily as unskilled laborers. They rarely held skilled positions; when Blacks did fill such jobs, they were almost exclusively in the coke plant. Negro foremen were highly unusual. Black workers protested to an Urban League investigator in 1944 that the lack of foremen resulted from an overt policy against promoting Blacks. Some departments refused to employ Blacks in any capacity.

In rebuffing Black workers attempting to secure positions in the chemistry division, a U.S. Steel official argued that Blacks would not fit in since whites could not invite them to worker-sponsored parties and other social events. He implied that discrimination conformed with society and therefore was acceptable to U.S. Steel. Last to be hired, the unskilled Black millhand found that he was laid off first and could be promoted only with the greatest difficulty; while at work, moreover, he faced such indignities as separate washrooms and locker facilities. A strong voice demanding racial justice did occasionally rectify minor grievances, but the Black community displayed little unity in tactics or in goals.

The Emerson School strike and the subsequent city council decision to build the segregated Roosevelt School, however, resulted in lengthy conflict involving the NAACP. The NAACP first organized a group to escort and protect the Black transfers to and from school each day. Later, it opposed Superintendent Wirt's decision to return the students to the deficient Virginia Street School. National headquarters provided money and expertise to carry out legal action. In the ensuing cases, the court declared the Virginia Street School unfit for students and unequal to local white schools. Thus, the city of Gary closed the Virginia Street building and built a new elementary school—also limited to Black students.

Local Black spokesmen, led by the NAACP, likewise opposed establishing segregated Roosevelt High School. A committee of Gary Blacks protested that the decision of the mayor and the city council on this issue was "discriminatory, un-American, prejudicial, unfair and unjust"; the new school plan, the committee contended, violated "both the letter and spirit of the Constitution." The NAACP publicized the Roosevelt School issue; one of its rallies attracted fifteen hundred protestors. The organization turned to the courts which delayed the school's construction with a temporary injunction, but this move failed to prevent the school's eventual completion.

The Roosevelt controversy illustrated divisions in the Black community. The emotional aspect of the issue could be seen as late as 1930 at a mass meeting called to protest the new school. Alfred M. Hall, a local Black union official and the meeting's principal speaker, argued that "all Negroes in favor of segregated schools should go back to Mississippi." In a similar vein, a Gary minister, Reverend Polk, declared "all those ministers not here at this meeting tonight are traitors to the race and should be exposed." The meeting ended in an uproar, as opposition speakers were shouted down, fights broke out, and guns were drawn. The segregated school received significant support from some Black politicians, from students who preferred a Black school to indignities at Froebel, and from the local chapter of Garvey's Universal Negro Improvement Association (UNIA).

The NAACP also attempted to end discrimination at Froebel. In 1934 it participated with the Communist party and the Gary Young Communist League in a mass meeting protesting racial discrimination at the school. The *Gary American* supported the movement, challenging Jim Crowism in the school's athletic and intellectual activities. The NAACP also attempted to integrate some of Gary's parks, successfully gaining Black entrance to a small park in the increasingly Black central city.

But except during the Roosevelt school crisis, NAACP activity appeared sporadic and its leadership uncertain. The organization avoided involvement in many obvious issues and failed to carry out a sustained effort in others. As late as 1945, it refused to support "Operation Beachhead," a campaign by Blacks and white allies to integrate Marquette Park and its beach area. Although the NAACP opposed this campaign because it claimed radicals were involved, integration continued as the organization's goal.

In contrast, Gary's UNIA promoted Black cultural identity, achievement, and institutions. The local press first mentioned Gary's UNIA in 1921. In the next three years the organization grew considerably, completely overshadowing the NAACP in the early 1920's. In October of 1923, Garvey gave a two-hour speech in Gary on race solidarity and the hope of Africa. He spoke in the city again a year later with, the *Gary Sun* noted, "fire and courage," urging his audience to achieve success through education. Between 1922 and early 1924, the UNIA reached the high point of its influence in Gary. It organized a band, a choir, Black Cross Nurses, and a paramilitary Black Legion. Although the number of UNIA members remained small, its following went well beyond the 185 dues-paying participants. The Gary UNIA prospered sufficiently to run classes and to purchase its own building with a large meeting hall. Hardy L. Keith, editor of a local Black newspaper, the *Gary Sun,* lauded Garvey; he called the movement "the vanguard of a bigger and more powerful revolution in the thought of Black people of the world." While red-baiting Garvey's critic, W. E. B. DuBois, the *Sun* offered its encouragement and assistance to the UNIA. The NAACP admitted the overshadowing influence of Garvey during this period, and later blamed its own inaction on issues on the Black community's enthusiastic reception of the Garvey ideology. Some NAACP spokesmen reacted to the sudden rivalry by accusing the UNIA of supporting the "Klux ticket" in municipal elections. Similarly, UNIA leaders were charged with membership in a Black unit of the KKK called the "Bow-tie Amalgamation."

Garvey lost some of his Gary support after the federal government indicted him for fraud in 1924, but the UNIA still functioned. However, local divisions in the organization and accusations of political graft resulted in expulsion and continued loss of membership during 1924. But while the *Gary Sun* condemned individual UNIA leaders as corrupt, it nevertheless remained faithful to the movement. It congratulated Garvey for his "nerve, grit, and stickability," and blamed Garvey's financial problems on some dishonest members of the UNIA. "The thoughtful Negro who loves his race and honestly hopes for its betterment," the *Sun* editorialized, "holds his criticism in abeyance with the undaunted assurance that Garvey will come back." The UNIA continued its activities: it raised money to build Liberty Hall (a meeting place for the UNIA), held contests providing Gary's outstanding Blacks with awards, and arranged for speakers on Negro history and racial pride.

In the 1927 school controversy over Roosevelt High School, the UNIA supported establishment of the segregated school because an integrated system would destroy "class and race consciousness." F. C. McFarland, principal of Roosevelt from 1923 to 1929, although officially not a member of the UNIA, emerged an acknowledged Garveyite spokesman on the Roosevelt issue. In speeches and discussions he stressed that the Roosevelt student learns "to value his own background with its African virtues." During the Black community's conflict over Roosevelt High School, the Klan issue was once again raised; but this time Garvey forces accused NAACP leaders of participating in the Bow-tie Amalgamation. The Garvey-oriented *Sun* hired a detective, Sherod Brusseaux, to investigate the charge. His claim of having evidence linking Gary's major Black politicians and prominent NAACP members to the Klan caused considerable publicity but was never substantiated. The NAACP denied the charges as an attempt to "discredit our efforts in the school fight."

The Roosevelt issue of 1927 revitalized the UNIA as the city's Black youth overwhelmingly supported the school's establishment. Gary's UNIA continued functioning for several years when most local units in cities of similar size had disintegrated. As late as 1931, the UNIA still demonstrated in the city. "As you watch them parading thru the streets of Gary, Sunday, be sure to notice the expression of pride worn on the faces of each one of Garvey's followers," suggested the *Gary American*. And the paper defended Garvey, by then in prison: "Paying no heed to those that laughed at him and considered his ambition ludicrous, Garvey defied hunger, criticism, and the most heart-breaking opposition to carry out his plan, to realize his vision." The Garvey movement in Gary all but disappeared by the mid-1930's, but many of his ideas did not die. "He is a shadow of the black leader of the future," said the *Gary Sun* of Garvey at the height of his influence. It added that Garveyism "is the vanguard of a bigger and more powerful revolution in the thought of black people of the world."

Discrimination and segregation were not outstanding issues in either election of Black candidates or in citywide elections for white candidates. Support of Black political spokesmen for white candidates in primaries and elections mainly depended upon the white man's selection of Black officials for city posts and Black workers for municipal jobs. In the 1940 mayoralty election, an exception to this generalization, Dr. Ernst L. Schiable, a Republican, ran for reelection. In 1938 he won as a reformer promising to rid Gary of political corruption and organized crime. Although Black political spokesmen supported the Democrats in 1938, the Black fifth ward went for Schiable who, however, did not respond with Black patronage for Blacks and the *Gary American* accused him of discrimination. It alleged that the administration assigned Black policemen to dog catching, that almost all other Black employees worked as laborers, that it prosecuted unlicensed Black cab drivers but let white ones off, and that it harassed small-scale gambling in the central district. Schiable did not receive the Black vote in 1940, but whether these complaints were as crucial as the Roosevelt presidential election or as New Deal public assistance policies is difficult to determine. In any event, politicians—Black or white—seldom addressed themselves to questions of local segregation and discrimination.

By World War II, Gary had a clearly defined Black ghetto, many segregated public and private institutions, and overt discrimination against Black residents—all explicitly condoned by local government. Racism was imposed on the community by those who controlled the city. U.S. Steel was primarily responsible through its promotion and hiring policies, its control of the Gary Land Company, and its influence on the school board and the park commission. Local politicians, through municipal policy and realty codes, reinforced trends established by the steel corporation. Immigrants were not immune to the examples set by Gary's opinion leaders. But even when Blacks were used as strikebreakers during the 1919 steel strike, racial conflict did not ensue. It took eight more years for seeds planted by the steel company and the city government to bear fruit in the Emerson student strike. By that time, the immigrants and their children had been Americanized; racism was part of their Americanization.

THE CITY OF BLACK ANGELS
Emergence of the Los Angeles Ghetto, 1890-1930

LAWRENCE B. DE GRAAF

The spotlight of national attention on Black ghettoes during the past decade has led historians to study a field which had previously been largely the preserve of sociologists and economists. Several excellent studies of the formation of major areas of Black urban concentration prior to the Great Depression have been written, and long-held interpretations of the causes and timing of ghetto development have been altered. To date, however, no historian has produced a scholarly study of the origins of the community in Los Angeles which, by 1960, ranked sixth among all Black urban populations in the United States. This neglect resulted partly from the fact that writers saw no substantial Black population in the West prior to the 1940's and concluded that the presence of Negroes was largely a phenomenon of wartime migration. Thus Gunnar Myrdal dismissed the role of Blacks in the development of the West by noting that in 1940 they constituted in all states west of the Mississippi, outside of the South, only 2.2 percent of the nation's Negro population. He was typical in neglecting to observe that one-fourth of this percentage resided in one county, mostly in certain sections of one city, Los Angeles, which already ranked fourteenth among the nation's cities in Negro population. It had been the largest Black community in the state since 1900, when the director of the census recognized it as one of only two substantial Negro centers in the West.

Reprinted with permission from the *Pacific Historical Review*, 39 (August, 1970), pp. 323-352. Footnotes and tables appearing in the original publication have been deleted in the present volume, and should be consulted for full documentation of the author's conclusions.

At what period in history this center of Negro population became a ghetto, and whether the Los Angeles Black community was a ghetto in the same sense as cities in the Northeast and South are questions which require a careful definition of terms and criteria. For many years most scholars worked from the premise that there had not always been a necessary relationship between a ghetto, "an area which houses a people concerned with the perpetuation of a peculiar (and different) culture," and a slum, a neighborhood characterized by poverty and physical and social deterioration. The concentration of Negroes into urban ghettos grew out of the Great Migration of 1915-1929. The subsequent deterioration of these ghettos into slums was largely the result of the confinement of Blacks to areas and structures whose size and age precluded adequate housing for the growing population. In emphasizing the recency of the Black slum-ghetto, many writers partially accepted the view of "old resident" Negroes that the post-1915 influx of southern migrants was a cause of deterioration. Robert Weaver wrote that, prior to 1915, "Negro housing . . . [in the North] did not differ from that of any other race." Black belts, ethnic segregation, and rent discrimination were evident, but these did not confine all Blacks to certain areas, nor to the poorest housing, nor did it dampen their belief that with higher income they could advance to better housing. But the Great Migration, by changing "the size and general characteristics of the migrants," transformed the Black ghetto from a section for poor Blacks to an area of racial confinement tightened by such new devices as restrictive covenants. By the late 1930's several studies of Black sections revealed that most housing—for poor and well-off alike—was old, lacked modern sanitation, had been neglected by white owners, and was often occupied by more persons or families than it had been designed to accommodate. Such overcrowded and deteriorating housing after 1915 bred the high sickness and death rates, high crime rate and police-resident hostility, poor educational and recreational facilities, and general deterioration which have come to characterize the Black ghetto.

In the past decade, scholars and public commissions have expanded this definition of ghetto and slum and challenged its recency in American history. To this school the ghetto is not only a restricted residential area but, even more, "an impressionistic phrase which summarizes the social, economic, and psychological positions of Black people in the city, and also the tone of urban race relations." The earlier distinction between a ghetto and a slum was replaced by a single phenomenon, the slum-ghetto, "an area within a city characterized by poverty and acute social disorganization and inhabited by members of a social or ethnic group under conditions of voluntary segregation." Several historians have challenged the "old resident" theory by noting that involuntary residential segregation and widespread racial animosity antedated the Great Migration to northern cities. Alan Spear writes:

By 1915, Negroes had become a special group in the social structure of prewar Chicago. . . . The systematic proscription they suffered in housing and jobs, the discrimination they often . . . experienced in public accommodations and even municipal services, the violence of which they were frequently victims, set them apart from the mainstream of Chicago life.

More recently, Gilbert Osofsky has used this broader definition to project the origin of New York's ghetto—and by inference all northern ghettos—back to colonial times. He states that in spite of the size of the Black population or the number of different residential areas, "by all the standard measurements of human troubles in the city, the ghetto has always been with us—it has tragically endured."

Both these interpretations give insights to the development of a Black ghetto in Los Angeles, but neither affords a complete answer. To ascertain when a ghetto developed, this historian will accept the distinction between a ghetto and a slum, for by 1930 Los Angeles did have a distinct physical ghetto with few opportunities for Blacks to live outside its boundaries. But the predominance of single-family dwelling units within that area, in contrast to the appearances of most other ghettos, led most writers to conclude that the city had no extensive Negro slum. Therefore, the broader definition, specifically measuring occupational opportunities, social discrimination, and racial hostility, must be employed to determine whether and when this ghetto took on the characteristics of a slum. These criteria must be augmented by considering several novel features of the Los Angeles area. Its development as an urban industrial metropolis was overshadowed by a continuous suburban expansion which provided much of the economic opportunity, particularly in the form of real-estate investment. Los Angeles also contained several racial minorities who rivaled Blacks in number. Therefore, low occupational status did not necessarily preclude the accumulation of wealth, and Blacks were not unique in the degree of racial animosity and social restrictions they suffered. Finally, since some of the earliest references to deterioration have come from old resident Negroes, the volume and characteristics of migration to Los Angeles will be examined to test the validity of that factor as a dynamic of ghetto formation. Only when all of these variables have been considered can the development of the Los Angeles ghetto be fully understood.

The origins of the Black community in Los Angeles have been traced to the founding of the city in 1781. Of the 44 original settlers, 26 had some African ancestry. However, they quickly lost their majority position. By 1790, the first census of Los Angeles revealed only 22 mulattoes out of a total population of 141; moreover, few Blacks came to the city during the remainder of the Spanish and Mexican periods. Thus the identified Negro element virtually disappeared, although recent research has found traces of African ancestry in several prominent landowners and political figures. The first three decades of American rule saw several families, especially those of Biddie Mason and Robert Owens, which would long be prominent in the Black community, come to Los Angeles. But the number of Negroes increased from 12 in 1850 to only 102 in 1880, less than 1 percent of the total population. The modern Black community began not with the founding party but with the land boom of 1887-1888 which increased the Negro population in the city to 1,258 or 2.5 percent of the total in 1890.

Had Negroes continued to come to Los Angeles at such a rate, a ghetto in the sense of an area of ethnic concentration might have developed by 1900. This possibility was averted by the collapse of the land boom in 1888, resulting in severe unemployment which spread throughout the state in 1893. Negroes in rural areas appear to have been particularly affected by the depression, and their population in California declined between 1890 and 1900. Los Angeles received much of the exodus from rural counties, and by 1900 it had surpassed San Francisco to become the largest Black community in the state. But the increase was smaller than that of the previous decade, and in 1900, Negroes numbered only 2,131, barely 2 percent of the population. Some writers have noted that during this decade Negroes developed their earliest residential concentration, particularly in rooming houses along First and Second streets, and that they established several businesses on nearby Weller Street. But these faint signs of a ghetto were overshadowed by the fact that they could and did live throughout the city and were much less concentrated in any one area in 1890 and 1900 than they would be after 1910.

Evidence that the Black community prior to 1900 constituted a ghetto is as difficult to obtain by the broader criteria as it is by the standard of migration and concentration. The employment conditions of Blacks showed signs of discrimination and poverty. They were hard hit by unemployment, and in 1893, when unions ignored their appeal for jobs, they formed an Afro-American Protective Association to secure work and lands. But unemployment was not unique to Blacks, and the effects of the depression were lessened by several factors. The full impact of the panic was not felt in Los Angeles until 1897, and considerable construction went on through the decade. Many Blacks held service jobs, and the influx of whites created a market for more such jobs, especially a demand for servants. Labor unions increased their membership among white workers, but they seem to have confined their racial hostility to the Chinese. The depression did not discourage several Black physicians from coming to the city, nor did it prevent Blacks from developing businesses. Some who owned real estate survived the collapse of the boom and increased their estates. In 1896 the heirs of Biddie Mason refused an offer of $200,000 for their property on Spring Street. The decade also saw little racial animosity toward Blacks. Such hostility had declined since the 1860's, when the city was a center of Confederate sympathy. By the 1880's, Los Angeles had desegregated its schools, and the state had passed a civil rights law. In an era when Chinese were being excluded from jobs and driven from cities, the small and relatively inconspicuous Negro population appears to have enjoyed a lessening of racial tension and a considerable degree of acceptance. At the turn of the century, the Los Angeles Black community showed few signs of its future history, except for being the focal point in the West for Black settlement and the logical place for a ghetto, if any city developed one.

Between 1900 and 1920 the volume of Negro migration to the city increased sharply, causing the Negro population to multiply more than sevenfold. This movement has obvious similarities to the Great Migration to northern cities after 1915. Most migrants came from southern states. There were also a few efforts at the mass importation of Negroes. The Southern Pacific Railroad brought nearly 2,000 to the area in 1903 to break a strike of Mexican construction workers, and in the following year hundreds of Negroes in Texas organized a flight from racial oppression to the Pacific Coast where they believed "there is no antagonism against the race." Over all, however, the movement of Negroes to Los Angeles was neither as voluminous nor as concentrated in any short time period as the Great Migration. The Black population grew from 1,258 in 1890 to 38,898 by 1930, yet as a proportion of the total population it increased from 2.5 to only 3.14 percent. Neither local employers, with the exception of the Southern Pacific in 1903, nor the Negro press solicited migrants; the main tribune, the *California Eagle,* said little about migration during World War I. When the growth of the Negro population is compared with overall trends, the movement becomes but a small part of a general migration to the area, not a distinctive racial phenomenon.

The attractions that brought most Blacks to Los Angeles during this period were similar to those which lured whites. The major motive was economic. Typical was the civil servant who attributed his decision to move from Georgia in 1904 to a series of contacts he had with persons who had been to California and found it was a place "to make more and easier money." A second factor attracting some was the climate. Its warmth convinced several visitors that this was a region where "Negroes belonged." A lawyer who arrived in 1913 exhorted his family to "come and dwell in God's country." The climate also offered the hope of relief from ailments which were particularly troublesome in damper weather, and there are indications that some Blacks participated in the "health rush" to southern California at the turn of the century. A Negro sanitarium was erected in Duarte during the early 1900's, and newspapers carried several letters from Blacks giving health as their reason for coming to California.

In personal characteristics, migrants between 1900 and 1920 were neither markedly elite nor proletarian, but many were optimistic about their ability to make a better life for themselves in the West. The one significant change during this period appears to be in their origin, though this conclusion must be drawn from data on the state as a whole, not on Los Angeles. In 1900, 37 percent of California's Negroes had come from the Pacific states, less than half were of southern birth, and the largest portion of these came from the South Atlantic states. While these proportions are obviously exaggerated for Los Angeles, which had few Negroes before 1887, they do suggest that many of its Black residents at the turn of the century were a "select" group, compared to most southern Negroes, in that they were acculturated to California by birth or had shown willingness to adapt to nonsouthern and urban cultures by long migration. Less than 10 percent had been born in the West South-Central states of Texas, Louisiana, Oklahoma, and Arkansas, the section from which Negroes, with a minimum of money or cultural change, were most likely to come to California. In the succeeding two decades, the origins of California Negroes changed considerably, and by 1920 less than 25 percent were born in the Pacific states, 58 percent came from the South, and 27 percent were from the West South-Central states. This shift in origins may be interpreted as indicating that between 1900 and 1920 an increasing percentage of the Negroes in Los Angeles retained crude southern mannerisms that may have elicited contempt and hostility from whites. This line of reasoning is not borne out, however, if occupational and educational status is measured by the jobs that Negroes held in Los Angeles. Migrants throughout this period were predominantly common laborers, janitors, porters, and domestic servants. Less than 5 percent of the males were in business or the professions. These jobs were not always an accurate reflection of educational or previous employment level, as many migrants who had worked as teachers or skilled laborers in other states accepted lower-status jobs in Los Angeles out of necessity. But such underemployment also appears quite constant between 1900 and 1920.

Documented observations from this period give a different impression of the caliber of migrants. Quite a few came to the state with money. Stories of parties leaving the South for California mention their taking with them up to several thousand dollars to invest in California land, and one Black pastor estimated in 1906 that his brethren had $600,000 "lying in the bank." Above all, commentators refer to the enterprising nature of the Black population and the ability of those who came with very modest means to acquire considerable wealth. A businessman who moved from San Francisco to Los Angeles in 1901 described his brethren in the latter city as "industrious, prosperous people who have an object in life." Another source notes that "while a great many have brought some money, the large majority have started with their strong, capable, willing hands and a determination to succeed as their only capital." This observation is supported by the testimony of two Tennessee migrants who arrived in the community destitute but by the end of the 1920's had managed to acquire eight houses.

In reviewing the nature of the migration, it is difficult to conclude that the newcomers contributed to isolation or necessarily caused the development of ghettos. At no time does there appear to have been a sudden, rapid influx of Blacks which would have produced white alarm or an invasion of white residential areas comparable to that of Harlem. There were no colonies of Blacks formed within Los Angeles during the period; on the contrary, most migrants came as individuals or as families desirous of becoming a part of a general Los Angeles community. While the percentage of southern migrants rose during this period, in both cultural and economic characteristics the average Black migrant was not so different from others in Los Angeles that he should have felt the need for confining himself to a ghetto or that he could only afford the poorest areas. In sum, it is difficult to see how either the volume or characteristics of these migrants could have produced a ghetto. Yet by 1920 most Los Angeles Negroes did live in a few restricted areas which amounted to a spatial ghetto and which had some of the social, economic, and psychological characteristics of a ghetto in the broader sense of the term.

Dispersal over several areas of the city remained characteristic of Black residence in Los Angeles during the early years of the twentieth century. In addition to the commercial settlement which had grown along Weller, First, and Second streets, Blacks resided in the northwest portion of the city, along West Temple Street, the northeast, in Boyle Heights, the Furlong tract in the southeast corner of the city, and the western area along Jefferson Boulevard between Normandie and Wester, as well as on numerous streets south of First Street and Central Avenue. In 1904 the editor of the local Negro monthly, the *Liberator*, emphasized an apparently prevalent attitude on the opportunity and wisdom of residential dispersal:

> The Negroes of this city have prudently refused to segregate themselves into any locality, but have scattered and purchased homes in sections occupied by wealthy, cultured white people, thus not only securing the best fire, water and police protection, but also the more important benefits that accrue from refined and cultural surroundings.

While Blacks living in railroad house courts could hardly consider themselves in "refined and cultural surroundings," the general impression conveyed by this quotation has been substantiated by interviews with Black residents of this period. It is also corroborated by the census statistics of 1910, which showed substantial Black population in all sections of the city and a difference of less than 700 percent between the districts having the highest and lowest proportions of Blacks. This broad distribution might be attributed to characteristics of Los Angeles as an urban area, especially its smaller population in comparison to many eastern cities, the rapid growth and expansion of its housing, and the relatively small amount of old housing in one area. However, these factors did not prevent a much higher degree of segregation among Japanese and Chinese than among Negroes in 1910. Moreover, these factors would not change so significantly in the following decade that they alone could explain the great increase in the degree of residential segregation of Blacks by 1920.

The formation of a distinct Black district may be traced to the beginning years of the twentieth century, when Blacks expanded from their centers of the 1890's and whites sold their homes and abandoned the area. The areas of greatest expansion were the commercial district along Weller Street and the segregated railroad houses adjacent to the old Arcade Station at Fifth Street and Central Avenue. By 1906, Negroes had established an area of settlement between Fourth and Ninth streets, from Central Avenue west to Maple. In 1910, the community expanded to the east when a Negro preacher purchased several acres of undeveloped land at Third and Traction for a commercial and cultural center and Bob Owens built a hotel in the area. Within a few years, however, white businessmen purchased the land at a considerable profit to the Blacks, who looked south for their next community center.

The street along which Black settlement subsequently advanced and which was to become the heart of the Black community, Central Avenue, had a history which in some respects is reminiscent of Harlem. It was established around the turn of the century as a neighborhood of houses and small businesses, including a legitimate theater. Even before the displacement of the Black community center described above, Blacks had been moving into the northern end of Central Avenue, attracted in part by the comparatively low rents. The decision of a real-estate dealer to open a hotel at Eleventh and Central seems to have triggered a large-scale exodus of whites after 1912 and a corresponding movement of Blacks steadily southward, displacing the Jewish residents, although in most cases not displacing their ownership of businesses on the street.

White exodus and Black concentration in the Central Avenue area continued, and by 1920 most Blacks were living in one physical ghetto stretching approximately thirty blocks down Central Avenue and several blocks east to the railroad tracks, or in a few detached islands, especially on West Jefferson, Temple Street, and just south of the city in Watts. Each of these communities was separated from the Central Avenue ghetto by blocks of solid white resistance. This concentration was accentuated by the location of most Black churches and businesses in the Central Avenue area, leading some persons who resided in other parts of the city to move to the ghetto for social contacts. It must be noted that this "ghetto" was still quite mixed in its population. A survey of areas of immigrant and minority-group concentration in 1919 found Mexicans and Italians living in and adjacent to Negroes in the area between Central Avenue and the Los Angeles River, while Negroes and Russian Jews shared the district immediately east of the river. Nevertheless, the increase in the concentration and segregation of Negroes between 1910 and 1920 was striking. By the latter year, nearly 75 percent of their population resided in three of the city's twelve assembly districts, while in five others, Negroes composed less than 1 percent of the population. These figures also suggest that after 1910 the major dynamic governing the location of Negroes shifted from their real-estate investments and white withdrawal to an increasing restriction of Negroes to certain areas and mounting resistance by Caucasians to their expansion.

Incidents of possible resistance to Black settlement and legal efforts to exclude them accompanied their earliest efforts to enter previously all-white areas in any substantial numbers. During the early 1900's, white residents on Central Avenue endeavored to restrict Blacks at Seventh Street, and one of the first Blacks to settle south of that street was threatened by a mob. A decade later, one of the first Blacks to settle on Eighteenth Street and Central had her house sacked by a white mob. Despite such occasional efforts at intimidation, Blacks continued to obtain houses along Central Avenue and in 1918 moved from their old westside community into the prestigious West Jefferson area east of Normandie Avenue. But by 1916 whites were publicly expressing their resentment of Black neighbors. One writer complained to the *Los Angeles Times* of "the insults that one has to take from a northern nigger, especially a woman, let alone the property depreciation in the community where they settle. . . ." Such feelings were most frequently expressed in the growing adoption of race-restrictive covenants on property deeds. Restrictive covenants had been placed on some lots in the nineteenth century and were widely used by the early 1900's. Technically they provided an absolute restriction against sale, lease, or rental to any person other than a white with penalties of loss of premises for violation. By 1917, one Black resident described his tract during World War I as "encircled by invisible walls of steel. The whites surrounded us and made it impossible for us to go beyond these walls."

This statement expresses the growing racial tension of the World War I period, but it exaggerates the extent of enforced segregation prior to the 1920's. Forcible exclusion of Blacks was confined to isolated acts, and there is no evidence of a sustained organized effort to confine Blacks to certain neighborhoods. The effectiveness of race restrictive covenants varied according to the determination of whites to enforce them and the resourcefulness of Blacks in finding means of circumventing them. The latter was quite evident. In several instances light-skinned Blacks posing as whites penetrated all-white neighborhoods, and whites sold to other Blacks in violation of their covenants rather than live with them. Negro real-estate brokers also made a practice of checking titles to see when covenants expired and then purchasing a house on a white block where the deed restriction had lapsed. Not all whites resented such expansion. In some older residential areas, they welcomed the arrival of Blacks as a means of getting rid of homes which "were nothing to brag about [but] . . . were veritable Edens to some of the Negroes." By the end of the World War I decade, however, the use of block protective association restrictions as well as individual deed covenants heralded a more rigid and efficient era of residential segregation. This movement received a considerable boost from a reversal of legal rulings on restrictive covenants.

Prior to 1919, local courts had ruled that race restriction clauses in property deeds were either illegal or unenforceable by court action. In 1914, two Blacks successfully sued a Los Angeles realty company for refusing to sell them property on account of color. Two years later, in *Title Guarantee and Trust Co.* v. *Garratt,* the municipal court ruled that a deed restriction "is not only contrary to the general policy of the law, and contrary to the express provisions of Section 711 of the Civil Court . . . but also is unenforceable in the courts under the State and Federal constitutions." An appeals court upheld the decision but rejected the broad conclusion that individual residential exclusion was *ipso facto* a violation of the Fourteenth Amendment. The same reasoning was applied in lower courts to a similar suit by the Los Angeles Investment Company against Alfred Gary. However, upon appeal to the California Supreme Court in 1919, that body by a three-to-two decision distinguished between a restriction against alienation (for example, sale or lease) of property to non-Caucasians, which was in violation of the state civil code, and the restriction against use or occupancy, which is found valid under law. This reversal provided a legal precedent for enforcement of restrictive covenants that would be followed and enlarged upon through World War II, with the result that residential exclusion and eviction became much more common and effective than it had been before 1920.

Such a pattern of Black migration, residential segregation, and racial hostility would logically be expected to result in substandard housing, excessive rents, and other characteristics of a slum in the developing spatial ghetto. This result would seem even more certain in such a rapidly growing metropolis as Los Angeles. The city housing commission reported in 1908 that wooden shacks and tents were being thrown up on lots in the heart of the city to create "a peculiar kind of slum" lacking adequate water and sanitation facilities. While the city had few multi-story tenements, it had many congested house courts consisting of several rows of small, poorly ventilated units with common outdoor privies and water facilities, "as vicious as the tenement condition in Eastern cities." A city council ordinance aimed at compelling landlords and railroad companies to improve these courts was only partially successful, and many were still occupied in 1920. The rents charged for such quarters were also analogous to conditions in eastern slums. Tiny lots for tents rented for $2.50 per month, and by 1910 a "mere shack of two or three rooms" cost from $10 to $15 per month. These rents led to doubling up and chronic congestion. Finally, studies agree that virtually all the tenants were "foreigners," persons other than native white Americans. From such evidence as this, Robert M. Fogelson could easily conclude that Los Angeles's Negroes shared with the city's Mexicans, Japanese, and southeast Europeans the common plight of being "confined to rented quarters in the deteriorating downtown district and outlying industrial sections."

While all these groups had poorer and more restricted residences than native whites, there were great differences between the proportion of their population which lived in slum conditions and the relative quality of housing inhabited by the majority of each ethnic group. Until the 1920's, Negroes appear to have had one of the smallest representations of the "foreign" groups in slum areas. Mexicans had the worst housing of any group. The poorest of all minorities, they composed most of the inhabitants of tent and shack colonies and occupied many of the poorest house courts, often dubbed "cholo courts." Prior to World War I, Chinatown and European immigrant districts—especially those of Russians, Italians, Slavonians, and Austrians—were cited as congested and lacking in sanitary facilities. Negroes were mentioned least of all minority groups. Some resided in the Southern Pacific house court on New High Street, "one of the largest and dirtiest courts," and some lived in shacks in the center of the city. They were also noted for being able to occupy new and improved house courts, while Mexicans were generally excluded.

By the time of World War I, Blacks' housing conditions drew greater notice. A 1915 study found that 68 out of 1,192 families in house courts were Black, a much higher ratio than the proportion of Blacks in the population. In 1918 an anonymous Negro wrote

there are two distinct Negro colonies. . . . In both of these quarters I found that the white people are making the mistake of leaving these Negro quarters with bad sanitation and insufficient street work. They are not helping the Negroes to make the most out of themselves.

This picture of Negro neighborhoods was quickly disputed by the *California Eagle*. "I should like to know just where these Negro quarters, with bad sanitation and insufficient street work are, in this city," asked the editor. "In fact, the Negroes here are exceptionally well housed by comparison with other cities." Studies in 1919 cite Blacks as residents of one "foreign district" which had many violations of state housing laws and a small percentage of ownership, but neither these nor other studies mentioned their presence in the most deteriorated areas. They were also never mentioned in connection with such ramifications of slum life as high crime rates, family instability, juvenile delinquency, prostitution, and gambling, which were noted in Mexican, European, and Chinese districts. Most significant is the near-unanimity among Black visitors and residents in extolling the beauty and viability of their community and making no reference to signs of deterioration:

They [Negroes of Los Angeles] are without doubt the most beautifully housed group of colored people in the United States. They are full of push and energy and are used to working together. . . . I saw the business establishments of the colored people. There was a splendid merchant tailor shop with a large stock of goods[,] . . . a contractor who was putting up some of the best buildings in the city with colored workmen; physicians, lawyers and dentists with offices in first-class buildings and, above all, homes—beautiful homes.

In their social relations and quest for employment, however, Los Angeles Blacks may have considered themselves living in a ghetto. Socially they suffered discrimination and faced barriers typical of their treatment throughout the nation in the early twentieth century. Many theaters and places of amusement refused to seat them with whites; others tried to discourage their attendance by charging them higher prices. Many restaurants outside the Black area refused to serve them; some insisted they use rear entrances and eat on stools rather than sit at tables. Women were refused service at some clothing stores; most hotels were closed to them; and Pasadena segregated its public playgrounds in 1918. Generally social segregation before 1920 stopped short of legalizing Jim Crow. Some Blacks filed successful suits against public accommodations discrimination, and there were no serious efforts to segregate public schools. But the extent of white hostility to racial equality and interracial association was seen when jitney buses appeared in 1914 with a policy of refusing to serve Negroes. For four years they flourished, despite efforts of street-car interests and local government to outlaw them as a public menace. Jitney owners openly appealed to voters to defeat regulation laws in order to keep a public transportation medium that served whites only. When the council did outlaw them, one Black observer reported that whites threatened a "near riot" and caused some Black families to flee their homes.

Blacks were similarly restricted from the start of the century in the areas of employment that were open to them. They were disproportionately represented in service jobs. In 1910 and 1920 nearly one-third of the employed males worked as janitors, porters, waiters, or house servants. Los Angeles did not have as many industrial jobs as northeastern cities, and Blacks were largely relegated to the position of laborer. They received some jobs as chauffeurs and draymen, but they were virtually excluded from positions as conductors, motormen, and other higher jobs in transportation. The most significant restriction was their absence from retail trade and nonprofessional white-collar jobs—the largest area of unemployment in the city. In 1910 there were 6,177 store salesmen, of whom 8 were Black; in 1920 Los Angeles had 11,341 salesmen, 28 of whom were Black.

Los Angeles lagged behind many other United States cities in the jobs it offered to Blacks, especially during the 1910–1920 period. In most other major cities, the percentage of Negro males and females holding industrial jobs sharply increased. In Los Angeles, however, the percentage of Blacks holding industrial jobs declined during the decade, and their overall job status by 1920 was more similar to that of northern cities before the Great Migration than after World War I. This occupational pattern was not the result of a lack of skill on the part of Blacks; college graduates, teachers, preachers, and other professional men were found holding custodial jobs. It was rather the result of extensive competition from European and Mexican immigrants and discrimination on the part of management.

Blacks were also largely restricted to the lower rungs of public service work, although they secured a disproportionate share of some of these jobs. In 1912 a Georgia migrant, L. G. Robinson, was given the position of head of the janitors' department of Los Angeles County, and by 1929 he had expanded the janitors' staff from 35 to 178, nearly all of them Black. Los Angeles was ahead of many cities in opening some public-service positions to Blacks. The first Black police were hired before 1900, and twenty-three were on the force by 1920, some in advanced ranks. Several authorities agree that Los Angeles was the first major city to employ Blacks in its fire department. But efforts of Black women to gain training and jobs as nurses in the county hospital during World War I caused threats of resignation by white nurses, and victory came only after a long legal battle. On several occasions, Blacks complained that they were barred from civil service jobs or examinations.

Such a catalogue of discrimination would today be diagnosed as part of a syndrome which results in chronic poverty, psychological debasement, and social deterioration. However, one must be wary of presuming such development in Los Angeles during the early twentieth century. Most Blacks received low wages; even the prestigious Pullman porters complained in 1912 that they earned only $25 per month. In a survey of families of Black delinquents done in 1919, it was found that they averaged only two-thirds of the United States government minimum family income—making theft of food a necessity. However, neither unemployment nor poverty are common themes in the literature and observations of the Black community prior to the Great Depression. The wage rates of even menial jobs were high by southern standards, a janitor's position returning three or four times what many Negroes made in farming.

The most important ameliorating factor was the opportunity to buy land and houses at a low price either for personal use or for resale in the boom of urban expansion that prevailed through much of this period. As one historian has described the scene,

Subdivision after subdivision was thrown onto the market until it seemed as if there would be no land left for farming between the city and the sea or between the city and the mountains. Investment companies, building associations, homemakers, home builders, and corporations of various kinds, limited and unlimited, were organized to furnish lots and houses to the homeless and lotless.

This "bungalow boom" was particularly noticeable in the Central Avenue area where most of the houses were four- or five-room "California cottages" which were advertised at prices ranging from $900 to $2,500 and usually sold for $100 to $200 down with monthly payments of $20.

Many Blacks of modest means and occupation found these homes within their reach. A female domestic wrote Booker T. Washington that after thirteen years she had already bought one lot. The chief custodian for the city of Los Angeles picked up several lots on the edge of the city which he subsequently sold for a profit of several thousand dollars and went on to raise $40,000 in an endeavor to organize a grocery store. A dining car porter, arriving in the early 1900's, bought several successive houses in various parts of the town with little financial difficulty. This real-estate boom and home ownership gave Los Angeles Blacks reason for optimism and enterprise despite discriminations in other aspects of life. But, considering the Black's low job status, they also held an ominous potential. For if real-estate prices rose beyond the ability of laborers to purchase lots, or if the most profitable areas of purchase were closed to Blacks—as would occur in the 1920's—then their low occupational status would contribute to the pattern of poverty and neighborhood deterioration already becoming evident in many northern ghettos.

If the story of the Los Angeles ghetto before 1920 is one of enterprise and economic opportunities prevailing over racial hostility, segregation, and discrimination, the record of the succeeding decade is in many ways the reverse. This change was partly rooted in the volume of migration to Los Angeles. The Negro community, like all of southern California, experienced growth of unprecedented magnitude during the 1920's. Its population increased from 15,579 to nearly 39,000, while the city as a whole grew from 576,000 to nearly 1,250,000. In their motives for migration, whites and Blacks remained similar, but their opportunities for settlement varied greatly. While whites built miles of residential tracts along the coast and into rural lands adjacent to the city, Blacks were barred from such expansion and had to absorb the influx in their existing community or in older residential areas on its periphery. The result was increased ethnic concentration, a deterioration of property values, and a less optimistic view of their community on the part of some Blacks. While this deterioration had not become as dominant a feature as it was in many eastern cities, the 1920's did establish the foundations for many of the problems of Los Angeles's Black community which became so noticeable in the 1960's.

Blacks entering the city met a pattern of racial discrimination and restrictive employment opportunities that differed little from conditions in earlier decades. Discrimination in public accommodations was less frequently reported, but the popularity of the Ku Klux Klan in southern California and the segregation of municipal swimming pools by the Los Angeles City Playground Commission created greater fears and uncertainties among Blacks than had been expressed in earlier decades. Employment patterns continued to be little different from the first two decades with most women employed in domestic service, and service work and common labor being the leading areas of male employment. The growth of industries proved of little benefit, for they were mostly light industries employing skilled labor. A 1926 study by the Urban League revealed that most employers refused to hire Blacks on the ground that they were unfit for such jobs or that whites would refuse to work with them. These conditions were no more proscriptive during the 1920's than they had been before. The crucial change was the tighter residential segregation and its effects upon alternative economic and housing opportunities and thus upon the condition of the entire ghetto.

The tremendous volume of migrants entering southern California in the early 1920's on the heels of the World War I housing shortage and the postwar depression contributed a major problem for the white population alone. This problem was magnified by widespread real-estate advertising which led migrants to enter the state with visions of immediate home ownership. Often unable to obtain funds, many of them rented lots and erected tent houses and shacks which "passed from one settler to another, constantly deteriorating, and [were] constructed without the minimum regard for sanitary necessities." Black realtors advertised Los Angeles as having a higher percentage of Black home owners than any other city, fully intending that such claims would "broadcast to colored Americans everywhere the opportunities, the welcome, the hope and cheer which free California, its hills and valleys . . . and always sunshine offer to the American Negro." Los Angeles in the 1920's had all the ingredients for both an expansion of its Black community into adjacent white areas and determined resistance to such penetration.

During the first years of the decade, Blacks were able to expand into several previously white areas. Older residents in the Central Avenue community moved southward, displacing over half of the white residents and leaving their old houses to the new arrivals. By 1925 the main Black community stretched down to the Florence district on Slauson Avenue.

Here, expansion was checked. Families moving south of that street were driven out with threats of violence and in some cases had their homes raided and wrecked. In contrast to the short-lived efforts at exclusion along Central Avenue in earlier decades, this intimidation, attributed by some to the Ku Klux Klan, maintained Slauson as a racial boundary until World War II. The small middle-class westside area expanded northward from West Jefferson to West Adams in 1923-1924, aided by many whites who had allowed their deed restrictions, initially put on in the 1880's, to expire. After a few persons had penetrated the area, a Black realtor used block-busting by moving in an "undesirable" family and spreading the rumor that more would follow. Blacks and Japanese also continued to move eastward in the vicinity of Jefferson Boulevard, where some whites broke their restrictive housing agreement in order to sell their property. Both of these "invasions" roused widespread fears of property depreciation which led to efforts to bind all white property owners in the area to a district-wide ban against nonwhites. While not fully effective, it limited the area of Black housing and so inflated prices—up to double what whites were charged—that this community was available only to the wealthiest class of Blacks.

South of Los Angeles lay a community whose name was a subject of derision in the early 1900's and of controversy in the 1960's—Watts. Some Blacks had settled there in the late nineteenth century and established a southern agricultural community, but the town was predominantly composed of white workers. The low rents and status of its citizens made the name a "sort of clowning synonym in showdom for everything that is pedantic, plodding or punk," but by 1910 it was incorporated and regarded as a prosperous and attractive suburb. During World War I southern Negroes began moving in, attracted by the low housing costs. Whites generally refused to buy near them, with the result that by 1924 the town was regarded as likely to have a Black mayor. This "Watts invasion" was cited by other suburban papers as illustrating the folly of allowing any Blacks to gain title to the land. In 1926, allegedly at the instigation of the Ku Klux Klan, an election was held in which a majority of the voters chose annexation to Los Angeles rather than remaining a separate city which might be predominantly composed of Blacks. The "lesson" of the Watts invasion apparently was heeded, for until World War II the Blacks in Watts constituted a lonely island in an otherwise white southeast Los Angeles.

By 1926, the substantial expansion of Blacks into adjacent neighborhoods of central Los Angeles had ended; their communities were surrounded by established white areas closed by restrictive covenants. New housing and long-range opportunities for residential expansion and race enterprise necessitated that they join the housing boom in suburban areas. In retrospect, perhaps the most significant turning point in the development of the Los Angeles ghetto was the several efforts Blacks made during the 1920's to join the urbanization of outlying areas and their complete rebuff in all these endeavors.

The most publicized attempts at suburban expansion were several recreational centers, mostly in beach areas, which generally had the dual aim of providing a "more cultured and sophisticated recreation" and of being nuclei for Black residential colonies. In 1925 an attorney established the Pacific Beach Club at Huntington Beach, Orange County, after a long battle with the local chamber of commerce over access routes. When the buildings were almost finished, they "caught fire and were totally destroyed." A nationwide appeal by the club for renewal funding only spurred greater local white opposition, and by the end of the year a white club took over the property. In 1922 rumors of a Black bathhouse and amusement center at Santa Monica led the city commission to pass ordinances prohibiting their construction and closing a Black dance hall. Property owners along the beach were urged to adopt covenants to prevent Negro purchase or occupancy. A white country club in Corona, between Riverside and Los Angeles, was taken over by Blacks in 1928 as an interracial recreation area, but it failed for lack of patronage. Equally hostile attitudes in other suburban areas were illustrated by Lomita, south of Watts, where signs were posted telling Negroes to stay out, Glendale's advertising the absence of Blacks from its schools, and the long battle that Booker T. Washington, Jr., had in retaining a home he had bought in the San Gabriel Valley. The epitome of suburban exclusion came in Manhattan Beach, where a combination of Ku Klux Klan pressure and white and Black real-estate ventures to open tracts to Negroes led the city to condemn property owned by Blacks since 1911 and close the beach to their swimming as well as occupancy. An NAACP suit reopened the beach to bathers, but by the end of the twenties virtually all Black residents had been terrorized out of the city.

Residential segregation and exclusion efforts owed their success in part to support by the courts. The most celebrated case came in 1925 when white property owners brought suit against the Long family for purchase of a converted house in the south Central Avenue area. The suit was an ominous one, for while the entire tract was covered by covenants, Negroes had lived there for as long as seventeen years. NAACP attorneys contended that this change in racial conditions invalidated the covenants, since to rule otherwise would pave the way for wholesale forfeiture. But the lower court ruled against Long, and when NAACP attorneys failed to file an appeal, suits were filed against all other Blacks in the area.

The effectiveness of restrictive covenants was further enhanced in 1928 when the California Supreme Court upheld neighborhood restrictive agreements even when Negroes had occupied the area and ruled that the Black families must vacate restricted properties in West Los Angeles. By 1930 the effect of such court decisions, restrictive covenants, and exclusion from outlying areas was to contain nearly all Negroes in Los Angeles in several isolated communities whose populations were becoming predominantly Negro. Out of fourteen assembly districts, one (the Sixty-second), running along Central Avenue, had 70 percent of the city's Negroes. In five districts, Negroes were virtually absent. So rigid had segregation become that the ghetto grew little during the 1930's, even though more Blacks came to Los Angeles than in any previous decade. The effects of such congestion on the quality of neighborhoods was accentuated by the lack of new home building—nearly all houses in the ghetto had been built before World War I—and the rezoning of the northern section of Central Avenue for manufacturing in 1922. Over a hundred industries were located there by 1939, and many owners lost interest in maintaining residential structures. By 1929 many of the older areas along Central Avenue had the structural characteristics of a slum— few sanitary conveniences, leaky pipes and roofs, patched windows and doors, and a general lack of house repair and good maintenance.

Widespread residential exclusion, employment discrimination, social segregation, and growing congestion and structural deterioration of housing were reflections of a pervasive racial animosity toward Blacks. They tempt the historian to classify parts of Los Angeles by 1930 as a slum-ghetto in league with most northern cities. This evaluation gains support from some contemporary observers. The comments about the Black community by its residents and visitors were less optimistic and had fewer references to the beauty of the area than the observations of earlier decades. Instead, residents spoke of the decline of neighborhoods, the rise of prostitution and crime, and the advertising of Central Avenue's night clubs as "ones which would make Monte Carlo or Sodom look like a Sunday School picnic." But the causes of this deterioration were attributed not to white hostility but to the influx of a "lower class" of southern migrants whose attitudes of superstition and irresponsibility contrasted with the older residents' ethic of work and self-improvement. A growing proportion of Blacks in both the state and the city of Los Angeles were of southern origin, and the majority of these came from the West South Central states. Texas was the birthplace of one-fourth of the city's Blacks by 1930. But any inference of "low caliber" which may be drawn from the shifting origin of migrants is rebutted by evidence that "color" alone heightened racial restrictions during the 1920's.

The condition of European immigrants is one case in point. They were singled out as late as 1919 for living in slums and being in danger of developing "ghettos" if their housing was not improved. During the 1920's they vanished as a subject of concern. The "foreign districts" of the state cited as slum areas in 1923 were "southtown," "Mexican village," and "Chinatown," racial rather than immigrant ghettos. In 1930 foreign-born whites had the highest percentage of home ownership in Los Angeles of any segment of the population. They had long enjoyed greater access to skilled industrial and white collar jobs than Blacks, and native hostility to their residence gradually diminished, especially where Blacks or Japanese also entered the neighborhood. Their record of emergence from ghettos in an atmosphere of diminishing discrimination is an interesting contrast to the Black experience. The "old resident" theory was similarly rebutted by events in the West Jefferson area where generally well-educated and well-to-do Blacks, whom the white residents recognized as "a good class of colored people," met widespread fears of property depreciation and organized efforts to prohibit whites from allowing them entrance to the area. An ominous sign of growing animosity toward Negroes was the remark of some residents that they preferred Japanese to Black neighbors.

While dismissing the old resident theory of the cause of deterioration, the historian must also modify the analogy between Los Angeles and eastern ghettos of the 1920's. The Los Angeles ghetto still retained many opportunities for Black migrants, chief of which was the promise of owning a home. In 1930 over one-third of the Black families owned their homes, in contrast to 10.5 percent in Chicago, 15 percent in Detroit, and 5.6 percent in New York. Only six cities of a hundred thousand or more exceeded Los Angeles in Black home ownership, and none of these had as large a Black population. There was also an exceptional degree of equality between whites and Blacks in their degree of home ownership. In 1930, Los Angeles had ten Blacks per Black-owned home as opposed to eight whites per white-owned home. Most other cities had ratios in excess of 2 to 1. In New York the ratio was 77 to 15; Chicago, 44 to 12; and Detroit, 31 to 10. Blacks were relegated to old and often deteriorating structures, but they did not have the extensive dependence on white landlords nor the excessive rents which plagued many other ghettos, or Mexicans in Los Angeles. Home ownership also provided a base for continuing pride in the Black community. Several important businesses and prominent buildings were established, culminated by the Hotel Somerville which was built in 1928 to host the NAACP convention. Throughout the decade, the Central Avenue district had a Black assemblyman, Frederick Roberts.

By 1930 the dynamics of the ghetto formation—in all senses of the word—were well established, and symptoms of deterioration and an emerging slum ghetto were evident. But it would take another decade of residential segregation, a major depression, and then a massive in-migration of Blacks to culminate the development of the Los Angeles ghetto.

7

CITY AND SUBURB
SINCE 1940

World War II set in motion a new wave of migration out of the South that was even greater in numbers and geographical dispersion than the Great Migration. Over a million and a half Blacks headed for urban centers in the 1940's, attracted initially by booming defense industries. For the first time West Coast cities were the recipients of large numbers of migrants. Los Angeles' Black population doubled in three years; other spectacular gains were registered in San Diego, San Francisco, Oakland, Portland, and Seattle, permanently transforming them from distinctly "western" cities into urban areas similar in racial and ethnic mix to most eastern and midwestern centers. Prosperity continued after the end of the war, and the flood of out-migrants from the South hardly abated, even during recession years, in subsequent decades. All told, four million Blacks moved from farm to city between 1940 and 1970, some to southern cities, but most to centers in other parts of the country. The results were striking. The overwhelming majority located in central cities, very few in suburbs. By the latter date, three-quarters of the nation's Black population lived in urban areas, making Blacks considerably more urbanized than whites. By the middle of the 1970's several cities had Black majorities—Gary, Atlanta, Washington, D.C., Newark, New Orleans, and Baltimore. And by 1978 Blacks were serving as mayors or had recently held that office in all these cities but Baltimore. In addition, Blacks had been elected or appointed mayor in three majority-white cities—Los Angeles, Cincinnati, and Cleveland. Not all Black migration was from South to North. By the 1970's a considerable "reverse migration" was underway in which northern Blacks, particularly middle-class, well-educated, younger individuals, were seeking careers and political opportunities in the booming cities of the "Sunbelt" of the South and Southwest. Atlanta not only had a Black mayor; to many it was becoming the capital of the modern, affluent Black middle class.

The central core of mid-century American cities remained, as it had been for previous generations, the point of entry for migrants. Unfortunately, it too often became the permanent location for Blacks. To many, the center-city ghetto became a trap, with no avenues out or upward. An insignificant number trickled into all-Black towns on the periphery of the cities, but this was not a viable alternative for most. And although there was also a modest movement to suburbia, particularly in the 1970's, this trend did not spell relief for the masses of urban dwellers. Although suburban housing was often no more expensive than inner-city dwellings, suburbs radiated little welcome for even middle-class Blacks, much less the masses of the urban poor. Where Blacks did enter suburbia, they often found themselves isolated in mini-ghettoes where little genuine integration could be noted.

"The ghetto" became, by the mid-1960's, a term familiar to all Americans, signifying a national base to Black militants, a "jungle" to frightened, uninformed, or racist whites, and to social scientists a separate city characterized by decaying structures, slum conditions, massive unemployment, and numerous other evidences of social pathology. White society, although it failed to acknowledge responsibility, had created the ghetto, maintained the ghetto as an urban colony, and condoned its continued existence. As whites moved in increasing numbers to the suburbs after World War II, they drew business and commerce and a healthy tax base with them, leaving behind an unbalanced employment structure, decaying properties, and expensive transit, health, and educational systems, which the city increasingly could not afford. Yet whites were not totally absent; many of them still staffed the police and fire departments and schools and came to be perceived by Blacks as an alien army of occupation. The court system, banking and credit institutions, employment and welfare services, still remained largely controlled by whites. And suburbanites who still worked from nine to five in the cities utilized municipal services for which they did not adequately pay. In short, distinctions between city and suburb had taken on an obvious racial dimension, as the National Advisory Commission on Civil Disorders (Kerner Commission) pessimistically noted in 1968.

To many Black Americans, the ghetto reflected the shattered promise of the American dream, the unattainable material goals and opportunities so alluringly displayed by the mass media. Rural dwellers were less exposed to the comforts, conveniences, and luxuries of modern America, although this does not lessen the amount of their comparative deprivation, but city living made it impossible to ignore the materialistic achievements of society. Yet whetted appetites could not be satisfied by inferior jobs, overpriced housing, and inadequate schooling and health care. Rising expectations, in other words, ran head on into the economic realities of an internal colony. Some Blacks, especially after 1960, were beginning to ascend the escalator of upward mobility through possession of college educations and subsequent white-collar and skilled jobs. But the majority couldn't even find the escalator. Despite the progress of the fortunate, Black incomes only approached 70 percent of the figure for whites, and this percentage began to slip in the mid-1970's. Factoring out the near-parity incomes of college-educated, upwardly mobile Blacks, and the income ratio for the masses was closer to 60 percent.

To many observers of both races these economic and mobility realities formed the important roots of the urban explosions in the mid-1960's. Some Blacks and most whites termed them riots, but younger and more militant Blacks proudly identified them as insurrections or rebellions. Between 1964 and 1968 the ghettoes of approximately seventy-five cities were convulsed by flame, looting, and death. No part of the country escaped. The peak occurred within a three-week period in 1967 when Detroit and Newark exploded. Certain factors were common to all these events. At least 10 percent of ghetto residents participated to some degree, which put the number of "rioters" in the hundreds of thousands nation-wide. The largest numbers joined in looting; those who felt personally the disparities between middle-class affluence and their own impoverished lives rationalized this opportunity to seize a slice of the American pie, even if it carried only a ninety-day warranty. To the surprise of many, the center cities did not erupt in such fury after 1968, although there was little comfort for whites in the rise of the paramilitary Black Panthers and avowedly murderous guerrilla-warfare groups like De Mau Mau in Chicago, the Black Liberation Army in New York City, and the Symbionese Liberation Army in California cities.

More constructive aspects of recent Black urbanization should also be noted. Cities, especially in the South, proved to be the launching pad for significant civil rights activities. By the early 1950's the southern Black population was poised for a new era of overt militancy. Not only the countryside, but cities as well were often ruled by police authorities responsible only to themselves and their militantly racist cohorts, men like police commissioner Eugene "Bull" Connor of Birmingham. Yet urban Blacks summoned both raw courage and the will to liberation necessary to challenge the status quo. Not every campaign was a success, but even failures advanced the civil rights momentum, and the names of Montgomery, Little Rock, Birmingham, Greensboro, and Memphis were etched in the consciousness of both white and Black Americans as a result. The cities also provided the context for Black capitalism, a panacea that some hoped would lead to liberation. Urban-development schemes based on seed money or "reparations" from white-dominated foundations, banks, churches, and government were seen by the optimistic as heralding increased employment, upgrading of skills, rejuvenation of center cities, and ultimately "community control." For a time, riots seemed beneficial in getting money and programs flowing, but all too often the financing was "soft" and disappeared once the "heat" was off or guilty consciences were assuaged. More often than not, the ghettoes remained burned and bulldozed.

The promise of politics as an avenue for ghetto liberation similarly proved only a limited success. Certainly the rising number of Blacks holding public office, particularly as mayors, was no small achievement. Several political victories led to city governments more responsive to the needs of impoverished residents. But without influence over the purse strings of the larger society, local political control had its limits. Blacks could dominate the political machinery of Detroit and Newark, but what did possession of bankrupt cities achieve in economic terms? Without far greater clout in Washington in terms of influence over job programs, the welfare system, and what remained of the war on poverty, gains would be limited. Increasingly by the late 1970's, the fate of older cities like New York was in the hands of a federal government only reluctantly interested in its social health.

Given these factors, which control the destiny of American cities today, it is little wonder that historians have recoiled from the uncertainties of the ever-changing present and left analysis of contemporary urban affairs to others. For informed commentary on the city since 1940, and more particularly for research and analysis of the dynamics of the nation's Black ghettoes, we must rely on the work of demographers, sociologists, anthropologists, economists, and students of mass behavior. Their conclusions are only as long-standing as the current census report or psychological study of riot participants. But they provide a starting point for an understanding of contemporary America. Far back in 1903, the young Black sociologist W. E. B. DuBois predicted that "the problem of the Twentieth Century is the problem of the color line." Today, seventy-five years later, the only amendment to that prescient statement would note that it is in the cities of America that the problem is most acute.

THE CHANGING DISTRIBUTION OF NEGROES WITHIN METROPOLITAN AREAS
The Emergence of Black Suburbs
REYNOLDS FARLEY

After World War II, many studies claimed that new life-styles were developing within suburbia. These life-styles demanded that suburbanites be very friendly to their neighbors, spend much time on child-rearing activities, and participate in many community endeavors. Some sociologists argued that the major reason for the development of these new social patterns was that suburbs contained a young, middle-class, native American population which shared common values, unlike central cities which contained a heterogeneous population.

Long ago some authors had shown there was a variety of types of communities in the suburban territory surrounding central cities, but further research was required to challenge the myth of suburban homogeneity. Schnore pointed out the differences in ethnic composition and socioeconomic status which could be found within the nation's suburbs. Further study found that suburban living did not completely change working-class life-styles and that middle- and working-class residents could be found within the same suburbs. The similarity of cities and suburbs was demonstrated by another investigation which showed that patterns of residential segregation common to central cities were also found in suburbs.

Recently much publicity has been given the idea that central cities are coming to contain a principally Black population while the surrounding

Reprinted with permission from the *American Journal of Sociology*, 75 (January 1970), pp. 512–529. Footnotes and tables appearing in the original publication have been deleted in the present volume, and should be consulted for full documentation of the author's conclusions.

suburbs are residential areas for whites. President Johnson's Commission on Civil Disorders stated succinctly in warning that if present trends continue there will be "a white society principally located in suburbs, in smaller central cities and in the peripheral parts of large cities and a Negro society largely concentrated within large cities."

This paper examines the hypothesis that cities and suburbs are coming to have racially dissimilar populations. First, historical trends in racial composition are reviewed. Second, data are examined to study the rapidity of Black population growth in suburbia in recent years. Third, the socioeconomic characteristics of Blacks in suburbia and those moving into suburbia are analyzed. Finally, the types of suburbs which have experienced Negro population growth are described.

HISTORICAL TRENDS

Changes since 1900 in the racial composition of central cities and the suburban area that surrounds them can be determined from census data.

Central cities outside the South contained relatively few Blacks prior to World War I; thereafter a cessation of European immigration combined with an influx of Blacks gradually changed the racial composition of these cities. As recently as 1940, however, the proportion Black was no greater than 6 percent. During and after World War II, the in-migration of Negroes continued, and, in many cities, the white population decreased. As a consequence, the proportion Black in these cities went up and by the late 1960's reached 18 percent.

Very different trends characterize southern central cities. Prior to the Civil War the number of Blacks in many southern cities actually decreased, but after emancipation freedmen left their plantations, and between 1860 and 1870 the proportion Black in southern cities rose. However, there was little change in the racial composition of these cities after 1870. While their Black populations grew, the cities annexed outlying territory, and their white populations have grown at about the same rate, effecting no substantial change in their color composition. Since 1950 there has been a slight rise in the proportion Black in the southern cities. If these cities, in the future, find it difficult to annex outlying areas which have rapidly growing white population, their color composition will change.

There have always been some Blacks in the suburban rings which surround northern and western cities. The proportion Black in these areas remained approximately 3 percent for many decades. As white suburban communities were growing, Negro suburban communities were expanding at a correspondingly rapid rate. Some of these Black suburbs date from the early years of this century and have histories similar to those of white suburbs. For instance, just before 1900, a tract west of St. Louis, Missouri, was subdivided, and lots were sold to Negroes. This suburb, called Kinloch, grew slowly for some decades but was incorporated in 1939, and by 1960 it had a population of 6,500, all but two of whom were Black. In the Chicago area, a Negro realtor secured land west of the city prior to World War I and sold homesites to Blacks. This suburb, Robbins, was incorporated in 1917 and has continued to grow, reaching a population of 7,500 in 1960. Near Cincinnati, Ohio, the Black suburb of Lincoln Heights developed during the 1920's, and by 1960 had 7,800 residents.

Suburban rings surrounding southern cities have undergone great change in racial composition. Early in this century, when these suburban rings contained extensive rural areas, at least one-third of the population was Black. Gradually but consistently this proportion decreased, for, as southern cities grew, suburbs developed, and whites moved into out-lying areas. In some suburban rings whites displaced Blacks; in other suburban rings the Black population continued to grow but at a slower rate than the white population. Nevertheless, Black suburbs have sprung up near some major cities. For example, after World War II a suburban development for Negroes was built near Miami, Florida, and by 1960 this suburb, Richmond Heights, contained some of the nicer homes available to Miami Blacks. In the 1950's, after an expressway cut through the Black ghetto of Shreveport, Louisiana, many inexpensive homes were put up in an area to the north of the city. In 1960 North Shreveport had a Black population of 8,000.

RECENT TRENDS

It has been almost a decade since the last national census was conducted, so it is difficult to know exactly what population changes have occurred since 1960. However, the Census Bureau's monthly *Current Population Survey,* which now involves a national sample of 50,000 housing units, provides increasingly detailed information about Blacks.

Since 1960 there has been continued growth of the Black population in the nation's central cities both within and outside the South, although growth rates for the 1960's are lower than those of the 1950's. The white population of central cities, with the exception of western cities, has decreased, and this too continues a trend which developed in the World War II era.

The Black population in suburban rings has grown quite rapidly. In the suburban rings of the North and West, the Black population has increased since 1960, not only more rapidly than it did during the 1950's but more rapidly than the white population. This had produced a slight change in the racial composition of these suburban rings. Within southern suburban rings, the white population increased at a higher rate than the Black, but the Negro population has grown more rapidly during this decade than during the last.

Despite the suburbanization of Blacks, central cities are becoming more racially differentiated from their suburban rings. The proportion of population which is Black is rising more rapidly in central cities than in suburban rings. This finding lends credence to the view of the Commission on Civil Disorders, but two facts should not be overlooked.

First, at present Blacks are a minority in most central cities. In 1965 only one of the nation's thirty largest cities, Washington, D.C., had a Black majority; and in only four others (Atlanta, Georgia; Memphis, Tennessee; New Orleans, Louisiana; and Newark, New Jersey) did Blacks comprise as much as 40 percent of the population. In the future some large cities in both the North and the South will have Black majorities, but these cities will be the exceptions rather than the rule. If the growth rates from central cities which were obtained between 1960 and 1966 continue to 1980, the proportion of population in central cities which is nonwhite will rise from 22 percent in 1966 to 32 percent in 1980. Since 1960 the rate of natural increase among Blacks has decreased for fertility rates have fallen, and by 1967 only a little more than one million Blacks remained on the nation's farms. The Black population is simply not growing rapidly enough, nor are there sufficient numbers of rural Negroes to radically change the racial composition of most central cities even if the whites continue to move away.

Second, suburban rings do contain Negroes, and some suburban Black communities, both in the North and the South, have grown in the recent past. A Census Bureau study indicates that within suburban rings the Black population increased much more rapidly between 1966 and 1968 than between 1960 and 1966, although sampling variability may affect this finding.

Aggregate figures obtained from national samples of the population give no indication of which specific suburban communities have growing Black populations. In both Illinois and New York, however, a number of communities have requested the Census Bureau to conduct special enumerations since 1960 because certain state appropriations are based upon the population of local areas as officially enumerated. This provides an incentive for growing suburbs to request special censuses, and in both the Chicago and New York metropolitan areas many of these have been conducted. This permits us to investigate racial change in the suburbs near the nation's two largest cities, New York and Chicago.

NEGROES IN THE CHICAGO SUBURBAN AREA

A total of seventy-six places within Cook County but outside the city of Chicago, that is, suburban cities, towns, and villages, were covered by special census enumerations between 1964 and 1968. These places, in 1960, contained about five-eighths of the suburban population of Cook County.

Chicago's suburban population increased rapidly after 1960. Among the places covered by the special censuses, the total population went up from about one million in 1960 to one and one-third million at the special census dates. The nonwhite population increased at a higher rate than the white, affecting a small change in the proportion nonwhite in these suburbs, a rise from 2.2 percent in 1960 to 2.6 percent when the special enumerations were carried out.

A closer examination of these data reveals that little integration has occurred. Rather than being distributed throughout the suburbs, the growth of Black population has concentrated in three areas; one in Maywood, one in and around Harvey, and a third area of Chicago Heights and East Chicago Heights.

Between 1960 and 1965 the Black population of Maywood doubled, increasing from five thousand to ten thousand. This is an older suburb which was settled after the Civil War and grew rapidly when rail lines linked it to Chicago. Maywood did not participate in the post-World War II boom; in fact, its peak growth followed World War I. It is a suburb of older, relatively less expensive homes. Maywood has experienced population replacement since 1950, for as its white population declined, its Negro population grew, while its total population has remained about constant.

The Black population of Harvey, another old suburb, and the nearby but newer suburb of Markham increased. Harvey was founded in the 1890's but has continued to grow, and in recent years manufacturing firms have located in this area. In 1960 the majority of Blacks in Harvey lived in older homes, but one-third lived in houses which had been erected after World War II. Since 1960 there has been a modest building boom in this suburb, and new construction as well as the conversion of older homes from white to Negro occupancy account for the growth of Black population. Markham is a post-World War II suburb. In recent years many new single-family homes have been built, and both the white and Negro populations have increased.

The third suburban area which had a growing Black population included a section of Chicago Heights and the village of East Chicago Heights. Steel and chemical plants have been in this area since the 1890's. During World War I, Blacks began moving into Chicago Heights, and their members rose during World War II. A pattern of intracommunity segregation emerged; and an area separated from the rest of the suburb by a major rail line contained the Black population. Bordering Chicago Heights is an area of older, low-quality homes. In 1960, 60 percent of them lacked indoor toilets and half were in deteriorating or dilapidated condition. This is the suburb of East Chicago Heights. During 1964, a public housing project was started, and this along with other new construction explains the rise of Black population.

NEGROES IN THE NEW YORK SUBURBAN AREA

New York City's suburban ring, in 1960, included four counties. Those closer to the city are Nassau, which lies immediately east of New York on Long Island, and Westchester, which is located just north of the city. The outer counties are Suffolk, on Long Island, and Rockland, which is northwest of the city and across the Hudson River. Between 1965 and 1968 the population of this entire area was enumerated by special census except for some small enclaves. These special census data make it possible to determine the number and age of recent migrants to the suburban ring.

The Negro population of the suburban ring has grown since 1960; by the mid-1960's, there were at least 175,000 Blacks in these suburbs. In each suburban area, except the outer towns of Suffolk County, the Negro population increased more rapidly than the white, producing a small rise in the proportion Black within the New York suburban ring.

Negro population growth has occurred not only because of natural increase but also because Blacks are migrating into these suburbs. Examination of the migration rates reveals that the highest rates were for the age groups 20-34 and 0-4 in 1960. This indicates that Black families headed by young adults along with their young children are moving into the suburban ring.

There are racial differences in growth rates and migration patterns. Population growth has been very slow in the suburban counties closer to New York. These counties attracted whites who were in the early stages of family formation but lost about an equal number of teenagers and older whites, so their net migration rates for whites were near zero.

The outer counties, Suffolk and Rockland, have grown rapidly and attracted whites of all ages. Black population growth has occurred in all counties, but the largest increases in numbers occurred within the suburban areas nearer New York City.

Long Island will be considered first in investigating which suburbs have growing Black populations. Although there are few incorporated cities on Long Island, census tracts—that is, geographical areas containing about 5,000 people—were defined for the entire area in 1960, and special census tabulations have been presented for these same areas. Twenty-two census tracts on Long Island had increases of 250 or more Blacks between 1960 and the special census date. They can be divided into two groups.

One group, located principally within the county near New York, gained Negroes and lost whites while the total population remained about constant. The homes in these census tracts were older than was typical for Long Island. Population replacement occurred in these suburbs. The second group of tracts, most of them within Suffolk County, gained large numbers of both Negroes and whites. Many new homes must have been built to accommodate these population increases, although it is impossible to determine from special census data the number of new homes or the race of their occupants. The census of 1970 will reveal more about these suburban areas which gained both whites and Negroes and will indicate whether Blacks have occupied new homes or have replaced whites in older homes.

Most of the recent growth of Black population within Westchester County has taken place within four suburbs. Mount Vernon, New Rochelle, White Plains, and Yonkers are large and older suburbs. World War I interrupted their period of most rapid growth. While the number of Blacks in each of these suburbs increased, their patterns of demographic change were quite different. These same patterns of change undoubtedly are occurring in central cities and suburbs throughout the nation.

Mount Vernon exemplifies a common pattern of change. This suburb lost whites and gained Negroes while its total population slowly declined. By 1965, one quarter of the population was Black. The tracks of the New York, New Haven and Hartford Railroad bisect Mount Vernon. In 1960 the area south of the railroad was racially mixed, but since then whites have moved away and Negroes moved in. If the patterns of racial change observed in large cities in the 1940's and 1950's are duplicated in Mount Vernon, whites will continue to leave and the southern half will soon be a Black ghetto of thirty thousand. North of the rail line there has been little population change. The area was 98 percent white in 1960 and 97 percent white in 1965.

Yonkers illustrates a second pattern of change. This suburb attracted relatively many Blacks, but among whites in-migration has been matched by out-migration. An area of older homes near the center of Yonkers has lost white and gained Black population. In the northern extremities of this suburb, new construction has taken place, and the increase in white population in one area offsets a loss in another area. If no vacant land for new construction remains, the color composition of this suburb will change as more Blacks move into older residential areas.

Other types of change, reflecting urban-renewal activities, occurred within New Rochelle and White Plains. New Rochelle's population and racial composition remained stable after 1960. An urban-renewal project was begun in New Rochelle which led to an out-migration of both Blacks and whites sufficient in size to offset the effects of natural increase.

Since 1960, the white population of White Plains decreased while its Black population grew slowly. This suburb has many of the same characteristics as Mount Vernon and Yonkers, and one might expect its Black population to increase rapidly. However, an urban-renewal project was started which will raze the homes of four hundred whites and four hundred Negro families. This involves only about 3 percent of the white but 21 percent of the Negro population. If the displaced Black families relocate outside this suburb, the process of racial succession will be slowed.

Rockland County had a sparse population in 1960, so census tracts in this county included very extensive land areas. The Black population in a number of tracts went up, but more detailed information is needed to ascertain which particular areas have attracted Black residents.

THE CHARACTERISTICS OF SUBURBAN IN-MIGRANTS

Data from the special census conducted in the New York and Chicago suburban rings indicate there is a growing Black suburban population and suggest that young Black families are moving into suburbia. However, the socioeconomic selectivity of these suburban in-migrants or the status of Blacks in suburbia, compared to that of Blacks in central cities, is not revealed by these special censuses.

Whites who live in suburbs, particularly suburbs near the large central cities, are typically better educated, hold more prestigious jobs, and have larger incomes than central-city whites. One of the reasons for this is the selectivity of migrants who move into suburbs. The Taeubers investigated metropolitan migration patterns for whites for the period

1955–1960 and discovered that suburban rings attracted large streams of high-status migrants from their central cities. In addition, there was a sizable stream of intermetropolitan migrants, many of whom moved directly into suburbs when they came into a new area.

The most recent data showing the socioeconomic characteristics of suburban Blacks pertain to 1960, and the latest period for which figures are available about the characteristics of migrants is 1955–1960. To describe the Negro suburban population, the ten metropolitan areas whose suburban rings had the largest Black populations in 1960 were selected.

Central-city Blacks rather than suburban Blacks had the higher socioeconomic status. Both in the South and in the North, men in the cities held proportionally more of the prestigious jobs than did men in suburbia. Only in Newark was there a reversal of this pattern. A comparison of differences in educational attainment revealed a similar finding. In each of these areas, save Newark, the proportion of Blacks who were high school graduates was higher in the central city than in the suburban ring.

The causes of this unusual pattern of city-suburban differentiation are difficult to specify. In the South, suburban rings still contain some Blacks who are farmers, and this tends to lower average socioeconomic status in southern suburban rings. Within the North it was thought that city-suburban differences in age composition might account for this finding. However, after age differences were taken into account by a standardization procedure, suburban Blacks still did not match central-city Blacks in social status.

Metropolitan migration patterns among Blacks are similar to those of whites, even though there are important differences in the volume of migration. In eight of the ten metropolitan areas whose suburban rings had the largest Black populations in 1960, the largest stream of Blacks moving into suburban rings were people leaving the central city. In each area except Birmingham, these city-to-suburb movers were higher in socioeconomic status than either the Blacks who remained in the central city or the other Blacks who lived in the suburban ring.

The suburbs attracted two other, but typically smaller, streams of migrants. Among Negroes, as among whites, there was a stream of higher-status intermetropolitan migrants who moved directly into the suburban ring between 1955 and 1960. There was also a stream of young migrants from nonmetropolitan areas who were low in socioeconomic status. Many of these migrants may have left southern rural areas or small towns for the economic opportunities of a large metropolitan area.

These central cities attracted two streams of migrants which were of approximately equal size. One stream came from other metropolitan areas and was high in socioeconomic status. The second stream came from nonmetropolitan areas, and few of the men held white-collar or craftsmen jobs. In addition, the central cities attracted migrants from suburbia, and these ring-to-city movers were generally high in socioeconomic status. This is similar to the Taeubers' finding that, between 1955 and 1960, cities and their suburbs exchanged relatively high-status white population. Unlike the situation for whites, however, among Negroes the number of city-to-ring movers did not always greatly exceed the number of ring-to-city movers. In some areas, New York or Miami, for instance, the number moving from the city to the ring exceeded the number moving in the other direction, but in other areas, such as Detroit, Michigan, ring-to-city movers were more numerous.

The data presented in this paper clearly indicate that between 1955 and 1960 suburban rings attracted higher-status Black residents from their central cities and also attracted a sizable share of the higher-status inter-metropolitan migrants. The growth of the Negro suburban population has increased since 1960, and the migrants to suburbia during this decade are probably of higher status as were the migrants during the last decade. This migration may already be of sufficient size to establish a pattern of city-suburban socioeconomic differences among Blacks, similar to that observed among whites. For instance, in 1959 median family income among Blacks in the suburban rings was far below that of Blacks in central cities, but by 1967 it was higher in the suburban rings. Among young adult Blacks, educational attainment levels in 1960 were lower in the suburban rings than in the cities, but by 1968 this was reversed, probably reflecting the migration to the suburbs of well-educated young Negroes. It is likely that the census of 1970 will find that suburban Blacks are higher in socioeconomic status than those in central cities.

THE PROCESS OF SUBURBANIZATION

The demographic data indicate that suburban rings are attracting Black migrants and that, while all economic levels are represented, the migrants to suburbia tend to be higher in socioeconomic status. It appears that three types of suburban areas have gained Black population. First, particularly in the North, there are older, densely settled suburbs often containing or near employment centers. Such places as Maywood, Yonkers, and East Cleveland, Ohio, have experienced population replacement—that is, decreases in white population but growth of Black—and in the future more suburbs will undergo similar change. Studies of residential change have found that the first Negroes to move into a white neighborhood are those who are financially able to purchase better housing than that which is generally available to Blacks. Such older suburbs contain housing units which are better than those Blacks can occupy in the ghettoes. On the other hand, because of the age of the homes and the small lots on which they were built, homes in these suburbs may not appeal to whites who move out from the central city. The causes of racial change in any particular older suburb may be idiosyncratic, but proximity to employment is probably an important factor.

The second type of area with growing Black population is the new suburban development. Some are built exclusively for Negroes. Richmond Heights, Florida, which was described previously, is one example; in recent years Hollydale has been built near Cincinnati, and new homes have gone up in Inkster, a Detroit suburb with a large Black population. In addition, it is possible that a small number of Blacks are moving into new and integrated suburban developments.

A third type of area with a growing Negro population is to be found in the suburban rings of many large cities. Areas lacking adequate sewer and water facilities, containing dilapidated homes of low value, and having exclusively Black populations could be located in 1960 in suburban areas. They have grown partly because of natural increase, partly because some public housing has been erected, and partly because low-income Blacks may find inexpensive housing close to their jobs in these suburbs.

Expansion of the Black suburban population will depend upon many factors; three of the most important are discussed here. First is the rate at which the economic status of Blacks improves. In recent years the income of Negroes has gone up much faster than have prices. For instance, median family income of Blacks increased about 6 percent each year from 1960 to 1967 while the cost of living went up by less than 2 percent annually. Negroes now have more money to spend for shelter and consumer goods. The migration of Blacks to suburbia reflects such economic gains, and if incomes continue to go up more rapidly than the cost of living, more Blacks will be able to afford better housing.

The second factor is the rate at which new housing is constructed and the housing policies which will be favored by the federal government. At present, a little over 1.5 million housing units are built annually. The President's Committee on Urban Housing estimated that 2.7 million new housing units were needed each year to provide for the growing population and to replace substandard housing. The Kerner Commission Report recommended numerous programs to encourage building new homes for low- and moderate-income families outside central-city ghettoes. If there is a great volume of new construction, and if clusters of low and moderately priced homes are spread throughout suburbia and are open to Negro occupancy, there may be a rise in the Black suburban population.

The third factor is the rapidity with which suburban housing becomes available to Blacks. Since 1960 the incomes of Negroes have increased more rapidly than those of whites. If this continues, more Negroes will be able to compete with whites for suburban housing. Perhaps when the federal open-occupancy law becomes fully effective, discrimination will be reduced, and more suburbs will include Blacks in their population. This is an optimistic view. Racial policies in the new suburb of Levittown, New Jersey, were described by Gans. Despite a state open-occupancy law, the developers announced plans to sell only to whites and turned away Black customers. Negroes were eventually accepted after a suit proceeded through the courts for two years. Even after this, special policies were instituted to screen Negro buyers and place them in isolated areas. If this is duplicated in other suburbs, Blacks who desire to move into the suburbs will still face immense difficulties regardless of their financial means.

THE CONSEQUENCES OF SUBURBANIZATION

The suburbanization of Blacks does not herald a basic change in the patterns of racial segregation within metropolitan areas. Cities and their suburban rings are becoming more dissimilar in racial composition, and the out-migrations of some Blacks from the city will not alter this process. It will do no more than slow the growth of the Black population of some cities while adding still greater diversity to the already heterogeneous population of suburbia.

It does indicate that Negroes, similar to European ethnic groups, are becoming more decentralized throughout the metropolitan area after they have been in the city for some time and improved their economic status. However, improvements in economic status brought about not only the residential decentralization of European immigrant groups but also reductions in their residential segregation. Negroes have deviated widely from this pattern for, despite economic gains and some decentralization of predominantly Black residential areas, the residential segregation of Negroes has persisted. Even during the prosperous period from the end of World War II to the present, there is no evidence that the residential segregation of Blacks decreased. It is possible that the suburbanization of Blacks will alter this pattern, and a future census may reveal integrated suburban neighborhoods. In the meantime, we can be certain that the residential segregation patterns of central cities are reappearing within the suburbs.

8

BLACKS
AND THE AMERICAN CITY
Conceptual Perspectives

This book began with several generalizations suggesting that the Black experience in American cities fits into common patterns in urban history. Blacks migrated to cities for the same reasons as did other immigrant groups, and like them quickly became part of the urban lower class. City life had similar impacts on family life, health, and the development of social institutions. But in addition to these similarities, there are important ways in which the Afro-American urban experience has been, and continues to be, unique, and our perspectives would be unbalanced if we did not recognize these areas of distinctiveness.

One of the most dramatic differences, which provides one of the chief rationales for the study of Black urban history, is the fact that Blacks have been present in American cities longer than any other identifiable ethnic group. It was only a very short while after English settlers began to group themselves into towns in the seventeenth century that Blacks were introduced into urban environments. The colonial urban experience cannot be understood without reference to the Black population, not only in the South, where pre-Revolutionary Charleston and Williamsburg were half Black, but even in cities of the northern colonies where the population ratio was far smaller. As persons of English background gradually ceased to be a visible immigrant group, Blacks remained. They are today the oldest ethnic group in the cities, sharing the urban core with the newest groups—Chicanos and Puerto Ricans. And if current trends continue, as Spanish-speaking groups gain upward mobility, the latter will leave the center cities while a significant Black population will remain. In addition, Blacks are more highly urbanized today than the non-Black population, and this phenomenon has been accomplished in a dramatically short time. At the turn of the present century less than one-quarter was urbanized; as late as 1950, less than half. But today, well over three-quarters of Afro-Americans reside in urban areas, with increasing numbers in southern and western cities. And the concentration in particular cities has been unique; no other ethnic group since the Civil War has comprised more than 50 percent of a major city's population, as Blacks presently do in a number of the nation's largest cities.

Another pattern distinctive to Blacks is the increasing urban ghettoization over time. Other groups inhabited ethnic enclaves, but their residence was commonly limited to two or three generations. Where the ghetto experience often provided the springboard for Irish, Germans, Poles, and Italians to attain upward mobility, it has not served that purpose for Blacks. The increase in residential segregation which accompanied Black ghetto development was, again, dramatic in the twentieth century. Although there were Black enclaves in many cities in the nineteenth century, in no case was the overwhelming majority of a city's Black population concentrated in one neighborhood with densities of 75 to 90 percent. Instead, Blacks inhabited several neighborhoods in modest numbers and shared territory with non-Black groups. But in the present century, while ethnics were enjoying residential dispersion, Blacks were being funneled into Hough, Watts, and the Black Belts of numerous other cities. For no other group has residential segregation increased so uniformly.

The denial of meaningful upward mobility to Blacks is another singular aspect of American urban history. Again, every other ethnic group which came to the city eventually found group mobility up and out of the central city. Today Chicanos and Puerto Ricans are more mobile than Blacks, although their sojourns in the city have been of short duration. Upward mobility can be measured in terms of housing, discussed above, as well as in economic and occupational parameters. In colonial cities, particularly in the South, Blacks filled many skilled craft positions. To a lesser degree, Blacks in cities of the northern colonies also were trained in the crafts, as well as performing semiskilled and unskilled work. Throughout the first half of the nineteenth century, both slave and free Black craftsmen dominated many of the skilled trades in southern cities; without their contributions to industry and commerce, that region's economy would have been even further retarded behind that of the North. But already in the same time period, the ranks of skilled Black craftsmen in northern cities were being eroded, and after the Civil War those Blacks with mechanical skills found it increasingly difficult to preserve their fair share of the labor market, much less expand it. By the time of the Great Migration, in the second and third decades of the twentieth century, entrance to skilled positions in northern cities was barred to all but the most fortunate few. And this trend has continued to the present. Despite affirmative action, federal job-training programs, and court agreements with entrenched labor unions, the number and proportion of skilled Black workers is far below equitable levels. The same discouraging trends are true for professionals. Despite preferential admissions to medical schools in the decade prior to the Bakke case, only 8,000 out of 400,000 practicing physicians in the United States are Black. Even though nearly all Black doctors practice in cities, they come far from meeting the needs of their race or of sharing equally in society's bounty. Similar comparisons and statistics could be repeated endlessly. They all point to the conclusion that while cities have generally provided a jumping-off point for economic and social mobility, Blacks have consistently been deprived the fruits of this process.

No other ethnic group has remained as highly visible, for so long, as have Afro-Americans, whether in the countryside or the city. For other groups urban life provided the opportunity to become first invisible, and then "American." The immigrant from abroad, speaking a foreign tongue, could learn English, pack away his Old Country costume, learn the word "nigger" and a few other necessary prejudices, and gradually meld into the dominant society and culture. He became socially invisible. He entered the melting pot and, if he desired, came out a new entity, deracinated, "Made in U.S.A." But Jamaican-born John B. Russwurm, publisher of the first Black newspaper (1829) would never, despite his Bowdoin College degree, be allowed to enter the American mainstream. Langston Hughes, who so feelingly described Black life in the cities during the Great Migration, was despite critical acclaim still a "Negro" poet, not an American poet.

Has any other ethnic group suffered such a long history of racial attacks in urban America? The Irish were assaulted, and their schools and religious institutions burned by bigoted nativists in the middle of the nineteenth century, but as they gained in social and political influence such attacks ceased. Chinese were the targets of cruel persecutions on the West Coast for the span of half a century, and Japanese for a shorter period. But an important thread of Black history is the repetitious narrative of racial assaults. Abstracting out only those that took place in cities, one could begin with the attack on New York City Blacks in 1741, and then recite numerous northern antiabolition riots in the 1830's, the Irish-led, so-called Draft Riot in New York City in 1863, southern revenge on the Memphis Black community in 1865, end-of-century mob assaults in New

York City, New Orleans, Atlanta, and Wilmington, North Carolina, and the wave of race riots initiated by whites between 1919 and 1921. Since that time northern urban riots have been characterized by Black assaults on white property and symbols of authority, although during the civil rights era in the South the "traditional" pattern of white versus Black reappeared with ugly frequency. The above listing is a reminder that Blacks have led hazardous lives in American cities, more so than any other group.

Finally, no other group in the history of American cities has been subjected to a colonial status. Urban colonialism is yet another twentieth-century phenomenon; it would be incorrect to use this construct to describe the Black experience in cities before then. Whether in psychological, economic, or military terms, the modern ghetto is exploited, dependent upon, and under alien rule. The ghetto is perpetuated by a system—racism. Like nonwhite colonies in the era of European imperialism, a portion of the "mother country" benefits from colonization, although the working masses derive at best only second-hand profits. America's Black ghettoes display the same characteristics seen in Algeria or Angola before decolonization: low per capita incomes; a high birth rate; an unskilled population; undercapitalized "native" businesses and more advantaged foreign-owned businesses; limited local markets; the need for imported goods and services; an economy dependent on the export of one raw material (unskilled labor); chronic unemployment; the necessity for government transfers (welfare, unemployment benefits) to prop up the local economy; "foreign" control of the governmental apparatus, although "natives" will be employed at lower levels of the bureaucracy. Finally, police (military) control of the ghetto (colony) is in "foreign" hands.

The prospects for decolonization of the Black ghetto, for liberation of the captive Black populations in America's cities, are not promising. Few whites in a position of power perceive the colonial relationship and analogy. Fewer still have solutions for ending it. Blacks possess the will to press for change, but the reins of power lie in other hands. If, as Robert Blauner asserts, white America feels little necessity for change, and only experiences urgency in propping up a threatened status quo, will nothing be changed by the twenty-first century? The long history of Blacks in the cities of America does not lend grounds for optimism.

INTERNAL COLONIALISM
AND GHETTO REVOLT

ROBERT BLAUNER

It is becoming almost fashionable to analyze American racial conflict today in terms of the colonial analogy. I shall argue in this paper that the utility of this perspective depends upon a distinction between colonization as a process and colonialism as a social, economic, and political system. It is the experience of colonization that Afro-Americans share with many of the nonwhite people of the world. But this subjugation has taken place in a societal context that differs in important respects from the situation of "classical colonialism." In the body of this essay I shall look at some major developments in Black protest—the urban riots, cultural nationalism, and the movement for ghetto control—as collective responses to colonized status. Viewing our domestic situation as a special form of colonization outside a context of a colonial system will help explain some of the dilemmas and ambiguities within these movements.

The present crisis in American life has brought about changes in social perspectives and the questioning of long-accepted frameworks. Intellectuals and social scientists have been forced by the pressure of events to look at old definitions of the character of our society, the role of racism, and the workings of basic institutions. The depth and volatility of contemporary racial conflict challenge sociologists in particular to question the adequacy of theoretical models by which we have explained American race relations in the past.

Reprinted with permission from *Social Problems*, 16 (Spring 1969), pp. 393–408. Footnotes appearing in the original publication have been deleted in the present volume, and should be consulted for full documentation of the author's conclusions.

For a long time the distinctiveness of the Negro situation among the ethnic minorities was placed in terms of color, and the systematic discrimination that follows from our deep-seated racial prejudices. This was sometimes called the caste theory, and while provocative, it missed essential and dynamic features of American race relations. In the past ten years there has been a tendency to view Afro-Americans as another ethnic group not basically different in experience from previous ethnics and whose "immigration" condition in the North would in time follow their upward course. The inadequacy of this model is now clear—even the Kerner Report devotes a chapter to criticizing this analogy. A more recent (though hardly new) approach views the essence of racial subordination in economic class terms: Black people as an underclass are to a degree specially exploited and to a degree economically dispensable in an automating society. Important as are economic factors, the power of race and racism in America cannot be sufficiently explained through class analysis. Into this theory vacuum steps the model of internal colonialism. Problematic and imprecise as it is, it gives hope of becoming a framework that can integrate the insights of caste and racism, ethnicity, culture, and economic exploitation into an overall conceptual scheme. At the same time, the danger of the colonial model is the imposition of an artificial analogy which might keep us from facing up to the fact (to quote Harold Cruse) that "the American black and white social phenomenon is a uniquely new world thing."

During the late 1950's, identification with African nations and other colonial or formerly colonized peoples grew in importance among Black militants. As a result the United States was increasingly seen as a colonial power and the concept of domestic colonialism was introduced into the political analysis and rhetoric of militant nationalists. During the same period Black social theorists began developing this frame of reference for explaining American realities. As early as 1962, Cruse characterized race relations in this country as "domestic colonialism." Three years later in *Dark Ghetto*, Kenneth Clark demonstrated how the political, economic, and social structure of Harlem was essentially that of a colony. Finally in 1967, a full-blown elaboration of "internal colonialism" provided the theoretical framework for Carmichael and Hamilton's widely read *Black Power*. The following year the colonial analogy gained currency and new "respectability" when Senator Eugene McCarthy habitually referred to Black Americans as a colonized people during his campaign. While the rhetoric of internal colonialism was catching on, other social scientists began to raise questions about its appropriateness as a scheme of analysis.

The colonial analysis has been rejected as obscurantist and misleading by scholars who point to the significant differences in history and social-political conditions between our domestic patterns and what took place in Africa and India. Colonialism traditionally refers to the establishment of domination over a geographically external political unit, most often inhabited by people of a different race and culture, where this domination is political and economic, and the colony exists subordinated to and dependent upon the mother country. Typically the colonizers exploit the land, the raw materials, the labor, and other resources of the colonized nation; in addition, a formal recognition is given to the difference in power, autonomy, and political status, and various agencies are set up to maintain this subordination. Seemingly the analogy must be stretched beyond usefulness if the American version is to be forced into this model. For here we are talking about group relations within a society; the mother country-colony separation in geography is absent. Though whites certainly colonized the territory of the original Americans, internal colonization of Afro-Americans did not involve the settlement of whites in any land that was unequivocably Black. And unlike the colonial situation, there has been no formal recognition of differing power since slavery was abolished outside the South. Classic colonialism involved the control and exploitation of the majority of a nation by a minority of outsiders. Whereas in America the people who are oppressed were themselves originally outsiders and are a numerical minority.

This conventional critique of "internal colonialism" is useful in pointing to the differences between our domestic patterns and the overseas situation. But in its bold attack it tends to lose sight of common experiences that have been historically shared by the most subjugated racial minorities in America and nonwhite peoples in some other parts of the world. For understanding the most dramatic recent developments on the race scene, this common core element—which I shall call colonization—may be more important than the undeniable divergences between the two contexts.

The common features ultimately relate to the fact that the classical colonialism of the imperialist era and American racism developed out of the same historical situation and reflected a common world economic and power stratification. The slave trade for the most part preceded the imperialist partition and economic exploitation of Africa, and in fact may have been a necessary prerequisite for colonial conquest—since it helped deplete and pacify Africa, undermining the resistance to direct occupation. Slavery contributed one of the basic raw materials for the textile industry which provided much of the capital for the West's industrial devleopment and need for economic expansionism. The essential condition for both American slavery and European colonialism was the power domination and the technological superiority of the Western world in its relation to peoples of non-Western and nonwhite origins. This objective supremacy in technology and military power buttressed the West's sense of cultural superiority, laying the basis for racist ideologies that were elaborated to justify control and exploitation of nonwhite people. Thus because classical colonialism and America's internal version developed out of a similar balance of technological, cultural, and power relations, a common *process* of social oppression characterized the racial patterns in the two contexts—despite the variation in political and social structure.

There appear to be four basic components of the colonization complex. The first refers to how the racial group enters into the dominant society (whether colonial power or not). Colonization begins with a forced, involuntary entry. Second, there is an impact on the culture and social organization of the colonized people which is more than just a result of such "natural" processes as contact and acculturation. The colonizing power carries out a policy which constrains, transforms, or destroys indigenous values, orientations, and ways of life. Third, colonization involves a relationship by which members of the colonized group tend to be administered by representatives of the dominant power. There is an experience of being managed and manipulated by outsiders in terms of ethnic status.

A final fundament of colonization is racism. Racism is a principle of social domination by which a group seen as inferior or different in terms of alleged biological characteristics is exploited, controlled, and oppressed socially and psychically by a superordinate group. Except for the marginal case of Japanese imperialism, the major examples of colonialism have involved the subjugation of nonwhite Asian, African, and Latin American peoples by white European powers. Thus racism has generally accompanied colonialism. Race prejudice can exist without colonization—the experience of Asian-American minorities is a case in point—but racism as a system of domination is part of the complex of colonization.

The concept of colonization stresses the enormous fatefulness of the historical factor, namely the manner in which a minority group becomes a part of the dominant society. The crucial difference between the colonized Americans and the ethnic immigrant minorities is that the latter have always been able to operate fairly competitively within that relatively open section of the social and economic order because these groups came voluntarily in search of a better life, because their movements in society were not administratively controlled, and because they

transformed their culture at their own pace—giving up ethnic values and institutions when it was seen as a desirable exchange for improvements in social position.

In present-day America, a major device of Black colonization is the powerless ghetto. As Kenneth Clark describes the situation:

> Ghettoes are the consequence of the imposition of external power and the institutionalization of powerlessness. In this respect, they are in fact social, political, educational, and above all—economic colonies. Those confined within the ghetto walls are subject peoples. They are victims of the greed, cruelty, insensitivity, guilt and fear of their masters. . . . The community can best be described in terms of the analogy of a powerless colony. Its political leadership is divided, and all but one or two of its political leaders are shortsighted and dependent upon the larger political power structure. Its social agencies are financially precarious and dependent upon sources of support outside the community. Its churches are isolated or dependent. Its economy is dominated by small businesses which are largely owned by absentee owners, and its tenements and other real property are also owned by absentee landlords.
>
> Under a system of centralization, Harlem's schools are controlled by forces outside of the community. Programs and policies are supervised and determined by individuals who do not live in the community.

Of course many ethnic groups in America have lived in ghettoes. What make the Black ghettoes an expression of colonized status are three special features. First, the ethnic ghettoes arose more from voluntary choice, both in the sense of the choice to immigrate to America and the decision to live among one's fellow ethnics. Second, the immigrant ghettoes tended to be a one- and two-generation phenomenon; they were actually way-stations in the process of acculturation and assimilation. When they continue to persist as in the case of San Francisco's Chinatown, it is because they are big business for the ethnics themselves and there is a new stream of immigrants. The Black ghetto on the other hand has been a more permanent phenomenon, although some individuals do escape it. But most relevant is the third point. European ethnic groups like the Poles, Italians, and Jews generally only experienced a brief period, often less than a generation, during which their residential buildings, commercial stores, and other enterprises were owned by outsiders. The Chinese and Japanese faced handicaps of color prejudice that were almost as strong as the Blacks faced, but very soon gained control of their internal communities, because their traditional ethnic culture and social organization had not been destroyed by slavery and internal colonization. But Afro-Americans are distinct in the extent to which their segregated communities have remained controlled economically, politically, and administratively from the outside. One indicator of this difference is the estimate that the "income of Chinese-Americans from Chinese-owned businesses is in proportion to their number 45 times as great as the income of Negroes from Negro owned businesses." But what is true of business is also true for the other social institutions that operate within the ghetto. The educators, policemen, social workers, politicians, and others who administer the affairs of ghetto residents are typically whites who live outside the Black community. Thus the ghetto plays a strategic role as the focus for the administration by outsiders which is also essential to the structure of overseas colonialism.

The colonial status of the Negro community goes beyond the issue of ownership and decision making within Black neighborhoods. The Afro-American population in most cities has very little influence on the power structure and institutions of the larger metropolis, despite the fact that in numerical terms, Blacks tend to be the most sizable of the various interest groups. A recent analysis of policy making in Chicago estimates that "Negroes really hold less than 1 percent of the effective power in the Chicago metropolitan area. [Negroes are 20 percent of Cook County's population.] Realistically the power structure of Chicago is hardly less white than that of Mississippi."

Colonization outside of a traditional colonial structure has its own special conditions. The group culture and social structure of the colonized in America is less developed; it is also less autonomous. In addition, the colonized are a numerical minority, and furthermore they are ghettoized more totally and are more dispersed than people under classic colonialism. Though these realities affect the magnitude and direction of response, it is my basic thesis that the most important expressions of protest in the Black community during the recent years reflect the colonized status of Afro-America. Riots, programs of separation, politics of community control, the Black revolutionary movements, and cultural nationalism each represent a different strategy of attack on domestic colonialism in America. Let us now examine some of these movements.

RIOT OR REVOLT?

The so-called riots are being increasingly recognized as a preliminary if primitive form of mass rebellion against a colonial status. There is still a tendency to absorb their meaning within the conventional scope of assimilation-integration politics: some commentators stress the material motives involved in looting as a sign that the rioters want to join America's middle-class affluence just like everyone else. That motives are mixed and often unconscious, that Black people want good furniture and television sets like whites is beside the point. The guiding impulse in most major outbreaks has not been integration with American society, but an attempt to stake out a sphere of control by moving against that society and destroying the symbols of its oppression.

In my critique of the McCone Report I observed that the rioters were asserting a claim to territoriality, an unorganized and rather inchoate attempt to gain control over their community or "turf." In succeeding disorders also the thrust of the action has been the attempt to clear out an alien presence, white men and officials, rather than a drive to kill whites as in a conventional race riot. The main attacks have been directed at the property of white businessmen and at the police who operate in the Black community "like an army of occupation" protecting the interests of outside exploiters and maintaining the domination over the ghetto by the central metropolitan power structure. The Kerner Report misleads when it attempts to explain riots in terms of integration: "What the rioters appear to be seeking was fuller participation in the social order and the material benefits enjoyed by the majority of American citizens. Rather than rejecting the American system, they were anxious to obtain a place for themselves in it." More accurately, the revolt pointed to alienation from this system on the part of many poor and also not so poor Blacks. The sacredness of private property, that unconsciously accepted bulwark of our social arrangements, was rejected; people who looted apparently without guilt generally remarked that they were taking things that "really belonged" to them anyway. Obviously the society's bases of legitimacy and authority have been attacked. Law and order has long been viewed as the white man's law and order by Afro-Americans; but now this perspective characteristic of a colonized people is out in the open. And the Kerner Report's own data question how well ghetto rebels are buying the system: in Newark only 33 percent of self-reported rioters said they thought this country was worth fighting for in the event of a major war; in the Detroit sample the figure was 55 percent.

One of the most significant consequences of the process of colonization is a weakening of the colonized's individual and collective will to resist his oppression. It has been easier to contain and control Black ghettoes because communal bonds and group solidarity have been weakened through divisions among leadership, failures of organization, and a general dispiritment that accompanies social oppression. The riots are a signal that the will to resist has broken the mold of accommodation. In some cities, as in Watts, they also represented nascent movements toward community identity. In several riot-torn ghettoes the outbursts have stimulated new organizations and movements. If it is true that the riot phenomenon of 1964–1968 has passed its peak, its historical import may be more for the "internal" organizing momentum generated than for any profound "external" response of the larger society facing up to underlying causes.

Despite the appeal of Frantz Fanon to young Black revolutionaries, America is not Algeria. It is difficult to foresee how riots in our cities can play a role equivalent to rioting in the colonial situation as an integral phase in a movement for national liberation. In 1968 some militant groups (for example, the Black Panther party in Oakland) had concluded that ghetto riots were self-defeating of the lives and interests of Black people in the present balance of organization and gunpower, though they had served a role to stimulate both Black consciousness and white awareness of the depths of racial crisis. Such militants have been influential in "cooling" their communities during periods of high riot potential. Theoretically oriented Black radicals see riots as spontaneous mass behavior which must be replaced by a revolutionary organization and consciousness. But despite the differences in objective conditions, the violence of the 1960's seems to serve the same psychic function, assertions of dignity and manhood for young Blacks in urban ghettoes, as it did for the colonized of North Africa described by Fanon and Memmi.

CULTURAL NATIONALISM

Cultural conflict is generic to the colonial relation because colonization involves the domination of Western technological values over the more communal cultures of non-Western peoples. Colonialism played havoc with the national integrity of the peoples it brought under its sway. Of course, all traditional cultures are threatened by industrialism, the city, and modernization in communication, transportation, health, and education. What is special are the political and administrative decisions of colonizers in managing and controlling colonized peoples. The boundaries of African colonies, for example, were drawn to suit the political conveniences of the European nations without regard to the social organization and cultures of African tribes and kingdoms. Thus Nigeria as blocked out by the British included the Yorubas and the Ibos, whose civil war today is a residuum of the colonialist's disrespect for the integrity of indigenous cultures.

The most total destruction of culture in the colonization process took place not in traditional colonialism but in America. As Frazier stressed, the integral cultures of the diverse African peoples who furnished the slave trade were destroyed because slaves from different tribes, kingdoms, and linguistic groups were purposely separated to maximize domination and control. Thus language, religion, and national loyalties were lost in North America much more completely than in the Caribbean and Brazil where slavery developed somewhat differently. Thus on this key point America's internal colonization has been more total and extreme than situations of classic colonialism. For the British in India and the European powers in Africa were not able—as outnumbered minorities—to destroy the national and tribal cultures of the colonized. Recall that American slavery lasted 250 years and its racist aftermath another 100. Colonial dependency in the case of British Kenya and French Algeria lasted only 77 and 125 years respectively. In the wake of this more drastic uprooting and destruction of culture and social organization, much more powerful agencies of social, political, and psychological domination developed in the American case.

Colonial control of many peoples inhabiting the colonies was more a goal than a fact, and at Independence there were undoubtedly fairly large numbers of Africans who had never seen a colonial administrator. The gradual process of extension of control from the administrative center on the African coast contrasts sharply with the total uprooting involved in the slave trade and the totalitarian aspects of slavery in the United States. Whether or not Elkins is correct in treating slavery as a total institution, it undoubtedly had a far more radical and pervasive impact on American slaves than did colonialism on the vast majority of Africans.

Yet a similar cultural process unfolds in both contexts of colonialism. To the extent that they are involved in the larger society and economy, the colonized are caught up in a conflict between two cultures. Fanon has described how the assimilation-oriented schools of Martinique taught him to reject his own culture and Blackness in favor of Westernized, French, and white values. Both the colonized elites under traditional colonialism and perhaps the majority of Afro-Americans today experience a parallel split in identity, cultural loyalty, and political orientation.

The colonizers use their culture to socialize the colonized elites (intellectuals, politicians, and middle class) into an identification with the colonial system. Because Western culture has the prestige, the power, and the key to open the limited opportunity that a minority of the colonized may achieve, the first reaction seems to be an acceptance of the dominant values. Call it brainwashing as the Black Muslims put it; call it identifying with the aggressor if you prefer Freudian terminology; call it a natural response to the hope and belief that integration and democratization can really take place if you favor a more common-sense explanation, this initial acceptance in time crumbles on the realities of racism and colonialism. The colonized, seeing that his success within colonialism is at the expense of his group and his own inner identity, moves radically toward a rejection of the Western culture and develops a nationalist outlook that celebrates his people and their traditions. As Memmi describes it:

Assimilation being abandoned, the colonized's liberation must be carried out through a recovery of self and of autonomous dignity. Attempts at imitating the colonizer required self-denial; the colonizer's rejection is the indispensible prelude to self-discovery. That accusing and annihilating image must be shaken off; oppression must be attacked boldly since it is impossible to go around it. After having been rejected for so long by the colonizer, the day has come when it is the colonized who must refuse the colonizer.

Memmi's book, *The Colonizer and the Colonized,* is based on his experience as a Tunisian Jew in a marginal position between the French and the colonized Arab majority. The uncanny parallels between the North African situation he describes and the course of Black-white relations in our society is the best impressionist argument I know for the thesis that we have a colonized group and a colonizing system in America. His discussion of why even the most radical French anticolonialist cannot participate in the struggle of the colonized is directly applicable to the situation of the white liberal and radical vis-à-vis the Black movement. His portrait of the colonized is as good an analysis of the psychology behind Black Power and Black nationalism as anything that has been written in the United States. Consider for example:

Considered *en bloc* as *them, they,* or *those,* different from every point of view, homogeneous in a radical heterogeneity, the colonized reacts by rejecting all the colonizers *en bloc.* The distinction between deed and intent has no great significance in the colonial situation. In the eyes of the colonized, all Europeans in the colonies are de facto colonizers, and whether they want to be or not, they are colonizers in some ways. By their privileged economic position, by belonging to the political system of oppression, or by participating in an effectively negative complex toward the colonized, they are colonizers. . . . They are supporters or at least unconscious accomplices of that great collective aggression of Europe. . . .
    The same passion which made him admire and absorb Europe shall make him assert his differences; since those differences, after all, are within him and correctly constitute his true self. . . .

The important thing now is to rebuild his people, whatever be their authentic nature; to reforge unity, communicate with it, and to feel that they belong.

Cultural revitalization movements play a key role in anticolonial movements. They follow an inner necessity and logic of their own that comes from the consequences of colonialism on groups and personal identities; they are also essential to provide the solidarity which the political or military phase of the anticolonial revolution requires. In the United States an Afro-American culture has been developing since slavery out of the ingredients of African world views, the experience of bondage, southern values and customs, migration and the northern lower-class ghettoes, and most importantly, the political history of the Black population in its struggle against racism. That Afro-Americans are moving toward cultural nationalism in a period when ethnic loyalties tend to be weak (and perhaps on the decline) in this country is another confirmation of the unique colonized position of the Black group. (A similar nationalism seems to be growing among American Indians and Mexican-Americans.)

THE MOVEMENT FOR GHETTO CONTROL

The call for Black Power unites a number of varied movements and tendencies. Though no clear-cut program has yet emerged, the most important emphasis seems to be the movement for control of the ghetto. Black leaders and organizations are increasingly concerned with owning and controlling those institutions that exist within or impinge upon their community. The colonial model provides a key to the understanding of this movement, and indeed ghetto-control advocates have increasingly invoked the language of colonialism in pressing for local home rule. The framework of anticolonialism explains why the struggle for poor people's or community control of poverty programs has been more central in many cities than the content of these programs and why it has been crucial to exclude whites from leadership positions in Black organizations.

The key institutions that anticolonialists want to take over or control are business, social services, schools, and the police. Though many spokesmen have advocated the exclusion of white landlords and small businessmen from the ghetto, this program has evidently not struck fire with the Black population and little concrete movement toward economic expropriation has yet developed. Welfare recipients have organized in many cities to protect their rights and gain a greater voice in the decisions that affect them, but whole communities have not yet been able to mount direct action against welfare colonialism. Thus schools and the police seem now to be the burning issues of ghetto-control politics.

During the past few years there has been a dramatic shift from educational integration as the primary goal to that of community control of the schools. Afro-Americans are demanding their own school boards, with the power to hire and fire principals and teachers and to construct a curriculum which would be relevant to the special needs and culture style of ghetto youth. Especially active in high schools and colleges have been Black students, whose protests have centered on the incorporation of Black Power and Black culture into the educational system. Consider how similar is the spirit behind these developments to the attitude of the colonized North African toward European education:

He will prefer a long period of educational mistakes to the continuance of the colonizer's school organization. He will choose institutional disorder in order to destroy the institutions built by the colonizer as soon as possible. There we will see, indeed a reactive drive of profound protest. He will no longer owe anything to the colonizer and will have definitely broken with him.

Protest and institutional disorder over the issue of school control came to a head in 1968 in New York City. The procrastination in the Albany state legislature, the several crippling strikes called by the teachers union, and the almost frenzied response of Jewish organizations makes it clear that decolonization of education faces the resistance of powerful vested interests. The situation is too dynamic at present to assess probable future results. However, it can be safely predicted that some form of school decentralization will be institutionalized in New York, and the movement for community control of education will spread to more cities.

This movement reflects some of the problems and ambiguities that stem from the situation of colonization outside an immediate colonial context. The Afro-American community is not parallel in structure to the communities of colonized nations under traditional colonialism. The significant difference here is the lack of fully developed indigenous institutions besides the church. Outside of some areas of the South there is really no Black economy, and most Afro-Americans are inevitably caught up in the larger society's structure of occupation, education, and mass communication. Thus the ethnic nationalist orientation which reflects the reality of colonization exists alongside an integrationist orientation which corresponds to the reality that the institutions of the larger society are much more developed than those of the incipient nation. As would be expected the movement for school control reflects both tendencies. The militant leaders who spearhead such local movements may be primarily motivated by the desire to gain control over the community's institutions—they are anticolonialists first and foremost. Many parents who support them may share this goal also, but the majority are probably more concerned about creating a new education that will enable their children to "make it" in the society and the economy as a whole—they know that the present school system fails ghetto children and does not prepare them for participation in American life.

There is a growing recognition that the police are the most crucial institution maintaining the colonized status of Black Americans. And of all establishment institutions, police departments probably include the highest proportion of individual racists. This is no accident since central to the workings of racism (an essential component of colonization) are attacks on the humanity and dignity of the subject group. Through their normal routines the police constrict Afro-Americans to Black neighborhoods by harassing and questioning them when found outside the ghetto; they break up groups of youth congregating on corners or in cars without any provocation; and they continue to use offensive and racist language no matter how many intergroup-understanding seminars have been built into the police academy. They also shoot to kill ghetto residents for alleged crimes such as car thefts and running from police officers.

Police are key agents in the power equation as well as the drama of dehumanization. In the final analysis they do the dirty work for the larger system by restricting the striking back of Black rebels to skirmishes inside the ghetto, thus deflecting energies and attacks from the communities and institutions of the larger power structure. In a historical review, Gary Marx notes that since the French Revolution, police and other authorities have killed large numbers of demonstrators and rioters; the rebellious "rabble" rarely destroys human life. The same pattern has been repeated in America's recent revolts. Journalistic accounts appearing in the press recently suggest that police see themselves as defending the interests of white poeple against a tide of Black insurgence; furthermore, the majority of whites appear to view "blue power" in this light. There is probably no other opinion on which the races are as far apart today as they are on the question of attitudes toward the police.

In many cases set off by a confrontation between a policeman and a Black citizen, the ghetto uprisings have dramatized the role of law enforcement and the issue of police brutality. In their aftermath, movements have arisen to contain police activity. One of the first was the

Community Alert Patrol in Los Angeles, a method of policing the police in order to keep them honest and constrain their violations of personal dignity. This was the first tactic of the Black Panther party which originated in Oakland, perhaps the most significant group to challenge the police role in maintaining the ghetto as a colony. The Panthers' later policy of openly carrying guns (a legally protected right) and their intention of defending themselves against police aggression have brought on a series of confrontations with the Oakland police department. All indications are that the authorities intend to destroy the Panthers by shooting, framing up, or legally harassing their leadership—diverting the group's energies away from its primary purpose of self-defense and organization of the Black community to that of legal defense and gaining support in the white community.

There are three major approaches to "police colonialism" that correspond to reformist and revolutionary readings of the situation. The most elementary and also superficial sees colonialism in the fact that ghettoes are overwhelmingly patrolled by white rather than by Black officers. The proposal—supported today by many police departments—to increase the number of Blacks on local forces to something like their distribution in the city would then make it possible to reduce the use of white cops in the ghetto. This reform should be supported, for a variety of obvious reasons, but it does not get to the heart of the police role as agents of colonization.

The Kerner Report documents the fact that in some cases Black policemen can be as brutal as their white counterparts. The report does not tell us who polices the ghetto, but they have compiled the proportion of Negroes on the forces of the major cities. In some cities the disparity is so striking that white police inevitably dominate ghetto patrols. (In Oakland, 31 percent of the population and only 4 percent of the police are Black; in Detroit, the figures are 39 percent and 5 percent; and in New Orleans, 41 and 4.) In other cities, however, the proportion of Black cops is approaching the distribution in the city: Philadelphia, 29 percent and 20 percent; Chicago, 27 percent and 17 percent. These figures also suggest that both the extent and the pattern of colonization may vary from one city to another. It would be useful to study how Black communities differ in degree of control over internal institutions as well as in economic and political power in the metropolitan area.

A second demand which gets more to the issue is that police should live in the communities they patrol. The idea here is that Black cops who lived in the ghetto would have to be accountable to the community; if they came on like white cops then "the brothers would take care of business" and make their lives miserable. The third or maximalist position is based on the premise that the police play no positive role in the ghettoes. It calls for the withdrawal of metropolitan officers from Black communities and the substitution of an autonomous indigenous force that would maintain order without oppressing the population. The precise relationship between such an independent police, the city and county law-enforcement agencies, a ghetto governing body that would supervise and finance it, and especially the law itself is yet unclear. It is unlikely that we will soon face these problems directly as they have arisen in the case of New York's schools. Of all the programs of decolonization, police autonomy will be most resisted. It gets to the heart of how the state functions to control and contain the Black community through delegating the legitimate use of violence to police authority.

The various "Black Power" programs that are aimed at gaining control of individual ghettoes—buying up property and businesses, running the schools through community boards, taking over antipoverty programs and other social agencies, diminishing the arbitrary power of the police—can serve to revitalize the institutions of the ghetto and build up an economic, professional, and political power base. These programs seem limited; we do not know at present if they are enough in themselves to end colonized status. But they are certainly a necessary first step.

THE ROLE OF WHITES

What makes the Kerner Report a less than radical document is its superficial treatment of racism and its reluctance to confront the colonized relationship between Black people and the larger society. The report emphasizes the attitudes and feelings that make up white racism, rather than the system of privilege and control which is the heart of the matter. With all its discussion of the ghetto and its problems, it never faces the question of the stake that white Americans have in racism and ghettoization.

This is not a simple question, but this paper should not end with the impression that police are the major villains. All white Americans gain some privileges and advantage from the colonization of Black communities. The majority of whites also lose something from this oppression and division in society. Serious research should be directed to the ways in which white individuals and institutions are tied into the ghetto. In closing, let me suggest some possible parameters.

1. It is my guess that only a small minority of whites make a direct economic profit from ghetto colonization. This is hopeful in that the ouster of white businessmen may become politically feasible. Much more

significant, however, are the private and corporate interests in the land and residential property of the Black community; their holdings and influence on urban decision making must be exposed and combated.

2. A much larger minority have occupational and professional interests in the present arrangements. The Kerner Commission reports that 1.3 million nonwhite men would have to be upgraded occupationally in order to make the Black job distribution roughly similar to the white. They advocate this without mentioning that 1.3 million specially privileged white workers would lose in the bargain. In addition, there are those professionals who carry out what Lee Rainwater has called the "dirty work" of administering the lives of the ghetto poor: the social workers, the schoolteachers, the urban-development people, and of course the police. The social problems of the Black community will ultimately be solved only by people and organizations from that community; thus the emphasis within these professions must shift toward training such a cadre of minority personnel. Social scientists who teach and study problems of race and poverty likewise have an obligation to replace themselves by bringing into the graduate schools and college faculties men of color who will become the future experts in these areas. For cultural and intellectual imperialism is as real as welfare colonialism though it is currently screened behind such unassailable shibboleths as universalism and the objectivity of scientific inquiry.

3. Without downgrading the vested interests of profit and profession, the real nitty-gritty elements of the white stake are political power and bureaucratic security. Whereas few whites have much understanding of the realities of race relations and ghetto life, I think most give tacit or at least subconscious support to the containment and control of the Black population. Whereas most whites have extremely distorted images of Black Power many—if not most—would still be frightened by actual Black political power. Racial groups and identities are real in American life; white Americans sense they are on top, and they fear possible reprisals or disruptions were power to be more equalized. There seems to be a paranoid fear in the white psyche of Black dominance; the belief that Black autonomy would mean unbridled license is so ingrained that such reasonable outcomes as Black political majorities and independent Black police forces will be bitterly resisted.

On this level the major mass bulwark of colonization is the administrative need for bureaucratic security so that the middle classes can go about their life and business in peace and quiet. The Black militant movement is a threat to the orderly procedures by which bureaucracies and suburbs manage their existence, and I think today there are more people who feel a stake in conventional procedures than there are those who gain directly from racism. For in their fight for institutional control, the colonized will not play by the white rules of the game. These administrative rules have kept them down and out of the system; therefore they have no necessary intention of running institutions in the image of the white middle class.

The liberal, humanist value that violence is the worst sin cannot be defended today if one is committed squarely against racism and for self-determination. For some violence is almost inevitable in the decolonization process; unfortunately racism in America has been so effective that the greatest power Afro-Americans (and perhaps also Mexican-Americans) wield today is the power to disrupt. If we are going to swing with these revolutionary times and at least respond positively to the anticolonial movement, we will have to learn to live with conflict, confrontation, constant change, and what may be real or apparent chaos and disorder.

A positive response from the white majority needs to be in two major directions at the same time. First, community liberation movements should be supported in every way by pulling out white instruments of direct control and exploitation and substituting technical assistance to the community when this is asked for. But it is not enough to relate affirmatively to the nationalist movement for ghetto control without at the same time radically opening doors for full participation in the institutions of the mainstream. Otherwise the liberal and radical position is little different than the traditional segregationist. Freedom in the special conditions of American colonization means that the colonized must have the choice between participation in the larger society and in their own independent structures.

BIBLIOGRAPHIC ESSAY

Black urban history did not claim the attention of more than a few trained historians prior to the 1960's, mirroring the general neglect of Afro-American studies by the academic profession before the modern civil rights era. Admirable studies of particular cities, in specific eras, have appeared in the last two decades, although works spanning the entire chronological history of one city's Black population have been rare, while a full scholarly overview of the total Black historical experience in American cities has not been written. Hence this Bibliography is lopsided, reflecting an abundance of work in some areas, a scarcity in others. No claims are made as to its definitiveness. Dissertations have not been included. Articles in regional or local-history periodicals may well have been overlooked in the computer-assisted search for appropriate titles. Very little of the sociological literature has been included; full coverage would warrant another separate bibliography. The reader should be aware, however, that the social sciences have produced a great quantity of studies of segregation, urban race relations, racial violence, and economic discrimination that illuminates the Black urban experience. In addition, the subject of all-Black towns has been ignored here, because most of them are essentially rural in character, even those "suburbs" of metropolitan areas. Finally, works which have been issued in paperback editions are so noted with an asterisk.

THE URBAN PARAMETERS

There are almost no works surveying, however briefly, the full three centuries of Black urban life, other than the article included in this volume by Reynolds Farley. A similar but less successful study is Faustine C. Jones, "Black Americans and the City: A Historical Survey," *Journal of Negro Education,* 42 (Summer 1973), 261-282; see also a popular history, Arna Bontemps and Jack Conroy, *Anyplace But Here* (New York, 1966).* Several older city histories are still valuable: James Weldon Johnson, *Black Manhattan* (New York, 1930);* Roi Ottley and William J. Weatherby, *The Negro in New York: An Informal Social History, 1626-1940* (New York, 1969);* John Daniels, *In Freedom's Birthplace* (Boston, 1914), on Boston; Robert Warner, *New Haven Negroes: A Social History* (New Haven, 1940); and Wendell P. Dabney, *Cincinnati's Colored Citizens* (Cincinnati, 1926). Recent studies of Blacks in Washington, D.C., are Constance M. Green, *The Secret City* (Princeton, 1967),* and Louise D. Hutchinson, *The Anacostia Story: 1608-1930* (Washington, D.C., 1976). See also Lionel M. Yard, "Blacks in Brooklyn, New York," *Negro History Bulletin,* 37 (Aug.-Sept.,1974), 289-292; and Daphne Spain, "Race Relations and Residential Segregation in New Orleans: Two Centuries of Paradox," *The Annals,* 441 (Jan. 1979), 82-96.

SLAVES AND FREEMEN IN COLONIAL CITIES

Rare is the study focusing specifically on Black life in colonial cities. Among the best are Jerome H. Wood, Jr., "The Negro in Early Pennsylvania: The Lancaster Experience, 1730-1790;" in Elinor Miller and Eugene D. Genevese, eds., *Plantation, Town and County* (Urbana, 1974), 442-452;* and Donald E. Everett, "Free Persons of Color in Colonial Louisiana," *Louisiana History,* 7 (Winter 1966), 21-50, focusing on New Orleans. See also Oscar R. Williams, "The Regimentation of Blacks on the Urban Frontier in Colonial Albany, New York City and Philadelphia," *Journal of Negro History,* 63 (Fall 1978), 329-338; Don C. Skemer, "New Evidence on Black Unrest in Colonial New York," *Journal of Long Island History,* 12 (Fall 1975), 46-49; and Michael Camerota, "Westfield's Black Community, 1755-1905," *Historical Journal of Western Massachusetts,* 5 (Spring 1976), 17-27.

BLACKS IN ANTEBELLUM CITIES

An increasing number of important studies of free Black communities in northern states before the Civil War is being written. For New England, see Julian Rammelkamp, "The Providence Negro Community, 1820-1842," *Rhode Island History*, 7 (Jan. 1948), 20-33, and Janis O. Horton, "Generations of Protest: Black Families and Social Reform in Ante-Bellum Boston," *New England Quarterly*, 49 (June 1976), 242-256. For New York, consult Leo H. Hirsh, Jr., "New York and the Negro from 1783-1865," *JNH*, 16 (Oct. 1931), 382-473; Daniel Perlman, 'Organizations of the Free Negro in New York City, 1800-1860," *JNH*, 56 (July 1971), 181-197; Robert Ernst, "The Economic Status of New York City Negroes, 1850-1863," *NHB*, 12 (Mar. 1949), 131-132, 139-143; and Arnett G. Lindsay, "The Economic Condition of the Negroes of New York Prior to 1861," *JNH*, 6 (Apr. 1921), 190-199. For the Midwest, see Carter G. Woodson, "The Negroes of Cincinnati Prior to the Civil War," *JNH*, 1 (Jan. 1916), 1-22; Richard C. Wade, "The Negro in Cincinnati, 1800-1830," *JNH*, 39 (Jan. 1954), 43-57; and Maximilian Reichard, "Black and White on the Urban Frontier: The St. Louis Community in Transition, 1800-1830," *Missouri Historical Society Bulletin*, 33 (Oct. 1976), 3-17. The Far West is seen in Philip M. Montesano, "San Francisco Black Churches in the Early 1860s: Political Pressure Group," *California Historical Quarterly*, 52 (Summer 1973), 145-152.

Two historians have surveyed the full scope of urban slavery in the South: Richard C. Wade, *Slavery in the Cities* (New York, 1964);* and Claudia Dale Goldin, *Urban Slavery in the American South, 1820-1860* (Chicago, 1976). For a shorter survey, see Jane R. Wilkie, "The Black Urban Population of the Pre-Civil War South," *Phylon*, 37 (Sept. 1976), 250-262. The nation's capital is covered in Letitia W. Brown, *Free Negroes in the District of Columbia, 1790-1846* (New York, 1972), as well as in Dorothy Provine, "The Economic Position of the Free Blacks in the District of Columbia, 1800-1860," *JNH*, 58 (Jan. 1973), 61-72, and Sammy M. Miller, "Slavery in an Urban Area—District of Columbia," *NHB*, 37 (Aug. 1974), 293-294. In addition to E. Horace Fitchett's article in this volume, see his "The Origin and Growth of the Free Negro Population of Charleston, South Carolina," *JNH*, 26 (Oct. 1941), 421-437; also of interest is C. W. Birnie, "Education of the Negro in Charleston, S.C., Prior to the Civil War," *JNH*, 12 (Jan. 1927), 13-21. New Orleans has been thoroughly studied by Robert C. Reinders, "The Decline of the New Orleans Free Negro in the Decade Before the Civil War," *Journal of Mississippi History*, 24, (Apr. 1962), 88-98; "Slavery in New Orleans in the Decade Before the Civil War," *Mid-*

America, 44 (Oct. 1962), 211-221; and "The Free Negro in the New Orleans Economy, 1850-1860," *La. Hist.,* 6 (Summer 1965), 273-285. See also Donald E. Everett, "Emigres and Militiamen: Free Persons of Color in New Orleans, 1803-1815," *JNH,* 38 (Oct. 1953), 377-402, and Roger A. Fischer, "Racial Segregation in Ante-Bellum New Orleans," *American Historical Review,* 84 (Feb. 1969), 926-937. Smaller southern cities are covered in Terry L. Seip, "Slaves and Free Negroes in Alexandria [Louisiana], 1850-60," *La. Hist.,* 10 (Spring 1969), 147-165; Edward F. Sweat, "Free Blacks in Antebellum Atlanta," *Atlanta Historical Bulletin,* 21 (Spring 1977), 64-71; E. Merton Coulter, "Slavery and Freedom in Athens, Georgia, 1860-66," *Georgia Historical Quarterly,* 49 (Sept. 1965), 246-293; and Jonathan Beasley, "Blacks—Slave and Free— in Vicksburg, 1850-1860," *JMH,* 38 (Feb. 1976), 1-32.

SOUTHERN CITIES AFTER THE CIVIL WAR

A number of informative studies illuminate the postbellum southern urban experience. Several cities are surveyed in August Meier and Elliot Rudwick, "Negro Boycotts of Segregated Streetcars in Virginia, 1904-1907," *Virginia Magazine of History and Biography,* 81 (Oct. 1973), 479-487; related in subject matter is William C. Hine, "The 1867 Charleston Streetcar Sit-ins: A Case of Successful Black Protest," *South Carolina Historical Magazine,* 77 (Apr. 1976), 110-114. A border-state city is surveyed in Carol E. Hoffecker, "The Politics of Exclusion: Blacks in Late Nineteenth Century Wilmington, Delaware," *Delaware History,* 16 (Apr. 1974), 60-72. For Raleigh, see Dorothy A. Gay, "Crisis of Identity: The Negro Community in Raleigh, 1890-1900," *North Carolina Historical Review,* 50 (Apr. 1973), 121-140. Savannah has been extensively studied by Robert E. Perdue, *The Negro in Savannah, 1865-1900* (New York 1973); see also Linda O. Hines and Allen W. Jones, "A Voice of Black Protest: The Savannah Men's Sunday Club, 1905-1911," *Phylon,* 35 (June 1974), 193-202. Florida cities are covered in Edward N. Akin, "When a Minority Becomes the Majority: Blacks in Jacksonville Politics, 1887-1907," *Florida Historical Quarterly,* 53 (Oct. 1974), 123-145, and Donald H. Bragaw, "Status of Negroes in a Southern Port City in the Progressive Era: Pensacola, 1896-1920," *FHQ,* 51 (Jan. 1973), 281-302.

The social history of Blacks in a New South city is explored in August Meier and David Lewis, "History of the Negro Upper Class in Atlanta, Ga., 1890-1958," *JNE,* 28 (Spring 1959), 128-139, and William Harris, "Work and Family in Black Atlanta," *Journal of Social History,* 9 (Spring

1976), 319-330. Excellent work has been done on New Orleans: John W. Blassingame, *Black New Orleans: 1860-1880* (Chicago, 1973);* David Rankin, "The Origins of Black Leadership in New Orleans During Reconstruction," *Journal of Southern History*, 40 (Aug. 1974), 417-440; and Dale A. Somers, "Black and White in New Orleans: A Study in Urban Race Relations, 1865-1900," *JSH*, 40 (Feb. 1974), 19-42. For the upper South, see Lester C. Lamon, "Progressivism Was Not 'For Whites Only': The Black Progressive Reformers of Nashville, Tennessee, 1906-1918," *Indiana Academy of the Social Sciences*, 9 (1974), 103-112.

THE URBAN NORTH BEFORE THE GREAT MIGRATION

Several book-length studies, as well as more limited articles, have greatly expanded our knowledge of late nineteenth-century northern city life for Blacks. Midwest coverage is spotty: see Jon Butler, "Communities and Congregations: The Black Church in St. Paul, 1860-1900," *JNH*, 56 (Apr. 1971), 118-134; Allan H. Spear, *Black Chicago: The Making of a Negro Ghetto, 1890-1920* (Chicago, 1967);* and William Tuttle, "Labor Conflict and Racial Violence: The Black Worker in Chicago, 1894-1919," *Labor History*, 10 (Summer 1969), 408-432. For the Ohio Valley, see Kenneth Kusmer, *A Ghetto Takes Shape: Black Cleveland, 1870-1930* (Urbana, 1975);* Larry Cuban, "A Strategy for Racial Peace: Negro Leadership in Cleveland, 1900-1919," *Phylon*, 28 (Fall 1967), 299-311; David L. Calkins, "Black Education and the Nineteenth Century City: An Institutional Analysis of Cincinnati's Colored Schools, 1850-1887," *Cincinnati Historical Society Bulletin*, 33 (Fall 1975), 161-173; and Paul Lammermeier, "The Urban Black Family in the Nineteenth Century: A Study of Black Family Structure in the Ohio Valley, 1850-1880," *Journal of Marriage and the Family*, 35 (Aug. 1973), 440-456. Michigan is well covered in David M. Katzman, *Before the Ghetto: Black Detroit in the Nineteenth Century* (Urbana, 1973);* see also Douglas K. Meyer, "Evolution of a Permanent Negro Community in Lansing," *Michigan History*, 55 (Summer 1971), 141-154.

Pennsylvania urbanization is covered in a classic of Black sociology and history, W. E. B. DuBois, *The Philadelphia Negro* (Philadelphia, 1899);* for additional Philadelphia detail see Frank F. Furstenberg, Jr., Theodore Hershberg, and John Modell, "The Origins of the Female-Headed Black Family: The Impact of the Urban Experience," *Journal of Interdisciplinary History*, 6 (Autumn 1975), 211-233. A study of a smaller town is John E. Bodnar, "Peter C. Blackwell and the Negro Community of Steelton, 1880-1920," *Pennsylvania Magazine of History and Biography*, 97 (Apr. 1973), 199-209. Black New York has received more scholarly attention than any other city. For this time period see Gilbert Osofsky, *Harlem: The Making of a Ghetto*, (New York, 1966);* Seth M. Scheiner, *Negro Mecca: A History of the Negro in New York City, 1865-1920* (New York, 1965);* George Psychas. "William L. Bulkley and the New York Negro, 1890-1910," *HJWM*, 1 (Spring 1972); Herman D. Bloch, "The New York City Negro and Occupational Eviction, 1860-1910," *International Review of Social History*, 5 (Part 1, 1960), 26-38; and Marsha Hurst, "Integration, Freedom of Choice and Community Control in Nineteenth Century Brooklyn," *Journal of Ethnic Studies*, 3 (Fall 1975), 33-55. For New England, see Elizabeth H. Pleck, *Black Migration and Poverty: Boston, 1865-1900* (New York, 1979). For a view of a small West Coast community, see Robert L. Carlton, "Blacks in San Diego County: A Social Profile, 1850-1880," *Journal of San Diego History*, 21 (Fall 1975), 7-20.

FROM GREAT MIGRATION TO GREAT DEPRESSION

No period in Black urban history has been more intensely studied than the teens and twenties. Important data on New York, Cleveland, and Chicago can be found in the works by Osofsky,* Kusmer,* and Spear,* mentioned in the previous section. New York in the twenties is also discussed in Johnson* and Ottley and Weatherby,* cited in "The Urban Parameters." The dynamics of the migration itself are studied in Emmett J. Scott, *Negro Migration During the War* (New York, 1920);* Clyde V. Kiser, *From Sea Island to City* (New York, 1932);* Florette Henri, *Black Migration: Movement North, 1900-1920* (Garden City, 1975);* and Dewey H. Palmer, "Moving North: Negro Migration During World War I," *Phylon*, 28 (Spring 1967), 52-62. For a general survey of the impact of the thirties on Black communities, see E. Franklin Frazier, "Some Effects of the Depression on the Negro in Northern Cities," *Science and Society*, 2 (Fall 1938), 489-499. Once again, New York City has been intensively studied. See Roi Ottley, *"New World A-Coming"* (New York, 1943);* Claude McKay, *Harlem: Negro Metropolis* (New York, 1940);* William Muraskin, "The Harlem Boycott of 1934: Black Nationalism and the Rise of Labor-Union Consciousness," *Labor History*, 13 (Summer 1972), 361-373; Dominic J. Capeci, Jr., *The Harlem Riot of 1943* (Philadelphia, 1977); and, for West Indian migration to East Coast cities, Ira De A. Reid, *The Negro Immigrant* (New York, 1939).

An excellent study of Newark is Clement A. Price, "The Beleagured City as Promised Land: Blacks in Newark, 1917-1947," in William C. Wright, ed., *Urban New Jersey Since 1870* (Trenton, 1975), pp. 10-45; for Philadelphia, see John F. Bauman, "Black Slums/Black Projects: The New Deal and Negro Housing in Philadelphia," *Pennsylvania History,* 41 (July 1974), 311-338. Midwestern cities are covered in David Allan Levine, *Internal Combustion: The Races in Detroit, 1915-1926* (Westport, 1976); Christopher G. Wye, "The New Deal and the Negro Community: Toward a Broader Conceptualization," *Journal of American History,* 59 (Dec. 1972), 621-639, on Cleveland; J. S. Himes, "Forty Years of Negro Life in Columbus, Ohio, 1900-1940," *JNH,* 27 (Apr. 1942), 133-154; Emma Lou Thornbrough, "Segregation in Indiana during the Klan Era of the 1920s," *Mississippi Valley Historical Review,* 47 (Mar. 1961), 594-618; William M. Tuttle, *Race Riot: Chicago in the Red Summer of 1919* (New York, 1970);* and Elliott M. Rudwick, *Race Riot at East St. Louis, July 2, 1917* (Carbondale, 1964).* Two classic studies of Chicago, from sociological perspectives, are nonetheless of unique importance to historians: Chicago Commission on Race Relations, *The Negro in Chicago* (Chicago, 1922); and St. Clair Drake and Horace R. Cayton, *Black Metropolis,* rev. ed. (New York, 1962).*

Studies of southern cities during this period are few. See Lester C. Lamon, "The Black Community in Nashville and the Fisk University Student Strike of 1924-1925," *JSH,* 40 (May 1974), 225-244; R. Halliburton, Jr., "The Tulsa Race War of 1921," *Journal of Black Studies,* 2 (Mar. 1972), 333-357; Robert V. Haynes, *A Night of Violence: The Houston Riot of 1917* (Baton Rouge, 1976); and Charles Carofalo, "Black-White Occupational Distribution in Miami During World War I," *Prologue,* 5 (Summer 1973), 98-101.

CITY AND SUBURB SINCE 1940

Sociologists, economists, and demographers have produced the bulk of the literature on Blacks in American cities since 1940. To begin to list the major works here would require a separate bibliography, and interested readers should consult the appropriate reference tools in those disciplines. Only a scattering of historically oriented works have been written: Howard A. Droker, "Seattle Race Relations During the Second World War," *Pacific Northwest Quarterly,* 67 (Oct. 1976), 163-174; Thomas C. Hogg, "Black Man in White Town," *PNQ,* 63 (Jan. 1972), 14-21, on Eugene, Oregon; Harvard Sitkoff, "The Detroit Race Riot of 1943," *MH,* 53 (Fall 1969), 183-206; Douglas K. Meyer, "Changing

Negro Residential Patterns in Michigan's Capital, 1915-1970," *MH*, 56 (Summer 1972), 151-167; Dominic J. Capeci, "From Different Liberal Perspectives: Fiorello H. LaGuardia, Adam Clayton Powell, Jr., and Civil Rights in New York City, 1941-1943," *JNH*, 62 (Apr. 1977), 160-173; John D. Reid, "Black Urbanization in the South," *Phylon*, 35 (Fall 1974), 259-267; C. Jack Tucker and John D. Reid, "Black Urbanization and Economic Opportunity: A Look at the Nation's Large Cities," *Phylon*, 38 (Mar. 1977), 55-64; August Meier and David Lewis, "History of the Negro Upper Class in Atlanta, Georgia, 1890-1958," *JNE*, 28 (Spring 1959), 128-139; and Alton Hornsby, Jr., "The Negro in Atlanta Politics, 1961-1973," *AHB*, 21 (Spring, 1977), 7-33.

BLACKS AND THE AMERICAN CITY: Conceptual Perspectives

Historical syntheses of the total scope of Black urban history are rare. The sociological literature contains several works on ghetto pathology, with a built-in negative bias. Economists have been carrying on a lively debate centered on Marxian and non-Marxian interpretations of the long-standing Black economic deficit. Three titles, although not the work of historians, are worth citing, as they challenge and complement Robert Blauner's article included in this volume: William K. Tabb, *The Political Economy of the Black Ghetto* (New York, 1970);* Donald J. Harris, "The Black Ghetto as 'Internal Colony': A Theoretical Critique and Alternate Formulation," *Review of Black Political Economy*, 2 (Summer, 1972), 3-33, a critique of the Tabb book; and William K. Tabb, "Marxian Exploitation and Domestic Colonization," *RBPE*, 4 (Summer 1974), 69-87, a reply to Harris, with a rejoinder by the latter. From a historical perspective, a controversial view is Gilbert Osofsky, "The Enduring Ghetto," *JAH*, 55 (Sept. 1968), 243-255. An excellent comparative study, which unfortunately could not be included in this volume, is Theodore Hershberg, Alan Burstein, Eugene Ericksen, Stephanie Greenberg, and William Yancey, "A Tale of Three Cities: Blacks and Immigrants in Philadelphia, 1850-1880, 1930, and 1970," *The Annals*, 441 (Jan. 1979), 55-81. Also consult Patrick Renshaw, "The Black Ghetto, 1890-1940," *Journal of American Studies*, 8 (Apr. 1974), 41-59.